A Good Enough Life After Freud:

Psychotherapy In Uncertain Times

Joyce Block

ISBN: 1461185351
ISBN-13: 9781461185352

TABLE OF CONTENTS

ACKNOWLEDGMENTS

Sometimes it seems that I have been breathing in all the material for this book since I was born. Over the years, I have accumulated relics from my childhood, fragments of wisdom from books I have cherished, as well as trace elements from innumerable conversations I have had with friends, family, and psychotherapy patients. After weaving together all of these disparate threads, I find it impossible to identify where one begins and another leaves off, but I want to separate out a few for special mention.

I am deeply grateful to all of the people who have come to my office and opened themselves up to me in their desire to gain a deeper understanding of what it means for them to live well. I have learned from their fears, hopes, disappointments, and victories to tolerate the unsettling experiences of knowing but also not knowing, of finding clarity but also uncertainty. In the secluded space of psychotherapy, they have illuminated for me the kaleidoscope of life's shifting meanings.

Victoria Shoemaker has been more than a literary agent to me. For years she has offered invaluable support for this project. Her enthusiasm, optimism, practical wisdom, and persistence have sustained my faith in the possibility of translating my multilayered experiences as a psychotherapist into a written form.

Ronna Kabatznick read a number of chapters when the project was in its very early stages, and I will always remember her loving encouragement, critical insights, and unwillingnesss to mince words.

Nancy Gulanick not only read the entire manuscript but has, throughout the past eighteen years, been alongside me as we have sifted through myriad problems as therapists, mothers, and women. Together we have delighted in our therapeutic victories, laughed at the unpredictability of people, and commiserated over the all-too-repetitive conflicts that play havoc with human life.

The endless conversations I have had with my dear friends Ruth Saada, Jane Elkoff, Lois Greenfield, Stuart Liebman, Karen Paull, Bobsie Levi Berliner, Jody Brown, Tom Parisi, Susan Taccheri, and Ann Rosen, and with my sister Diana Block have both stimulated and fed my appetite to think more deeply and broadly about the meaning of a good enough life. Sharing with them the contradictions and uncertainties of how to live has transformed an impossibly complex problem into a simple pleasure.

My husband Henry Weinfield has gone through the manuscript painstakingly. He has brought to the task his sensitivity to language and his desire for clarity; he has prodded me to bridge the gap between what I am thinking and feeling and the written words on the page. As he is at least as stubborn as I am, we can fight like cats and dogs over a word, let alone a metaphor or meandering free-association, so it is miraculous that we have both survived the process. After thirty plus years of being together, it must be love.

Finally, my children Paul, Saralena, and Vera have always cheered me on to keep writing, despite their jokes about my long-winded New Year's Resolutions and my tendency to veer off onto some psychological tangent at every opportunity. Their love, growth, and beautiful spirits are what has made my life more than good enough.

PROLOGUE

> "You sit there as if you were inside a giant kaleidoscope, but this time the glass fragments are you, the different parts of you . . ."
>
> David Grossman, *See Under: Love* (1989)

"Discontent that casts a shadow grey/ Upon the likeness of a summer's day" was one of my melancholic father's favorite aphorisms, and even he would not deny that he spoke from personal experience. For whether he was gazing out the window at the stragglers from the Single-Room Occupancy hotels that lined our Upper-West-Side New York City street, or dreamily contemplating the ocean waves from a solitary bench upon a Jersey seashore boardwalk, or spinning electrifying tales of people and places long ago and far away, my father wore his characteristic "lean and hungry look." Indeed, he was the personification of unrequited desire, a living proof that lived life is all too frequently not "good enough."

Not surprisingly, my mother was my father's oppo-site, that is, his mirror image, who saw everything in reverse. Whereas he was an exotic "sensitive plant" who suffered visibly from wanting more than what his meager life had offered, she was a "contented cow" (of "Russian peasant stock"), who suffered inconspicuously from accepting less.

I admired my mother's serenity, her dignity and her unwillingness to scramble for her equal share; but when her modesty disappeared behind a veil of quiet resignation, it weighed as heavily on my heart as my father's unabated yearning, his anxious sense of deprivation for which there was no salve. And so I oscillated between their two perspectives, unable to settle permanently for either one. (Which is probably why I was nicknamed "little Luba" and accused of having Austen's "worried look.") His restless pacing, her unworldly equanimity, prompted me to question the limits we idiosyncratically impose on desire and the boundaries we construct in our efforts to separate the "good enough life" from both the idealized life which is forever out of reach and from the unimaginative life which could have and should have been better.

In middle age my internal world is a kaleidoscope of meanings that are continually re-configuring, but this is not only a reflection of my personal history, loving and hating two very different parents. Contradictory values are colliding along the horizon of our contemporary American landscape, and every individual labors with uncertain success, to reconcile shifting definitions of self-fulfillment, strength, and virtue.

As a practicing psychologist I listen each day to diverse stories of life as it is experienced, stories that also include questions and assertions about life as it ought to be. And while there is no obvious connection between the story told by a twenty-four year old, ascetically-inclined artist/web-page designer, who speaks in awe of Mother Teresa's capacity for self-sacrifice, and the story told by a forty-three year old, two hundred pound "soccer mom," who is having a love affair as her husband engages in cyber-sex in the alcove off the kitchen, the overt differences sometimes obscure the underlying similarities. Both the young man who is disenchanted with his job and the middle-aged woman who is disillusioned with her marriage yearn to be elevated, to infuse ordinary life with extraordinary meaning. And if they are both anxious not to sacrifice their personal integrity for security, that is, not to settle for less than what is good enough, they are also both anxious not to mistake the fleeting pleasure of a quick fix (a new job, a different husband) for liberation or courage. A plunge into the vast unknown can reflect an inflated sense of invincibility if not delusions of grandeur, an exhilarating high may precede a humiliating fall.

My purpose in chronicling my psychotherapeutic encounters with meaning is two-fold. First and foremost I wish to pay homage to the creative and moral impulses that inspire the symptoms and the complaints, the delinquencies and the self-destructive behaviors of the people who show up at my office in search of a "cure." Protected beneath the cloak of a written narrative, in that transitional space between reality and make believe, I am at liberty to expose my own uncertainties as a therapist and express my admiration and empathy for unclaimed stabs at heroism that would otherwise go unmemorialized. And then secondly, I wish to translate those shamelessly idiomatic conversations that fall under the rubric of psychotherapy into a common language of hopes and constraints, ideals and compromises, certainties and ambiguities. When our contradictory human desires to have more than what is given, and yet feel sufficient unto ourselves are dignified, we are freed to imagine new definitions of the Good Life, to re-consider the lived value of old ones, and to find relief from the twinned burdens of feeling "I want too much, but what if I am settling for too little?"

PSYCHOTHERAPY AS A LABORATORY OF MEANING

"And unless we can answer this larger question of how our lives are to be lived, we may not be able to answer the most immediate practical question: 'What shall I do next'?"

Jonathan Lear, *Love and Its Place in Nature* (1990)

The Problem of "How to Live"

What the Good Life is and how we go about living our individual lives to the fullest are age-old dilemmas, and traditionally we have turned to philosophers, religious thinkers, artists, and poets in hope of finding clarity. We want our happiness to be authentic not counterfeit, our attachments to be worthy, not foolhardy, our pleasures to be meaningful not transient. Moreover, moral conceptions of the Good Life frequently do not correspond to experiences of living the good life, which may have less to do with fulfilling some larger purpose, than with fulfilling some individual desires or ambitions. As the philosopher and psychoanalyst Jonathan Lear suggests, before we can proceed confidently with our individual lives, we have to know what life itself is about. And, I might add, before we can settle gracefully into one particular life we have to believe that it is better (more courageous, more honest, more expressive of our essential nature) to accept its particular set of limitations (its promises, prohibitions, and traditions) than to pursue some alternative life that beckons to us over the horizon.

Without insight into the "true" nature of human existence, without the vision to discriminate between surface appearances and essential realities, and without the faith that "truth" or "reality" is constant not merely provisional, the individual battles we wage for meaning threaten to be interminable; these battles pit reason against passion, flights of the imagination against negotiated compromises, the desire to create ourselves and to shape the world as we would have it against the desire to be contained within a well-ordered, "intelligently designed" universe.

We are continually admonished to accept the limitations of our lives with equanimity, to not play at being God, but rather to be satisfied with our lot in life. But we also know from personal experience that active resistance to perceived injustice, despite the risk and whatever the outcome, can be of immeasurable value. And if it is true that without emotional engagement life is colorless and not worth living, it is equally true that "care" can turn upon itself and become destructive: without the capacity for emotional detachment we lose our bearings and our vision of the future. Thus the ideal of self-expression competes for our allegiance with the ideal of self-mastery, playing on our hopes and fears.

While human beings have always had conflicting desires and fears that have been a source of suffering, today more than in previous times these conflicts are reflected back to us as differences in perspective rather than as a battle between the forces of good and evil. Indeed, the multi-cultural world we live in, read about, log onto, and shut out by retreating into "gated communities," mirrors the confusion we normally generate on our own from inside. How do we cast lots in the battle between "family values" and "creative self-expression," between the morality of the superego, the common-sensibility of the ego, and the raw honesty of the id? How do we choose between what the psychologist Carol Gilligan identified as the ethic of individual rights and the ethic of care? What if we refuse to make a choice? Is it presumptuous to think that we can suspend indefinitely our wishes for certainty and closure and insist that we can, and, moreover, should, "have it all?" Ironically, the desire for closure, which is tantamount to the desire to settle down, competes with the desire to remain open to endless possibilities, and this is just one more example of our contradictions.

Flooded by images of what human beings can do, the question of what human beings should be is often bracketed or, worse yet, dismissed as moralistic, unsophisticated, old fashioned. Yet, outside the realm of scientific or social scientific analyses, this question cannot be postponed indefinitely. For unless one is willing to be carried along indiscriminately by the currents of cultural relativism – according to which there are no absolute truths ever, and everything is not only possible but also equally permissible (including female circumcision, racist ideology, or sado-masochistic sex) – the question of how best to live and what kind of life is worthy of our time and energy, love and respect, nags at us unrelentingly.

Dizzied by the kaleidoscopic shifting of possible ways to live our particular lives, we, no less than our forebears, look for anchors. Sometimes we find them in our work, in our churches or temples, in our families, or in our private and sometimes all-consuming obsessions with money, status, sex, or the shape of our bodies. And yet, flights of the imagination live on, albeit unconsciously, within the confines of our aging bodies, and we are leery of the limits imposed by holding fast to any single one of these anchors, unsure of what we stand to gain or lose in exchange for our commitment. Thus paradoxically, we are anxious to settle (settle down and settle in) and anxious when we do. What, we ask ourselves, have we settled for in our familiar, ofttimes familial, comfort zone? Is it good enough?

Psychotherapy: Alchemical and Archeological Metaphors

As a psychotherapist I am inadvertently thrust into a position of authority concerning questions concerning how much to want, how much to forgo, how best to live, and expected to formulate answers or prescriptions for what are essentially existential and ethical conundrums. This is ironic because psychology as a discipline has attempted to distance itself from philosophy, art, and religion, and, since Freud, has espoused neutrality with regard to moral issues. To be sure we have been warned of the dire consequences that come when we distort reality to avoid anxiety, or refuse to renounce our childhood wishes for the impossible and the forbidden. But as far as what we are supposed to do with that information – adjust, invent distractions, or fight heroically to the bitter end – good luck, says Freud and his post-modern progeny, you're on your own!

Identifying himself as an "archeologist" of the mind, Freud intended psychoanalysis to be regarded as a science, not a religious cult or art form, and the explicit aim of the talking cure was to ferret out the truth, not to judge or beautify it. The theory held that through laborious excavations into the Unconscious, it would be possible to discover fossilized fragments of psychic life, mend broken connections, and reveal meanings that were purposefully obscured. Indeed, as a voice of the Enlightenment, Freud offered the modern world a rationalist's alternative to ancient oracles and religious revelation, one that promised to release us from the stranglehold of infantile dependency and neurotic misery by acknowledging our essentially irrational nature. (In the world of unconscious fantasy, we are not qualitatively different from adulterers, sexual perverts, and murderers; they do what we only dream about.)

But as moral distinctions that separate the good life from the fallen life have blurred and receded into the background, certain psychological distinctions sharpened and became the basis for a new hierarchy of value. "Co-dependency," Bi-Polar Disorder, and all variety of addictive behaviors (including sexual) have emerged as "diseases" of the mind that need to be contained if not entirely cured, as they limit our potential to lead productive lives and wreak havoc on our relationships. Emotional integration, inner balance, and the self-conscious pursuit of mature as opposed to regressive forms of happiness (whatever that is supposed to mean) has become the gold standard of good mental health and by extension of how to live.

And yet, these answers beg the question, for embedded in the solution that psychology has offered is another set of problems, as people persist unrelentingly in their search for transcendent experiences and symbolic meanings that extend beyond themselves and the immediacy of their daily lives. As a psychotherapist I try to help individuals make wise and healthy choices about how to live within the actual, as opposed to the imaginary, constraints of their lives. However, two obvious questions remain unresolved and unresolvable. The first has to do with what constitutes good mental health, given the vast array of differences that exist in culture and religious beliefs. And the second has to do with whether good mental health, as it is conceived at any point in time or place, should be the first priority in determining our life choices.

Why should we value an individual's well being over the good of the community? And if psychic turmoil can be a catalyst for creativity and change, what value should I and my patients place on adjustment or inner peace?

Usually people who come to therapy are not as transparent in their hopes for revelation as one of my devoutly religious patients, who suffered from a myriad of physical ailments for which there was no discernable physiological basis. "I want to find out the *Truth* so I can be *Normal*," Amy implored without a trace of irony.

A tall order of business I should say, since she doesn't mean just "facts" about her early childhood experience: was she really sexually abused when she was three or did her imagination embellish what was actually a harmless incident? She wants the facts that will guide her to the right approach to take with her meddlesome neighbors: should she let their insults roll off her back, should she stand firm as a "sentinel" and fight fire with fire, or should she sell her house, cut her losses, and move elsewhere? And what's more, how *should* she respond to her husband's sexual fantasies and requests, which he claims are normal, and she finds repugnant? Indirectly Amy is challenging me and the entire psychotherapeutic enterprise either to affirm her idiomatic enactment of integrity or offer her an authoritative substitute. I have become the latest in a series of what psychoanalyst Jacques Lacan identified as "the Subject Supposed to Know."

Amy is not interested in simply creating new coping strategies – she has managed, albeit with difficulty, to live with her mysterious symptoms and irrational fears for more than twenty years. Rather, she wants me to provide her with a sense of closure about the origin and meaning of her suffering and her symptoms, and to reconstitute her uncertain faith in her own faltering judgment and God's justice.

So while it is not that unusual for a patient to ask me, with a mixture of hope and frustration, "How much should I compromise? How much disappointment should I accept? How much should I depend on other people, including you? How open and honest should I be?" it is far from self-evident how I should respond. Having for years wrestled with unruly feelings, alternately expressing and suppressing them, my patient Amy is literally sickened from going nowhere but around in a circle, and yet she is afraid of going somewhere straight, over the familiar and containing edge. But when she turns to me for direction, wishing I were a hypnotist or a prophet, or at the very least a good-enough parent, should I offer to give an answer (my provisional answer) even if the questions are unanswerable and her eagerness for suggestions may be part of her problem? At the risk of increasing her hopelessness, disappointment, and frustration, should I defend the twinned ideals of autonomy and freedom, and foist upon her, whether she wants it or not, the power to decide for herself? How open and honest, how uncompromising, and how disappointing should *I* be for her and for myself? My questions run parallel to my patients'. I want to know what it means to do good psychotherapy, but in order to know that, I need to know what it means to live a good life, if there is not a best life, and when to settle, without the need to apologize, for a life that seems good enough.

Without the authority of revelation, Talmudic argument, or traditional ritualized practice, without even the confidence that anyone can ever gain access to a practicable compendium of adaptive-living procedures, much less a universal code of ethics, the psychotherapist, unlike the pastoral counselor or philosopher, is limited to what may turn out to be just a subjective interpretation of a subjectivity which is itself divided. The tension that exists between the "spontaneous self" of childhood and the "reflective self" that represents adult maturity cannot be eliminated, anymore than we can honestly choose between the values of emotional engagement and emotional detachment when it comes to living a full life.

Thus, at the level of the individual self, our internal world has always been analogous to the "multi-cultural" world we currently inhabit. Which means that the question of how to live in the greater world among people who think and act differently from us, is essentially the same question as how to live more or less harmoniously with our own internal disjunctions. (I believe the term multi-cultural is an apt one when referring to intra-psychic experience, since at the source of our internal conflicts are competing ideals, prohibitions, and experiences of reality, in other words, competing systems of meaning that regulate behavior)

Is a Cigar ever Just a Cigar? The Encrypted Meanings of Sexual Desire

If, as Freud suggested, we routinely disguise our wishes, feelings and anxieties, and express ourselves symbolically in waking life as much as in our dreams, then arriving at an accurate interpretation of desire is essential to cure. However, as soon as we reject a one-size-fits-all approach to meaning (and Freud certainly did), there is a problem as to how to determine what meaning among many is true for this particular patient at this particular time. As symptoms are over-determined, and as such, the result of many factors not simply one cause, there are bound to be a myriad of true interpretations of any particular behavior. Hence sexual desire is not, in itself, a sufficient explanation for behavior, anymore than its fulfillment or containment is a sufficient solution to the problem of how to live. I sit with a patient who is sexually frustrated in his marriage, contemplating leaving it, and ask him and myself time and again, "What does it all mean?"

Although they grew up in the Sixties, Steven and Sharon were virgins when they fell passionately in love in college and, as Steven tells it, they have been loving and faithful partners ever since. ("I couldn't hope for a more devoted wife and mother.") However, for the past four years, since she began her own therapy, Sharon has not wanted to have sex or even to cuddle with Steven on the couch. In explaining why, she vaguely alludes to a hitherto unexplored experience of sexual abuse as a child. Although Steven has tried to be sympathetic, loyal, and respectful, and to subdue his mounting frustration and impatience with his wife of three decades, as the months have turned into years and Sharon's prohibitions against sex have turned into prohibitions against their customary back rubs and casual hand-holding, he has become increasingly agitated and despairing and has described to me in confidence how he obsesses about sex and Sharon throughout the day. Something has to change, but what? In the marital counseling sessions Steven attends dutifully every other week with my colleague Susan, he maintains that he is fully committed to working things out. "I'm an optimist, maybe a little bullheaded," he says, "but I have never been known to give up on a person." However, in the privacy of my office, he expresses uncertainty as to whether he should seek fulfillment for his increasingly pressing need for intimacy and disentangle himself from a marriage that is sexually dissatisfying, or whether he should question the "need" (one that resembles a compulsion) and untangle the knotted desires within himself that make sex an all-consuming obsession and his wife's limitations feel so punishing and debilitating. "Am I too controlling, too dependent on her approval?"

Were I to sum up the psychological and existential questions that he wishes I would answer as he searches my eyes with a look of hunger and determination, they would sound something like this:

"If I want to be 'healthy,' should I be expecting more from my current wife or (life) or needing less? Should I take pride in my ability to delay gratification indefinitely, manage my needs on my own, and remain true to my marriage vows? Or should I be ashamed of my reluctance to pursue my desires, take risks with my life, and break free of the shackles that make me feel emasculated?" Some of these questions he has openly shared with me, others are implicit in his conversations with his wife and Susan. None of us, however, is able to answer them definitively, and his uncertainty about the deeper meaning of his experience is mirrored by Sharon's, mine, and Susan's.

I reproduce below an imaginary dialogue in which I free associate with Susan about my patient Steven's dilemma. An uninvited Rabbi (who could just as well be a minister or priest) is a disembodied voice echoing from the corner who interjects commentaries on our patient's experiences and choices. These serve as footnotes to the experimental narratives we spin out, and they reflect traditional religious values. Because we ourselves have not rejected these values, even though they are not explicitly a part of our therapeutic mission, they provide yet another perspective on the good enough life.)

Susan's Narrative (which defends an ethic of self-expression and fulfillment and suggests that "settling" is a product of insecurity, an obsessive personality, or existential guilt):

Not only haven't they had sex for four years but Sharon won't even let Steven take her hand in the movies without first asking her permission. She says that she feels pressured as soon as she senses that Steven wants anything of her, and that at fifty-two she is finally resisting her lifelong tendency to give in to his wishes. She's struggling to be completely honest about her feelings, but that ends up leaving Steven feeling painfully self-conscious about expressing his own – he's even afraid to say where he might like to go out for dinner. I see him holding himself back continually so as not to overwhelm Sharon, and the result is that he feels anxious and insecure and you've told me that he is constantly obsessing about sex. To me he looks like a little boy at the edge of a sand box, fidgeting but trying to be patient, as he waits for his mother to bring him a shovel so that he can jump in, get dirty, and play. What a straitjacket to have to wear! Of course the question I haven't asked him, because I'm supposed to be neutral, is why on earth he feels he has to live like this indefinitely, all bottled up? Nobody should have to live such a truncated life; his sensitivity may be very appealing but it undermines his freedom to choose.

Joyce's narrative (which locates the primary source of conflict within the individual and his personal history, and suggests that "settling" means negotiating a "reasonable" compromise between infantile desires and real life limitations):

Sharon's rigidities and sexual restrictions are pretty gruesome – I think I'd go nuts if I was always monitoring myself the way Steven does – but I suspect that they are just the most obvious, *external* sources of Steven's frustration and unhappiness, the tip of the iceberg. And I have to ask myself why Steven's sense of well-being hinges on

Sharon's responses to his sexual wishes. He has always looked like the strong one who needs nothing and gives limitlessly, but if he were really so secure and so independent, would her unwillingness to have sex or cuddle on the couch color his mood for the entire day? He looks to her to fill him up and, right now, for her own reasons, she refuses to do it. Now that Sharon is beginning to create a life for herself outside of Steven's orbit, she has knocked him off the pedestal which he apparently needed to feel worthwhile. It is this blow not the absence of sex in and of itself, that unsettles him. Steven's personal happiness *should* not depend so much on being loved and admired or being sexually attractive to Sharon. He has to focus more on himself and be more self-sufficient, not try to wedge himself back into the center of Sharon's world, or anyone else's, for that matter.

The Rabbi (defends the values of self-sacrifice and care):

Hey, wait a second, Steven is what I'd call a real *mensch*! He's the kind of guy who steps up to the plate and gives to the community, he's not always calculating what's in it for him. You women speak as if his selflessness and willingness to assume some responsibility for Sharon's happiness were a character flaw, something he needs to work out in therapy! He's human, so of course he is wavering, but give him the credit he is due.

Susan (responding to Joyce's unempathic, overly analytical injunction to delay gratification even longer and look inwards, she passes over the Rabbi's reproachful remarks):

I'm not saying that Sharon is the source of all of Steven's problems, and I'm not denying that he might have even played a role in her feeling overwhelmed – his protectiveness and sensitivity can be suffocating, I suppose. However, my question remains as to why Steven is so willing to deny himself what seem to me to be normal wishes. Why does he tolerate the starvation diet Sharon has put him on for an indefinite period of time, indeed maybe forever? Her needs have become everything and his are blotted out. And this happens to him time and again – he's the universal defender of the underdog, the one who takes care of all the fragile people who can't take care of themselves. Steven has become totally obsessed with sex because Sharon, along with everyone else, assumes that he has no needs or desires of his own. But he does. You seem to imply that Steven wants and needs too much, but I think he doesn't ask for enough. How long should he wait for her to soften? How much should he laboriously try to put himself in her shoes? How much should he be expected to compromise?

Joyce (persists in digging deeper in search of childhood sources and also passes over the Rabbi's ethical challenge):

I have no doubt that Sharon's refusal to be intimate would disappoint any man, and I feel badly for Steven that he feels he has to tip toe around in an effort to be understanding. But should he really be focusing all his attention on if and when Sharon will soften, if and when to leave the marriage? He should be figuring out why he feels so totally dependent on her emotional availability.

It looks like she is the problem but maybe he is too needy for anyone to satisfy – in which case he'll just re-invent the same kinds of problems he has with Sharon in any intimate relationship. You ask why he stays with her: Well, maybe on some level he knows that about himself. Her strict rules prevent him from feeling altogether out of control. Sharon and sex have been a kind of drug for Steven which he has relied on to feel worthwhile and alive. Therapy should be encouraging him to wean himself of his various addictions (his childhood fantasies and fixations), not encouraging him to find a new supplier, in the form of another idealizing relationship.

Susan (insists on returning to the here-and-now):

Steve hardly allows himself even to fantasize about what it would be like with another woman, and says that as long as he is in a committed relationship with Sharon he would never have an affair. He's likeable, attractive, and financially comfortable and knows that there are lots of women out there who would be only too happy to fill her place. But he's loyal and I think that loyalty is not only a virtue but his fatal flaw. His willingness to sacrifice and follow Sharon's regimen may be some sort of a repetition from early childhood; he may be trying to win the love of an overly critical or idealized mother or father figure. But whether that is the case or not, he should realize that right now, as an adult who gives a lot and has a lot to give, he deserves more than what Sharon can give him. I agree with the Rabbi; he really is quite a *mensch*, but that's why I wish he'd let himself be happier.

Joyce's compromise:

Steven is a wonderful and generous human being, and you know he is one of my favorite patients, so don't you think I want him to be happier too? The question is how?

The Rabbi (his parting questions which cannot be ignored):

What chance is there for happiness if we lose our enduring connections? What monsters would we become if we forgot our histories?

If we accept Susan's perspective, with all its implicit assumptions as our frame of meaning, the goal of therapy would be to help Steve realize that his emotional and sexual desires are legitimate, not "too much," and that he has the right to express his needs and seek their satisfaction. His feelings of deprivation are justifiable, given Sharon's behavior, and, moreover, it is not his ethical responsibility to restrain himself indefinitely in order to protect Sharon's fragile sense of herself. If it turns out that Sharon can't or won't respond to Steve's normal desires for sexual intimacy and emotional support, he should feel free to leave her and find someone else who is more able and willing to appreciate him for who he really is. That would be the healthiest and most dignified choice for him to make.

If, however, we accept Joyce's perspective, with all of its implicit assumptions, the goal of therapy would be defined somewhat differently. Within this frame of meaning, therapy should help Steve understand that his all consuming sexual dependency on Susan is symbolic and rooted in his early childhood relationships and internal conflicts; moreover, therapy should help him construct a more mature and more autonomous self that is stable and does not rely on other people's idealizing responses, sexual or otherwise, for a sense of his own value and vitality. Indeed, it is only after he has recognized and renounced all extravagant and childlike desires for unconditional love and continuous attunement that he will be capable of making a realistic choice as to whether or not he wishes to remain with Sharon, for better or for worse, sex or no sex.

Each narrative is compelling. Each provides us and the patient with a sense of coherence. Each orients the therapy towards a specific end. Since both stories, along with the Rabbi's commentaries, say something true about Steve and about human life in general, neither I nor my colleague nor Steve is willing to commit to one to the exclusion of the other. How then does the therapy proceed? What encrypted meaning do we unearth and examine in the next session, knowing that these perspectives are just two of a multitude?

By surrendering spurious claims to objectivity when it comes to values, and yet at the same time refusing to surrender to an ethic of "anything goes" as long as the system runs smoothly, the contemporary psychotherapist creates for himself a unique and paradoxical position. By providing a temporary space in which to explore for a finite period of time the symbolic dimensions of commonplace and idiosyncratic experience, the psychotherapist validates and nurtures his patients' desires to make meaning and live lives they consider worthwhile. But at the same time, he assumes the responsibility for disappointing their hopes for absolute certainty about how and when this is best achieved. (Since most therapeutic hours end without even an inkling of closure, the limits within the session are a mirror for the limits that exist outside.) Ambiguities and discontinuities are inevitable when hammering out a life that isn't the good life but that is, nevertheless, "good enough." Thus, just as the search for meaning is increasingly legitimized and integrated into the psychotherapeutic dialogue, meanings themselves increasingly appear as "free radicals," conditional and unstable.

The Good Enough Life: The Mirroring Anxieties of Settling and Not Settling

For a symbolizing creature, who, in the words of Ernest Becker, is "out of nature and hopelessly in it," the question of what constitutes a good life or even a good enough life goes beyond the narrow frame of pragmatism, which considers only what works for the individual, or evolutionary psychology, which considers only what is adaptive for the species as a whole (as if even that could be determined in some objective fashion). Indeed, the problem of how to live well can only be partially obscured by focusing exclusively on the possibilities of what we know we can do well if we squarely confront material reality and capitalize on opportunity. (The myth of Horatio Alger is emblematic of this ethic. The mere fact that he raised himself up by his bootstraps renders him a hero. What he did with himself is not the primary message of the story; that is insignificant compared with the fact that he did it. The virtue of self-improvement (making an effort, whatever the end result) is, moreover, implicit in contemporary American politics, as presidential candidates compete as to whose roots were more humble and whose obstacles to success were more insurmountable)

As middle age sets in, and with it the disappointment that comes from unmet expectations, the ideal of self-containment and the ideal of self-fulfillment alternately coincide and diverge. Each proves insufficient unto itself (and not solely because each is unattainable). In Erik Erikson's stage theory of psycho-social development, middle age and beyond is a time for extending beyond the self, for forging connections to the next generation, and for generating extra-personal forms of meaning. Without a capacity for "generativity" we are destined to fall prey to despair. Thus naturally we ask ourselves, self-containment at what sacrifice? Self-fulfillment for what purpose?

Reductive answers that assume the primacy of instinctual over spiritual cravings, individualistic over interpersonal goals, or biochemical facts over diffuse subjective yearnings are alluring but ultimately fail to satisfy us. To be sure, the parameters of the good enough life would be less ambiguous and we might feel less anxious if our desires were so circumscribed, so utilitarian – if only unconscious guilt or serotonin uptake was the sole source of neurotic suffering; if only stabilizing our moods was our exclusive concern! But the proliferation of myriad addictions and compulsions – related to work, exercise, sex, drugs, television, food, success – suggests that we are not so easily sated. To the contrary, as we write our social, economic and political histories of the twentieth century, we may conclude that "the more we ate, the hungrier we grew" (Henry Weinfield, *Without Mythologies*).

Except for the most die-hard Freudians, psychologists today do not speak of human desire as something that exists independently of a social context, or interpret spiritual yearnings, political activism, or the capacity for empathic responsiveness as nothing other than ingenious defenses against libidinal or aggressive drives. Thanks to post-modern skepticism, we have lost some of our glibness, along with our faith in who we are and what we know. (In his book *Open Minded,* Jonathan Lear argues that the early Freud believed he could explain the irrational in rational terms. As long as the pleasure principle prevailed, then even the most mysterious of behaviors had a logic behind them which only needed to be deciphered. However, with the death instinct and the repetition compulsion this reductive tendency had to change. Neither the drive to self-destruct (Thanatos) nor the drive towards ever more complexity (Eros) could be accommodated within the classic psychoanalytic frame or any other existing frame for that matter. And so, more than one hundred years after Freud began his "archeological" excavations of the mind, we are left more enlightened but less certain about the significance of what has been uncovered.)

Indeed, now that feminism has entered the cultural mainstream, the traditional "feminine" perspective – a perspective that has been both idealized and devalued throughout history – has been incorporated into contemporary images of the "healthy" human being and the well-balanced life. (The ideal husband and father can no longer get away with being just a "good provider," any more than the ideal woman can get away with living vicariously through a husband or children.) The individual's desire for intimacy and validation, connection and mutual self-sacrifice is no longer automatically assumed to be more or less authentic or more or less developmentally sophisticated than his desire to reach his earning potential or a sexual climax, or to win the Nobel prize.

Carol Gilligan's critique of traditional models of social development, that equate maturity with individuation, was part of a broader challenge within the field of academic psychology to what has been described as a "masculine bias." Analogously, infant researcher Daniel Stern argued that, contrary to Mahler's original formulation of attachment and separation, normal development includes a heightening recognition and responsivity to the Other that parallels a heightening recognition and differentiation of the self. Thirty years ago, when I was in graduate school, this opening up to new perspectives of what is healthy and normal and what is not seemed revolutionary. But whether we believe, as some psychologists do, that all our desires are "hard-wired" or believe as others do that, unbeknownst to ourselves, we are socially constructed, it may not matter in the end if, as others would argue, human desire is an expression of a fundamental lack and is, therefore, impossible to gratify!

As essentialist assumptions about gender identity, not to mention human "nature," are increasingly challenged (from every corner we are encouraged not only to improve ourselves but to make ourselves over entirely), universal existential conundrums may turn out to be the only bedrock of truth to fall back upon. But certainly, there is no possibility of settling in there. We exchange the instability of limitless possibilities offered by consumer culture for the sobering realization that we are limited by our mortality and our embeddedness in the world. Paradoxically, at a time when scientists are mapping the human genome, increasingly confident of their ability to identify, isolate, and eventually control the individual proteins responsible for how we think and feel and how our lives unfold, psychologists, philosophers, and social scientists, increasingly uncertain of the boundaries of psycho-analysis and psychometrics, are arguing that the individual mind may be less a discoverable reality than an inter-subjective construction that is constantly being re-configured.

If there is no such place as an "isolated mind," no such thing as a baby without a mother, and no perspective that is objective or free of unconscious transferences, then the ways in which our lives unfold are as much an expression of how we think about feelings, feel about thinking, and who we do it with as a reflection of determinate characteristics, genetic, biochemical, or intra-psychic. Self psychologists George Atwood and Robert Stolorow speak of the "myth of the isolated mind" and challenge the boundaries that have been presumed to exist between the self and other. They argue that one person's subjectivity is of necessity informed by their experience of others' subjectivities and that this interpenetration is not pathological but normal. But what then is *not* normal, I ask myself when I see a patient disintegrate and then explode with rage when his much admired supervisor ignores him or hands him a mediocre evaluation. Psychoanalyst and pediatrician D.W. Winnicott is famous for saying that there is no baby without a mother, meaning that it is impossible to speak of the internal life of a child without acknowledging the ground in which it is nurtured. But what about an adult? What kind of boundaries can we expect to hold us secure? How much outside life can we and should we allow inside?

But as we flirt with various paradigms, and experiment with thinking of the self as either infinitely malleable (imaginatively, surgically, and biochemically) or more fixed than we are consciously aware, we search for fresh metaphors to satisfy our desire to create meaningful lives that are neither disposable nor preordained. We need to find a way to settle into one life, even if it is partial and our commitment is conditional, without feeling that we have sacrificed too much and just settled for something less than we should.

Engagement and Detachment: Which is the Cure and which the Disease?

> "Is success satisfying your desire or escaping from it?"
> Adam Phillips, *On Flirtation* (1996)

When people come to psychotherapy they bring with them a myriad number of unarticulated prejudices and expectations concerning the goals of treatment and the process of change and this applies to therapist and patient alike. In light of the contradictory models of self-improvement that coexist within the culture, the notion that psychotherapy can be value-free is as preposterous as the idea that a therapist can leave his or her personality at the door and serve as a blank screen upon which a patient projects his fantasies. So, although almost everybody hopes to become happier and maybe also less "crazy," some expect to accomplish this dual purpose by modifying an internal world which may include enduring personality characteristics, self-limiting beliefs, and unruly emotions, while others expect to develop more effective strategies to alter aspects of the external world that are unduly limiting and thwart their desires. Thus, there are those who expect to find amelioration of suffering through the expression of "strangulated" feelings and the fulfillment of ungratified wishes, ("I *shouldn't* feel guilty doing something just for myself, like going to the gym once a week after work, or cutting short a conversation with a friend, but I do"), and others who expect to find it through their secure containment and ultimate transformation ("I hate myself for being so needy – I'm a real wimp. I *shouldn't* look forward so much to when Jim calls me or be so disappointed if he has to work on Christmas and New Years.")

Today, as uncertain of the value of spontaneous self-expression as they are uncertain of the value of rational self-restraint, people oscillate between the one response to their desires and disappointments and the other. Lacking confidence in the virtue of either solution, they feel tethered to the ancient pendulum that swings back and forth between two imaginary worlds: the world of limitless possibility, which challenges them to expand their horizons and gobble up new experiences, and its mirror image, the world of inviolable limits (the world of our forefathers), which promises to protect them from their insatiable appetite for illusory pleasures. Within the one sphere they feel compelled to pursue an ideal of self-expansion/self-actualization that includes an unbridled search for more and better experiences and opportunities; within the other, they feel compelled to pursue an ideal of stoical self-sufficiency that includes an unbridled quest for more and better control over the undigested, unassimilated experiences inside.

Depending upon whether or not a patient's conscious and unconscious agendas match up roughly with the therapist's, he will either drop out of therapy after a couple of sessions or return for an indefinite period of time. (Despite the dreams or admonitions of managed health care "cure" is an ambiguous term that has dropped from the vocabulary of most therapists, except as an ironic reference to the naiveté of the past.)

Ironically, a fixed commitment to either solution sows the seeds of new problems. When the natural dialectic between desire and limitation is aborted, the result is a vague experience of incompleteness and loss, which then creates the conditions for what Freud referred to as the "return of the repressed." The ideal of total containment and detachment transmogrifies into the desire for unlimited freedom and gratification, and vice versa; and though they appear as polar opposites, psychologically they are equivalent, as each represents an all-consuming striving for the unattainable – for life beyond the body. Since either grand solution to the problem of human desire generates feelings of emptiness and insatiability, guilt for wanting so much and shame for never feeling full enough, the self-fulfilling prophecy that justifies each moral universe simultaneously threatens to destroy it from within.

But just as people bring different prejudices and expectations to therapy, so too, in the contemporary world, therapists bring their own very different therapeutic paradigms into play. A strict Freudian, for example, will have a very different understanding of how reality impinges upon a person's desires than an existential psychotherapist. A family systems theorist will be sensitive to different kinds of inter-personal dynamics than a self psychologist whose focus is largely intra-psychic. Living amidst a multitude of contradictory therapeutic paradigms, subsisting on a scant diet of only a few remaining "universals," the psychotherapist no less than his clients finds himself caught between competing narratives of the healthy person and the ideal of human potential, wondering how to choose among them without over-simplifying and shutting off possibilities. Should we encourage our patients to push against the limits and aspire to greatness of one form or another despite the risk? Should we oscillate perpetually between mutually exclusive ideals which inspire but also disappoint? Or should we try to dispense with idealizations of any kind, knowing that attempts to do so may leave us vulnerable to feelings of discontinuity, confusion, and insignificance? "Normal adjustment" may be too mundane a goal to settle for; it seems almost un-American. Which is the better way to live? Which is the better way for a psychotherapist to practice?

Experiments in Meaning and in the Meaning of Psychotherapy

> ". . . what we do may be only provisional. But that is all right. In the terrifying time in which we live and create, eternity is not our immediate concern."
> Yehuda Yerushalmi, *Zakhor. Jewish history and Jewish memory* (2005, p.103)

The meaning of the "good-enough" life is inevitably unclear now that our faith in the transcendental or the absolute is qualified by our (qualified) faith in the sciences (hard and soft) and our own personal explorations within the World Wide Web. Should it be surprising, then, that the meaning of the "good enough" therapy is equally unclear? Family systems theory, self psychology, and cognitive behavioral therapy (to name just a few), compete with classic psychoanalysis, Gestalt-type therapies, and psychopharmacology for our allegiance and our dollars.

Explicitly eschewing slippery questions of value does not eliminate the implicit moral imperatives that are enacted in the psychotherapeutic encounter itself. If psychotherapy has something to do with finding, restoring, consolidating, and identifying what we call a self, then the therapist's own subjectivity must not be overly obtrusive. And yet, shouldn't her perspective on the good enough life somehow be acknowledged? Must I offer my patients, who are trying to figure out how to be safely intimate, nothing but a mirror?

No family photos, no political debates, no reproaches for moral lapses, but . . . Where do we draw the line between woodenness and professionalism, between personal care and a personal relationship, between respectful discretion and hypocritical hiddenness?

The contradictory idealizations that coexist unharmoniously within our culture and within each of our individual psyches are mirrored in the ongoing controversies within the profession concerning the nature of the therapeutic process itself. One treatment approach emphasizes insight, autonomy, and adaptation to reality; another speaks of empathy, mutuality, and narrative cohesiveness; and yet another suggests that an amalgam of corrective emotional experience and cognitive restructuring provides the tools with which people can construct a better life. In any case, there are always moral as well as pragmatic considerations that define the nature of pathology and the method of cure.

So, for example, because Freud was convinced that patients idealize their therapists for the same defensive reasons that primitive peoples create idols or worship totems, he warned against the power and the dangers of transference love. Patients may press for direction and support from their analysts but, as long as gratification is believed to encourage rather than cure their regressive and illusory relationship to reality, it is to be resisted on ethical as well as on pragmatic grounds. Patients may take a "flight into health" in covert compliance with the presumed desires of their analysts, but since such "transference cures" by definition fail to cure them of their self-serving illusions, they are no "cure" for the "disease" Freud believes that they are suffering from!

If the classically trained analyst aspires to neutrality on principle, and on principle offers his patients neither gratification for their wishes nor reassurance for their anxieties, it is also on principle that other therapists (including many contemporary psychoanalysts) offer themselves as "mirrors," "containers," or even models ("auxiliary superegos") in the hope that they can gratify their patients' frustrated needs for mirroring, containment, and idealization. And so, as patients puzzle over what the proper limits of their desires should be and over the value of attempting to gratify their unmet childhood needs in their adult lives, therapists argue in parallel fashion about the proper limits they should place on their desires to influence and the parameters of their talking cures.

As a psychotherapist, my loyalty is perhaps even more divided than that of my patients, all the more so as during one hour

I listen closely to this person's timid questions and guilty confessions, and during the next to that person's bitter memories and uncompromising judgments, all the while listening with my "third ear" to a cacophony of voices representing diverse theoretical perspectives on the "optimal" way for a hypothetical therapist to respond to a hypothetical client living in a hypothetical world.

I allude to Theodor Reik's classic, *Listening with the Third Ear.* But more recently, psychoanalysts have referred to the "analytic third" as the felt presence of the professional community within the therapeutic relationship. The implication is that the dialogue between the therapist and patient always includes this Other, which is how this relationship is different from all other one-on-one relationships.

So, I ask myself, how can I respond consistently when client #1 seems shrunken and ravenous from demanding too little of the world outside, and client #2 seems shrunken and ravenous from demanding too much? Ever aware of my own prejudices (having grown up with a timid, self-effacing mother and a bitterly defiant father), I am dizzied by the interpretive possibilities!

Sometimes I hear a patient's story as the fragment of a coherent "narrative construction," which I do my best to empathize with, but which I believe could and maybe even should be modified through the process of mutual recognition and open dialogue. After all, as certain theorists have argued, the experience of a sense of self, which is essential to my understanding of what it means to be healthy, depends on the recognition from the Other as well as on recognition of the Other's subjectivity. At other times, however, I respond to an autobiographical account as if it were an ancient hieroglyphic relic, which needs to be dated, catalogued, and interpreted. On these occasions, it would be both naive and presumptuous of me to empathize or express any of my personal responses – a therapist is neither a substitute friend, a human rights attorney, or a surrogate parent, and, moreover, neither I nor my patient may be grasping the real significance of what is being said.

Looking across the room through my classic psychoanalytic lens, I see transferential fears and wishes; I detect hidden meanings when my patient complains repeatedly of feeling trapped by his wife or by life's circumstances; and when he says he is overcommitted, and yet refuses to slow down, I privately search my memory for relevant childhood antecedents he has hinted at in previous sessions, with an eye to their repetitions and his reaction formations. But just as I am ready to offer an interpretation that understands his present dilemma as a compensation for or projection of the real or imagined past, my social psychological conscience reminds me of the influences of present-day external "reality," and of the forces outside the individual (workplace expectations, family demands) that actually impinge upon his freedom to act in his own best interests. When the search for intra-psychic determinants of emotional distress prevents us from identifying significant interpersonal or situational influences, it becomes the equivalent of "blaming the victim." It is a blurry line, but it needs to be drawn, nonetheless, between holding an individual responsible for his behavior and his choices, and implying that he is guilty for whatever unhappy circumstances he finds himself in. In Freud's early topological model, it is in the deepest layer of the psyche – the Unconscious – where our latent wishes and fantasies reside. The analyst as archeologist digs beneath the surface to uncover the truth that is obscured by rationalizations and other forms of defense. Hence, the deepest interpretation is the one that extends back to the most primitive drives and associated anxieties, which are presumed to be the origin of present-day experience and behavior.

My loyalties are divided. Freud prompts me to work hard and never settle for the obvious, but before "blaming the victim" and sacrificing the interpersonal dimension at the altar of the intra-psychic one, I hesitate. The "deepest" interpretation – that is, the one that is farthest removed from conscious experience and that is held in highest regard by classical analysts – may not always be the truest or the best.

And when I find myself speculating about the influence of a "family system" on an individual's behavior, my watchful companions in relational theory remind me that it is the internalized family – the family inside a person's head – that *really* matters, not any actual family that existed or continues to exist today. I proceed cautiously, heeding their warnings.

No doubt, because of my own personal history, an attitude of quiet resignation on the part of the patient is more likely to make me feel anxious and impatient than an expression of righteous indignation. The former appears unnecessarily despairing to me (my mother was too passive!), while the latter seems like a normal response to a perceived injustice. Since I am aware that my soft-spoken colleague in the neighboring office might not have the same experience as I do or make the same judgment about what is *too* passive, the best – that is, the most therapeutic – way to respond is far from self-evident. And while there is always a danger of over-identifying with a patient's anger or despair in response to identifiable disappointment, and as a consequence misunderstanding its personal meaning to him in his life, there is also a danger in assuming an emotionally distanced posture – the bird's eye view. The interpersonal psychiatrist, Harry Stack Sullivan quotes Saint Augustine's famous adage, "Nothing human is alien to me," arguing that psychotherapists must make a conscious effort to integrate this understanding into their practice.

Some would argue that a psychotherapist should always suspend his or her subjectivity as best she can. By clearing a space she creates a "holding environment" that allows her patient to finally discover and express *his* subjectivity freely and in an unadulterated form. Others would argue, however, that there is no such thing as unadulterated subjectivity, and that the psychotherapeutic ideal of "the isolated mind" is but a myth to be exploded. According to this perspective, a psychotherapist should not aspire to be without qualities or, for that matter, to be unaffected by those of her patients. Indeed, as she introduces him to alternative perceptions of himself, his life circumstances, as well as to all sorts of unpredictable experiences that fall under the rubric of otherness (an interpretation of unconscious motives, a contextualization of a personal dilemma, or the therapist's authentic reaction expressed in words or a facial expression) she should, above all, be comfortable acknowledging her own humanity, insufficiencies and all.

Thus, from the standpoint of one approach to therapy, the therapist's presence as a person unto herself contaminates the process of self-discovery, and from that of another it is an essential element in a collaborative experiment with ambiguous meanings; the "uncontaminated" self resides only in a world of fantasy. If I am inconsistent, though not unself-conscious, in my therapeutic outlook, and my responses and techniques vary unpredictably, if not unself-consciously from hour to hour, should I be ashamed of myself? Certainly the "anything goes" attitude will not work for psychotherapy, but, just as certainly, there are no hard and fast rules about what does "go" and when.

None of the perspectives – neither those of my patients nor of my phantom colleagues – should be excluded from the conversation that continues, long past the originating hour, inside my head. But though I think "multi-culturally" (in the sense that I think about my patients and myself in several different "languages"), I find that it is as much a source of relief as it is a source of frustration that at any given moment, I am obliged to speak with only one voice, an idiosyncratic amalgam that is just my own.

Thus this blend of relief and frustration, this process of learning to live with "split screens" before ordering them, if only temporarily and with reservations, into one kaleidoscopic mix, is the compromise I have struck with myself and, when all is said and done, the only honest piece of advice I can offer my patients. Like the famous Gestalt figure that one moment resembles two women in profile facing one another, and the next a Grecian urn, every life looks different as different relationships are foregrounded. Without changing a single "fact," meanings metamorphose into other meanings and hierarchies of value topple and reconfigure themselves. Unless we consciously fix our gaze either on the two women or the urn, we naturally oscillate between the mutually exclusive but equally real perceptions. Developing the ability to tolerate this naturally recurring reconfiguration of meaning is an alternative to the post-modernist illusion that nothing is real, that we can perform anything, and that an interesting, de-formative performance is the best we can hope for. Thus, the problem of how to live the good life (and how to do good therapy), is transformed into the problem of how to create a "good enough" life (and a "good enough" therapeutic space) out of the materials we have.

A Great and Noble Life . . .

"To endure ambiguity and to make light shine through it" is a quotation from a Jewish High Holiday service I recently attended. As the message is itself ambiguous, it offers believers and skeptics a moral agenda compatible with our age of relativism. "To stand fast in uncertainty, to prove capable of unlimited love and hope" (which is how the prayer continues) prompts each one of us to make judgments, and yet at the same time to leave open the possibility for revising our life narratives, reversing our trajectories, and negotiating with disappointment. Ambiguities and uncertainties should be acknowledged and not rationalized away, forgiven but not forgotten, and yet we should never waver in our efforts to create beauty and find clarity even if the fog will invariably roll in time and again.

When psychotherapy is conceived as a laboratory of meaning rather than a cure for "neurotic misery," an aphrodisiac for the psyche, or a guide to an earthly paradise, it forces us to temper our appetite for polarizing idealizations that simplify life choices but deny us our possibilities, our limitations, and our contradictions. Ironically, as our desire to live purposefully and to express all of our human capabilities is both encouraged and disappointed, the psychotherapeutic encounter serves as a perfect microcosm for life.

Since every psychotherapy session brings to light unarticulated assumptions about the nature of desire and its proper limits, I shall begin my "experiments in meaning" with a young man who aspires to the selflessness of Mother Teresa and finds himself "mindlessly" crunching numbers as an artist-turned-web-page-designer in a small midwestern town.

DESIRE AND LIMITATION

"I saw a woman standing in a darkened door, and she cried out to me, "Hey, why not ask for more?" Then a young man leaning on a wooden crutch, he whispered to me, "Hey why ask for so much?"
(Leonard Cohen, "Bird on a Wire")

The Heroics of Self-Restraint

It's a frigid thirty degrees outside, which is not unusual for mid-November in South Bend, but Kevin is wearing just a thin, worn-out, corduroy jacket when he arrives ten minutes late for our regular lunch-time appointment. Since he is customarily late, I have come to expect and enjoy the extra few minutes he gives me between clients. But I know that the "gift" is not a gift at all, for there is a price to pay. If I don't understand and then don't try to help him understand why he is routinely late and why routinely he feels he has to apologize for being so "distractable," my pleasure will turn to guilt, and then I would be no better off than he.

"You're a closet revolutionary," I think with affection that I hesitate to reveal, "or like those Catholic missionary workers you read about in the *Catholic Worker*, whose hands are roughened by honest labor, and who can't spare the time or money it would take to protect themselves against the elements. You are only impersonating an "attentionally deficient" graphic designer who is incapable of getting to a regular appointment on time, focusing on a computer screen, or creating art-for-profit according to some faceless monad's marketing schedule." After weeks of asking mostly neutral questions and deliberately keeping my personality out of our conversations, I want to take some risks, maybe in the form of a tease, though I am more than half serious. As he proceeds to mumble something about last minute snafus with an overnight Federal Express delivery, a meeting that went on interminably, or unusual traffic, I hear the strains of another voice, the imperious voice of Kevin's conscience, which admonishes us that the minute hand on the office clock, the inclement weather, and the prevailing fashion conventions *should* not exert any noticeable influence on his and maybe even my behavior. Which voice should I be addressing now that Kevin is fumbling with his buttons and has leap-frogged onto an apparently unrelated topic? Which one among the several different voices will be ready and willing to be drawn into a meaningful (but not always so rational) dialogue?

Meanwhile, I shiver for Kevin inside, noting that his ears are bright red, his neck is bare, and his hands are chapped. And yet, my concern for this incorrigibly impractical young man who, in all likelihood, could not only get to my office on time but could also afford a warmer winter coat, is mixed with irritation and curiosity, amusement and admiration, as I imagine the gossip at his office and his time-sensitive colleagues' raised eyebrows. I try to follow the train of his associations, which take us from his being late to his feeling alienated from office politics, but I am also wondering whether, fifty minutes from now I will give into my temptation to run over and be a few minutes late for my next session in order to give him back what he unconsciously gave to me. Does he expect me to return what I experienced as the unsought-after "gift" of time because after all we both realize he needs the lost minutes more than I do? Would he think more or less of me, of himself, and of our work together if I broke my rules and did?

Kevin knows that his impractical reflectiveness, his quiet but prickly social analyses, and his less than enthusiastic involvement in the proliferation of computer art, sex, and football irritate and confuse his cohorts at work, just as he knows that his endless theological queries set his parish priest's teeth on edge. I can well imagine his office mates humourously needling him to "lighten up!" and join them at the local happy hour. "Why do you have to take everything so seriously?" must be the response this intense young man receives on a regular basis from his peers, if not yet from me. Even at church, he is too dark, he tells me. "Kevin, where's your faith? Let the light of the heavenly host fill up your heart."

But Kevin hasn't yet decided what to make of his failure to meld with the culture of the Internet or follow the traditional rituals of Sunday Mass, which is what prompted him, an ascetically-inclined religious Catholic, to indulge at least one of his appetites – his appetite for grueling introspection – with a psychotherapist who, from her appearance and office decor, clearly does not share his feverish other-worldliness. Maybe he's hoping that the culture of psychology has something fresh to offer. The "forbidden apple," I think, as he smiles at me impishly and circles around nervously for fifty minutes after arriving ten minutes late for our session.

Unable to accept the terms of his current life with equanimity, to join the fold (any fold), and defer to the greater wisdom of his elders (his father is painfully stoical except when he drinks, his priest is empathic but passive to the point of inertia, and his supervisor at work is far too pragmatic to be imaginative), he wonders, should he? If he always aspires to get more out of life, as he bears witness to the pain of having too little, where would this ultimately lead?

What would it mean to be a "real" artist without a steady income or an established audience, who at the age of forty may still be scraping together his rent money by working the evening shift at Barnes and Noble? Or if he were to work as a missionary in the tradition of Mother Teresa, abandoning family and friends, home, and the twenty-first century's version of multi-culturalism to minister to malnourished and illiterate children from an alien culture? Do his passions inspire him to act selflessly and heroically, seduce him into pursuing a dream of transformation that he will never attain, or facilitate an anxious flight from a competitive world in which he feels guilty when he isn't feeling inadequate?

At the crossroads of tradition, New Age, and post-modernism, Kevin, twenty-three years old, depressed, and uncertain about what sort of life is worthy of his emotional investment, asks himself if he suffers from insecurity, grandiosity, or from the courage of his convictions; from an underprivileged childhood or from a chemical imbalance? If he is not interested in the latest electronic design products, and recoils from the predictable conversations around the bar at "happy hour" or the health club Saturday mornings, is this because he is unconsciously self-destructive, hopelessly romantic, or sexually inhibited (thanks to his Catholic upbringing and gloomy father), or because his desires are more spiritual and less prosaic than the average person's, and (thanks to his Catholic upbringing and gloomy father) because he is not willing to strike a bargain with his soul?

There are many possible interpretations of Kevin's unhappiness, and all have a ring of truth. Hence, his (and now my) confusion as to what is of value in life: what appetites are worth trying to satisfy, what frustrations are worth struggling to endure, and what he should do next.

Competing Narratives of Appetite

> "It is appetite that makes things edible."
> Adam Phillips, *The Beast in the Nursery* (1998)

According to Greek mythology, Zeus, the father of the gods, jealously denies humanity access to fire for fear that man's creative impulses might pose a threat to his own power. But then Prometheus, a titan, sympathetic to man's desire to rise above the level of the beasts, defies Zeus' stern decree and steals for us the fire that was beyond our grasp. In fury, Zeus chains him to a rock where a vulture comes to devour his liver which each day grows back, prolonging his torment indefinitely. Prometheus remains unrepentant, however, and, most significantly, is ultimately vindicated. Unbound by Heracles, he is forever memorialized by the poets as "man's benefactor."

In the book of Genesis, Adam and Eve also disregard God's injunction when she eats of the fruit from the Tree of Knowledge. Not unlike Prometheus, they refuse to accept the limitations imposed on their desires. But whereas the Greek myth of Prometheus tends to be interpreted as an allegory of courage, creativity, and idealism, the story of Adam's and Eve's transgression is most frequently interpreted as an allegory of prideful greed, weakness, and seduction; imagination and desire have led them astray, and as Adam and Eve venture out into the world beyond the garden, they are ashamed and humbled and bear no trace of the heroic spirit.

Icarus' abortive flight and Oedipus' incestuous marriage are two other classic tales of appetite gone amok, stories in which the innocent (if prideful) breach of boundaries leads to tragic outcomes. But even within the myth of Prometheus the desire for access to the Forbidden (which is also the powerful and the sublime) leads to problems, and what was an heroic gesture for the Titan, reappears as an amusing but ultimately self-destructive adolescent rebellion when cast in human form. Ironically, it is Pandora, the "all gifted," who robs humanity of its equanimity. At birth she was blessed with every talent and virtue a child could wish for, which is perhaps why she could not imagine the necessity of curbing her appetite as an adult! Sent by Zeus to spoil the happiness Prometheus bestowed on mankind with his gift of fire, she is, by design, too inquisitive, too voracious, or within the language of psychology, too narcissistic and full of a sense of entitlement. By failing to heed the admonitions of her well-tempered husband Epimetheus, she opens the single box forbidden her, and like Eve, ushers misery into the world. Thus, "giftedness" is no gift at all but turns upon itself, Zeus is avenged for Prometheus' defiance, and mankind is collectively punished for its grandiose dreams.

Of course there are other interpretations to the myth of Pandora as well as to the Biblical story of Adam and Eve eating the apple. Without the transgressions there would be no suffering, but there would also be no self-consciousness, and we wouldn't be fully human. Yeats has a poem in which he poignantly alludes to the grandiose dreams of beggars; his tone, as I read it, is not one of condemnation but of profound empathy

Positioning ourselves in relation to our frustrated desires is perhaps the central human problem in constructing a life or a moral philosophy. And whether it is for moral or for pragmatic reasons, most religious and philosophical traditions caution us against pursuing our dreams or gratifying our appetites. Indeed, the implicit message that reverberates from every corner is that we should recognize our blindness and exercise restraint – in other words, that we should staunch rather than heed our inchoate, idiosyncratic, internal promptings.

Such a message is antithetical, however, to the thrust of contemporary psychology, particularly the version disseminated in the popular culture, which celebrates the spontaneous and challenges the impossible, which invites us to question the legitimacy of received authority and to pry open the boxes that our ancestral patriarchs have marked forbidden. Indeed, self-exploration and self-expansion have become psychological imperatives that orient us to a particular model of mental health, one that emphasizes authenticity over self-restraint and encourages us to divulge our darkest secrets so that we can be "all that we can be" and accept all that we are, as if what that actually means were fixed and self-evident.

Given these competing perspectives on desire, desire as creative inspiration and desire as blinding temptation, how are we to discriminate between "good" impulses, those we should trust as animals trust their instincts, and "bad" ones, those we should be wary of lest we allow ourselves to be seduced, degraded, and dehumanized? Promethean heroics of the kind that Kevin dreams of but has not permitted himself to act upon overtly can be interpreted as a reflection of healthy ambition, naive idealism, or unresolved narcissism; his desire for more recognition and more happiness may be life-affirming or self-consuming, it may catalyze latent potentialities or foment a destructive form of disquietude. How do we know which perspective to take? How could Kevin?

Post-modernist skepticism and the politics of multi-culturalism do not eliminate the hunger for authoritative and enduring answers to our existential conflicts between what is false and what is true. And so self-help programs, alternative therapies, and inspirational literature proliferate, reflecting but also creating an ever-expanding appetite for "meaning." Paradoxically, as the best sellers come and go, and no single solution proves itself worthy of an exclusive, long-term commitment, hope, feeding on a surfeit of disillusionment, continues to spring eternal.

Modest in his demands for physical comfort or personal recognition (to the point at which I feel tempted to say "Kevin stretch out your legs, raise your voice, and at least for the remaining fifty minutes make yourself comfortable"), Kevin sees little that he shares in common with the fast-paced, fashion-driven culture of the dot-com marketplace. But like those of his office-mates, who congregate at the Sports Bar after hours to compare design portfolios, stock options, and women's chest-sizes, Kevin's hopes are simultaneously quashed and regenerated by a vision of endless possibilities rather than a commitment to any one. In fantasy he will check everything out, including the benefits of monk-like abstinence and psychotherapy, and since he is hesitant to settle for second best or for less than what may be possible, he runs the risk of being as fickle as the celebrity mongers he abhors, unable to commit himself fully to any one person or vocation.

The Heroics of Instability

The paradox that Kevin brought to our sessions was that he felt both paralyzed and liberated by his own unsettledness, his apparent inability to carve a niche for himself in the world. His idealism was inspiring, but his nagging wish to transcend the prosaic concerns of the "here and now" was also dispiriting and alienating to him. Moreover, he suspected that there was something fundamentally contradictory about his aspiring to feel "holier than thou." Wasn't he applauding himself for his efforts to deny himself applause? Consequently, he vacillated between the heroics of Prometheus and his presumptuousness and the heroics of Christian missionaries and their humility: he always wanted more passion and more purpose, only to insist that less was more sublime and not just good enough.

These were the contradictions that Kevin brought to our sessions, contradictions that, initially, I was given hints of only indirectly through his lateness, his chapped hands, and his ability to seduce me into extending the session as he lingered at my door with a twinkle in his eye. So while Kevin sacrificed his lunch hour so that he could talk freely about himself to a stranger, and possibly a godless one at that, he was not about to sign on to the value system implicit in psychotherapy (which includes the values of self-exposure, self-acceptance, and individual striving for personal happiness); not any more than he was about to exchange his holey (holy) Salvation Army winter jacket for one without holes (or holiness) from Nordstrom's or Macy's. Indeed, he attended psychotherapy in the same fashion as he did Catholic mass and company gatherings at the local bar – regularly, but not every week and not within the specified time frame.

It took several months for us to decipher Kevin's secret codes of honor, but in the process of playing hide and seek with him I experienced in living color how intractable and ingenious the "psychopathology of everyday life" can be. The Science Section of *The New York Times* may insinuate that Freudian-based therapies are "passé," an embarrassing part of our Victorian great grandparents' pre-scientific heritage, but I would argue that the parapraxes that Freud paid homage to a hundred odd years ago (which include lateness, slips of tongue or pen, and assorted kinds of forgetting) only go by different names. Kevin may find support for his claims that he is late because of "poor time management," or an undiagnosed case of Attention Deficit Disorder, but whenever he arrives for our sessions ten minutes past the appointed hour, and then dawdles getting out the door fifty minutes later, I see him re-enacting his uneasy relationship to commitment of any form, which, if I am to be honest with myself, forces me to re-examine my own incompletely analyzed commitments. Indeed, his "acting out" stimulates my own inclination to bend the rules that I inherited from my psychoanalytic ancestors, and to resist giving into that inclination. This was another element in the "gift" that Kevin entrusted to me – a private staging of forbidden desires. Indeed, his tentativeness in making a commitment to what we were doing together, his challenging the limits of desire and its fulfillment, gave us a point of entry into the very heart of his life's dilemma and the dilemma we all face in one form or another. This can be summed up as the question "How much should I commit myself to the "pursuit of happiness," and how do I best respond to the personal and extra-personal obstacles I encounter along the way?"

Fifteen minutes into that cold November session, we see how this question can play itself out. In an effort to compensate for his less-than-faithful commitment to our appointed hour, and commit himself to something (to me and to the psychotherapeutic scriptures he skims surreptitiously at Barnes and Noble), Kevin offered to exchange his morally laden language of self-reproach, self-effacement, and self-purification, into a morally "neutral" language of psychological disorder. "Do you think I'm ADD or that I *have* Depression? Could I be Bi-Polar?" he asked, as he fastened upon one diagnosis and then another, all of which sounded clinically "correct" and cast him as an innocent sufferer of some psychiatric condition rather than as a guilty sinner. Kevin is not alone, however, in his eagerness to label himself according to the popular clinical terminology. Attention Deficit Disorder, which tends to be referred to by its shorthand abbreviation, ADD, is often used as an explanation rather than a description of symptoms, and depression is spoken of as a "thing" as in "I have depression" or "maybe it's my depression."

But whether I detected a trace of irony in Kevin's eagerness to be "objective" and solve his case scientifically, or was projecting my own sense of irony at the mass produced, inconclusive evidence that he dutifully supplied me, I refused to be pulled into the labeling maelstrom. As much as Kevin pressured me for a definition that might enable him to settle into a single life as a "recovering . . . " he seemed as relieved as he was frustrated when I stubbornly resisted his invitations. (The same applies to the psychiatrist I referred him to at his request, who rattled off a string of numbers from the DSM IV but waffled about the benefits of medication.) This office was not a "chat room" for Vacillators Anonymous any more than it was a confessional; he was not paying me to substitute generic forms of psychological disorder for original sin, or to enable him to surrender his volition under the aegis of his new-found faith in the authority of psychology.

No psychiatric label, no popular or sophisticated psychobabble could do justice to the variegated meanings he attached to his particular forms of mindlessness, his repudiation of his desires for comfort and success, his alienation from his peers. Even the most perfect classification ("I'm reading this new book and I have all of the symptoms") could not help him answer the question of whether there was greater value in a refusal or in a willingness to submit (or commit), be it to God, to his own father, to the culture of the workplace, or to his sexual and acquisitive urges.

Thus, without the prospect of settling upon a clear etiology for the "illness" that ailed him, let alone a name-brand prescription for self-respect, happiness, or the optimal state of mental health, we were left to ponder the problem of whether Kevin should renew one or the other of the unused prescriptions in his medicine cabinet (non-commercial art or liberation theology), or substitute a hybrid of provisional meanings. Kevin came to me complaining of feeling lost, but he had to think seriously about where he wanted to locate himself and whether there were hidden advantages to living nowhere and not being found.

Although I was his therapist, I couldn't help but privately sympathize with his suspicions of his colleagues' unreflective enthusiasm for computer pyrotechnics, the contemporary fashions in the art scene, and sexual adventure, but I could also well imagine how, confined within a chaste and colorless existence, he would be envious of them as well. No doubt his restless dreaminess, his quiet subversiveness, and philosophical inclinations held some appeal for me and served an important purpose for Kevin. They were amulets that preserved his ideals: unlike many of his friends and co-workers he would not fall prey to temptation or settle for empty and transient pleasures. And yet, what was the value of an existence such as his, chaste and colorless as a monk's, emptied of love and joy along with sex and aggression, detached as it was from God's other, less thoughtful and more earthy, creatures? The Anti-Christ takes many forms, he learned in Sunday school: sometimes he holds a Blackberry and shops at Barney's, and other times his eyes burn with the cold wearing a thin cordoroy jacket.

Local Colors and Personal Meanings

The first in his family to have graduated from college and moved from the cornfields of Indiana to the "big city," Kevin is ambivalently "white collar," having worked for the past year as a graphic designer in the mid-west office of a national advertising firm. As Kevin tells his story, his worldly accomplishments – which include a marketable degree, a regular salary, and two weeks of paid vacation – have earned him the admiration of high school friends, parents, and relatives, but have brought him little in the way of personal fulfillment. Indeed, from Kevin's description, his post-college days have been filled mostly with drudgery – mindless "number crunching" and marketing web-based products to faceless consumers. While going back to his "humble" roots is neither an attractive nor realistic option – his father's weekend drinking is embarrassing to witness and the family farm is barely sustainable – making new and enduring connections at bars, fitness centers, and sports events doesn't seem attractive either. Which is why Kevin feels unhinged and has an attention problem, going by himself to Barnes and Nobles most Saturday nights "just to browse" but never finishing any of the books that pile up alongside his bed, books on philosophy, religion, personality, and yoga, even though they confront him each morning and evening reproachfully: "You took us home and then abandoned us, and you couldn't really afford to buy us anyway!"

The world is sorely lacking (and not just Kevin's world but everyone's, his father would argue along with his priests). So should Kevin be faulted for being unhappy and ungrounded? As he dreams of extravagant adventures as a traveling troubadour in Wales, an indigent artist in a New York City tenement, a Peace Corps volunteer in Guatemala, or a missionary in the tradition of Mother Teresa, the numbers on the spread sheets lose their meaning. But does that really matter? What is significant and who really cares? The relief he finds in fantasies from the tedium of the office routine is short-lived, for when he catches himself weaving visions about a better life somewhere else, he feels ashamed and guilty. Guilty because one voice says, "Who is he to ask for more?" And ashamed because another counters, "Why isn't he going out and getting it?"

Indeed, Kevin's fantasies are no more reconcilable with the values of the poor rural community in which he was raised than they are with the market-driven culture in which he is currently situated. And so, he lives incognito in both worlds, subsisting on a bittersweet diet of daydreams, irritable awakenings, and scathing self-reproaches. Ironically, Kevin's unhappy but lucrative career path expresses his deeply rooted commitment to the Christian ideals of humility and service, sacrifice and penance, as much as it expresses his departure from them. Because he derives little pleasure from the money and status his current position offers, the "mindlessness" of the work coupled with his own "absentmindedness" are Kevin's compromise between sacrifice and indulgence: On a daily basis he reins in his unwieldy appetite for creative self-expression (and convincingly blames his unsated hunger on the corporate culture), but then compensates by "spacing out," wearing unstylish clothes off the racks of the Salvation Army, and failing to become a proper dot-com "soldier." Thus, the artist turned demoralized and faceless technocrat doubles as a secret agent of revolution who martyrs himself for the ideal of humble servitude.

As the son of poor and disheartened cattle farmers who expected little out of life and got what they expected, Kevin's material success and its attending compromises with free-wheeling desire simultaneously fulfill his parents' dreams of "more" (a carpeted office, a billable hour, an electronic "bridge to the twenty-first century"), and reproduce their experiences of making do with "not enough." Just as they do, he feels stagnant in his work and impinged upon by impersonal forces greater than himself. "I'm deathly bored moving the same old shapes on my computer screen; is that all there is?" is not that different a tone from his father's weariness in relation to the family farm: "It's subsistence, nothing better." However, unhappy as Kevin is with the ingenious compromise he has negotiated all by himself, I ask myself what kind of compromise can we come up with by putting our heads together? If he speaks eloquently, but out of both sides of his mouth for the inevitability of limitation, should I speak earnestly in counterpoint for the value of desire?

With embarrassment, Kevin confesses that in college he flirted with majoring in Studio Art and minoring in Religious Studies before stumbling into the advertising business and graduating, one semester late, with a patchwork quilt of twenty unrelated credits and an extra $5,000 of debt. Averting his eyes and blushing as he describes how his fellow classmates used to refer to him with admiration as "the Man," Kevin evidently takes pleasure in his former notoriety as a radical voice on a small midwestern college campus, and also feels foolish in that pleasure. ("Where do you draw the line, Dr. Block, between wanting to be creative and being an exhibitionist? Is it just a question of the audience's response?") Thus, he regards his fugitive fascination with art, fame and revolution as illicit. In my office every second Monday (not every Monday, mind you), lunch hour, I become another partner in his search for its legitimacy. He wants to know from somebody "objective," whether he should try to temper his subversive impulses or capitalize upon them, and whether it is idealism or mere hubris to imagine that the rules that governed his modest parents' drearily routine lives do not also apply to him.

But I'm not objective! I identify with Kevin when he tells me that he identifies with the high-spirited child he saw in the park, balancing precariously on a rock, shouting "Look at me" in the direction of his prematurely aged and dispirited mother. "She's so cynical, so worn out by life, that she can't even appreciate her son's energy." Yet, more often than not, he mirrors her and not her son, unable to enjoy the "normal" kinds of fun available to young men his age. Does he know too much for his own good about suffering and transience? Can a person feel too deeply or think too complexly?

When Kevin describes to me how he instantaneously and involuntarily translates his Saturday night experience of sexual attraction to a woman at a dance club into a documentary film-strip of monkeys humping in an African rainforest, I am at a loss for words. In his translation, the ordinary mating rituals that his office buddies follow when the lights are low and the liquor is flowing do appear "ridiculous" and debasing. But the question remains, if this is his mother('s) tongue, can he become fluent in another language and write a new translation?

In the theological debates he initiates with his parish priest on Sundays, he tries out different words than the words he tries out with me the following afternoon, but I suspect that there aren't any words that can adequately capture those "Saturday night fevers" or Monday morning doldrums, those diffuse aches and yearnings that are embodied fragments of spirit and are essentially wordless? Confused about what he *should* feel as much as about what he does feel, he loops back to the same impossible questions that nobody can answer. Is he too big for his breeches or are his breeches not big enough for him?

Kevin reminds me periodically that though the books on my shelves reveal that I prefer Freud, and that on some days he does too, Christ remains his model. The Jesus his priest worships is humble and selfless, but the Jesus Kevin admires is bold and unconventional; he speaks in metaphors like a poet, and, like Freud's, Christ the poet's messages are unpopular. So when it comes to the question, "What would Jesus do?" neither religion nor psychology can presume to provide Kevin with a definitive answer.

Laboratory Conditions

When I was training to be a psychologist during the 1980's I worked in various psychiatric hospitals where the "real" doctors – that is, the ones with the M.D.s not the Ph.D.s after their names – wore unbuttoned, calf-length white coats over their business attire. Since the psychiatric residents and attending physicians were not responsible for performing physical examinations on their patients, the uniform that distinguished them from the rest of us served no practical purpose. (There were no bodily fluids to protect against, no need to ensure a sterilized environment.) And yet, the tradition continued, despite the rumblings among the non-medical doctors (but maybe because of them as well). Some of my colleagues resented the exclusivity of the attire, and argued that in order to avoid invidious comparisons, all of the doctors should conform to a uniform dress code. Others opposed the coats on philosophical grounds – they thought they created a psychological barrier that ultimately interfered with the establishment of a good therapeutic relationship.

Regardless of the perspective, however, no one seemed to disagree that the white coats carried symbolic significance, and signaled to staff and patients alike that certain, but not all, of the experts were unlike ordinary folks, that their opinions and prognostications were scientifically purified, and, for better or for worse, that their relationships with their patients were uncontaminated by stray remnants of subjectivity. ("I am the Father who knows best, trust me.")

I never wore that controversial jacket, and now, years later, my personal taste, and probably even my politics, are expressed deliberately, though I hope unobtrusively, in the clothes I wear and the objects with which I decorate my private office. I have no interest in purposefully disguising my human qualities by overemphasizing my neutrality. If this muddies what psychoanalysts call the transference, it also demystifies my relationship with my patients, and diminishes my authority as an objective "voice from nowhere," and thus it is not unintentional. Negotiating boundaries, recognizing and not erasing differences, and working through the inevitable experiences of love and disillusionment without becoming too worshipful or too disillusioned are as essential to psychotherapy, as they are in ordinary circumstances to sustaining hope while living within the frame of a good-enough life.

Thus, the problem of how to practice good psychotherapy and the problem of how to live well raise similar concerns, and what happens inside the office between me and my patients serves as a rehearsal for what happens outside and vice versa. Kevin's internal conflicts about wanting and not wanting to be anonymous (selfless and bloodless beneath his own white jacket), about trusting his instincts or transcending them, have revived my memories of the factionalism I witnessed and participated in at the hospital around the wearing of white coats. Kevin is in crisis (just as our staff was polarized) because he believes that he has to choose between the "simple" animalistic pleasures of spontaneous self-expression, and the "difficult" intangible pleasures of reflective self-restraint, between the charming egocentricity of childhood and the moral imperatives of maturity.

As a matter of principle, I consciously refuse to make this choice, a choice that pits one problematic ideal against another, and because I want to let Kevin know that he too can refuse, I aspire neither to a disembodied neutrality nor to a naive version of authenticity. If psychotherapy is to serve as a laboratory of meaning, Kevin needs to feel comfortable experimenting with his contradictory desires – to be spontaneous *and* responsive to the needs of others, passionately engaged *and* dispassionately reflective – and I must be comfortable experimenting with such contradictions as well when I listen and respond honestly to him. The value of deliberate self-containment and the pleasures of mutual self-expression can only be evaluated if we live them in the real time and space we share together.

Responsivity and Restraint: (In Which the Containment of Desire Inside the Office Parallels the Containment of Desire Outside)

Because Kevin denies himself a winter coat, he brings to our encounter a memory of cold that makes both of us shiver. And because Kevin arrives late for his appointment, our time together runs out, just when this memory is beginning to fade and the conversation is beginning to flow. As he prepares to leave, and I feel a mixture of frustration and relief, I wonder whether this is what he feels (has felt) throughout his life. Are my cold and hot "counter-transference" reactions a window into his psyche – some internal thermostat he has projected onto me – or something I am projecting onto him? Perhaps Kevin experiences only the frustration of not having had enough time or only the relief of not having given up too much space, or perhaps a different blend of feelings entirely. It's too late to ask him about it, but as I am left guessing, I wonder if my experience of suspended animation is not unlike Kevin's chronic experience of confusion and anxiety about the pleasures of intimate connection and intimacy's limitations.

As Kevin lingers a couple of minutes, writes out his check, and formalistically confirms our next meeting (two weeks, twelve noon), I consider the possible meanings of his self-imposed abstinence, his short-lived but passionate outbursts, his semi-abortive stabs at self-disclosure. Aware that on occasion I have indulged my own inclination to extend the hour a few extra minutes, I vacillate as to whether this time I should allow him to linger longer, as he seems inclined to do, knowing that either choice – the choice to stand firm or the choice to yield – makes a statement and thus involves a risk. (I know what the "white jackets" would tell me I should do!) Does Kevin ask for less than what is offered (fifty minutes not my sixty minute hour), and secretly hope that unlike his abstemious parents I will give him more than what he explicitly asks? Or am I misinterpreting his meaning and mixing it up with my own? Does Kevin feel that less is sufficient and more is excessive, perhaps even smothering and de-humanizing – in which case he might see the movement of the minute hand on the clock as a finger of caution, a wise reminder that each of us has limits, and that we had better stick to the rules and bid each other good-bye?

As these questions rattled around inside my head that frigid November afternoon, and as I jockeyed back and forth between my impulse to be flexible and my conviction that I should interpret and not sneakily "act out" unconscious wishes, I became convinced that the amalgam of contradictory thoughts, values, and feelings I was having were analogous to the contradictions inside Kevin. Intimacy is exhilarating when our individual desires correspond, but frustrating as well as embarrassing when we find ourselves stepping clumsily on our partner's toes. In Kevin's enthusiasm to express himself beyond the customary limits of the session, is he taking up too much time or space? And does the answer depend on my particular feelings that day or if I have another patient waiting?

The hour was over five minutes ago, a stern voice admonishes me, even if he did arrive ten minutes late shivering, apologetic, and distracted; he mustn't get special treatment, and I mustn't be an overly indulgent mama who, afraid to set clear limits, infantilizes her son. Moreover, just because Kevin reminds me (and maybe himself as well) of a stray puppy, doesn't mean that I should treat him as if he were one, even if he would like me to. And yet, he has actually gotten less than what he has agreed to pay for, I reply in a softer tone, and though rules are rules, "who made those rules?" I ask with irritation. Don't I have the authority and good judgment to choose when to bend them?

And so, Kevin shrinks the hour by coming late, and then stretches it out by stalling over his checkbook. He may be unaware of his ambivalence, but I am acutely aware of mine, and, despite my inner critic's reproachful poking, choose not to hurry him out the door. I am the "shrink," but (I argue plaintively with myself) he is already shrunken and needs all the encouragement he can get to expand not disappear. As I give in to my impulse not to be rigid, hoping that once he leaves the office he will grant himself permission to follow suit, I am cautious, however. There are definite boundaries to my giving, as there are unavoidable limits on his desires, and I would have to be a martyr or an "enabler," a seductress or a naive romantic, not to acknowledge and defend them for us both.

"How much giving over of one's life is enough? Why I should spend a hundred dollars on a pair of shoes when I could pay thirty-five and give the rest of the money to the homeless shelter? Where do *you* draw the line, Dr. Block?" With no introductory bridge, Kevin begins our next session with a jolt by alluding to the newspaper reports on the recent death of Mother Teresa: "Her entire life was giving; she comes as close as humanly possible to being a saint."

While once again I found myself momentarily distracted by the redness of his ears, by the bareness of his neck, and by my wish to protect him against the cruelty of the elements, "distractable" Kevin, the boyish-looking young man who is routinely teased by family and office-mates for having his head in a fog, sat at the edge of my couch, with his eyes sharply focused. Still wearing his jacket, he made it clear through his dismissive response to the signals of his body that he was not about to waste our time worrying about his ears or commiserating with me about the weather. So, despite my misgivings, I filed away my observations and misplaced empathy to join him in his pressing philosophical reflections. Leery about where they might take us (what accusations was he about to hurl my way?) I suspected, nevertheless, that they would lead us back to the problem of how to respond to cold ears, to the constraints of time, and to personal and inter-personal suffering generally.

Kevin was inspired but also troubled by Mother Teresa's limitless capacity for self-sacrifice, and like a mirror I was inspired and troubled by his mixed responses. I thought, "How many young men in his position would even take notice of her passing, let alone pay homage to her unprofitable virtues? Surely he deserves to be respected, rather than teased or analyzed, for his idealistic inclinations." And yet, in my comfortably heated office, looking at Kevin's raw, wind-chapped hands, I sensed that there was a darker purpose to his bringing me the news, and that if I wasn't careful both of us could be vulnerable to blistering attacks.

So, although a part of me identified with Kevin's wish to extend himself beyond the narrow boundaries of his workaday world (one that involved designing formulaic web products and collecting what he believed to be an inflated paycheck), I was wary of how he imagined he (or we) should translate idealistic desires into our actual lives. Defensively, I wanted to protect us both from his stark asceticism, and yet I also wanted to support him in his worthy passions; Kevin's eyes were flashing, and in contrast to his customary vagueness and abstraction, he was referring to himself in the first person and beckoning me to do the same. In essence he was pleading with me to stop the polite stop-and-start shuffling that he suffers from repeatedly everywhere he goes and get real! "Where do *you* draw the line Dr. Block?"

Indeed, when Kevin shifted the conversation from the abstract moral to the personal realm, I was confronted head-on with a therapeutic dilemma (a variation on the white coat dilemma), and my thoughts began to race. I am not Mother Teresa and do not aspire to a love that is unlimited and selfless, but neither am I Sigmund Freud, who interpreted all idealism as a defensive and dangerous obfuscation. I am, however, Kevin's alternative to the lunchtime conversations at the Sport's Bar, and, as such, have a chance to offer Kevin another perspective on inner and outer reality. This being the case, should I or should I not accept the shift that edged us into the realm of *my* personal perspective? Should I be honest and tell him what I think about drawing lines or not?

If I were to see his crossing over the boundary that separates the professional from the personal as a childlike wish for reassurance and direction or else an adolescent challenge to my authority that should be interpreted rather than gratified, the answer would be a resounding no. But it would be yes if I were to see his question as representing a healthy and ageless desire for authentic engagement, an opportunity for mutual recognition and the construction of new meanings. Depending upon my understanding of what constitutes a normal amount of dependency and how this is achieved through a therapeutic relationship, Kevin would either stand to lose or to gain by my throwing the question back to him to consider for himself with classic analytical flourish. Thus, as much I was uncertain as to what my honest response would be to Kevin's ethical conundrum, I was also uncertain about whether (or how much) I should be communicating this honest response to Kevin.

Although psychotherapy has attempted to distance itself from the moral imperatives associated with religious ethics and cast itself as value-free, in practice each psychotherapist follows his own implicit moral agenda that reflects his understanding of the "good-enough" therapy and the "good-enough" way to live. Therapy is as much an expression of a particular set of values as anything else is, and if the therapist didn't have an implicit moral perspective on what is a better way to live his interactions with patients would be haphazard and unreflective. That being acknowledged, the question remains, whether (or how much) the implicit ethos of the therapist should be made explicit to the patient. Kevin's wish to hear my personal opinion about Mother Teresa and the limits of giving, and my wish to engage with him in an open dialogue about desire and human limits should not be gratified if he were to hear my voice as prophetic or interpret my beliefs as injunctions; my candid self-expression must not inadvertently discourage his. And yet . . .

Without warning, Kevin had poked his head out from behind the screen of intellectual rumination and prodded me to "draw the line" for him between enough and too much giving. My immediate impulse was to poke my head out too and speak passionately in defense of compassion: "Kevin, give yourself a break! At least buy yourself a winter scarf. You draw lines that are like barbed wire – you don't leave yourself room to take a deep breath!" But, I contained myself (less than some therapists might have, and more than others), realizing only later, when I reflected on how the session unfolded, that a modicum of self-restraint had kept us honest in a way that my uncensored self-expression could not have. For though I suspect that at the moment, both of us might have been relieved if I had confidently swept away the ambiguities, it would have been naive if not grandiose of me to presume that I could. Indeed, how could anybody know precisely just how much self-centeredness is healthy, or which forms of self-sacrifice are masochistic and which spiritually enriching?

Kevin's unsatisfying efforts to make peace with his contradictory desires – to soar ahead and yet to leave no one behind – could not be reduced to his particular obsessional inhibitions any more than those inhibitions could be understood without taking his contrary desires into account. His ethical quandary was unsettling to both of us, not just to him, and thus challenged me to ponder the limits of what I can give emotionally and the limits of my practical knowledge and inarticulate understanding both inside and outside the therapeutic relationship.

So while I refrained from expressing my personal distaste for Kevin's disembodied asceticism, lest either of us mistake it for objective, psychological truth, I could not be reconciled to retreating behind a screen of therapeutic neutrality. For if I had masked my subjectivity altogether, and answered his questions opaquely with other questions, I would have been implicitly advocating another version of asceticism (under the aegis of scientific professionalism) and sending Kevin the message that open dialogue is too entangling, authenticity too private to be shared, and limitation too embarrassing for me as well as for him. That was not a therapeutic message I could stand by. Kevin had unnerved me, and I felt I owed it to him to let him know that he had, and that his maneuver, as provocative as it was, heightened rather than fractured our connection.

"If by asking me where I would draw the line you are saying it's hard for you to know where you want to draw it, I would have to agree . . . it is hard to know. On the other hand, since I'm not God and I don't see much value in pretending to be, I do know that I have to draw it somewhere – I'd feel too overwhelmed or too resentful if I didn't."

"Mother Teresa didn't feel resentment, she was a completely selfless human being who gave out of her love for humanity. I don't think it's just a pretense to try and improve ourselves and to take Christ as our model."

"I guess for me it depends on what you mean by 'improve'; if it means trying to eliminate having a self and all the ordinary feelings connected with it . . . "

"By 'improve' I mean to be able to get outside your own little box and not be so concerned about promoting your personal ambitions."

"Okay, but what do you mean by *so* concerned? If you're asking me how I can justify having more than other people, and still wanting more for myself, I have to say that a lot of the time I can't, there is no justification. But that doesn't mean I have to condemn myself for it either." The silence was pregnant, and, retrospectively I had to admit to myself that my efforts to clarify were as much an outgrowth of my own anxiety to create meaning as of my concern for him. I had said: "Is there always a direct connection between what you have and what someone else has or does not have?"

At this point Kevin cast me a plaintive but dubious look which made me realize that I was in danger of rationalizing away my growing discomfort. (Who is the therapist now and who the patient?) In order not to betray my commitment to facing the truth and not massaging it to make it look simple, I felt a need to confront the narrow perspective of self-fulfillment and pay respect to its opposite – Mother Teresa's perspective, as articulated by Kevin.

"Sure," I continued. "If a homeless person asks me for some spare change and I give it to him, then my having less allows him to have more, but often there isn't that connection. For example, your wanting to be happier with your life doesn't have to take happiness away from someone else – unless you believe that there is a limited quantity of happiness floating around in the world."

"Well, that depends. If only one person can get the leading role in a play or the most interesting assignment on a project, then your gain is my loss, your pleasure is at my expense, and if you're so involved with your personal fulfillment that you become insensitive to how I'm doing, then it's just the survival of the fittest, Social Darwinism, and we're no better than monkeys in the jungle . . . " Kevin's sentence trailed off, but his allusion to Darwin recalled to me Freud's hydraulic model of the mind in which a limited quantity of psychic energy is available for distribution, and narcissism is inversely related to the capacity to love. This was not where I was heading, but it was a credible perspective with significant moral implications, and I had to take it seriously.

"Yes, that can happen," I responded. "If you were to become completely self-absorbed or self-righteous and blame those less fortunate than you for their misfortune, you would be merely justifying the fact that there really is inequality and unfairness in the world. But would you say it is necessarily the case that by you taking good care of yourself you will become callous to the next person's misery? Hasn't it sometimes worked in the reverse, so that when you're feeling frustrated and caged in you can't focus on anything else?"

Silence. At this juncture, Kevin looks to me like a boy hesitating by the cookie jar, and since I have lured him to that spot by my questions, I feel I need to back away and give him space to decide where he wants to go next. But he seems paralyzed, not knowing for sure which moves are possible, which are forbidden, and which are heroic. Uneasy at what has tranpired, I offer both of us a temporary way out.

"Spending a hundred dollars on shoes may feel unnecessarily extravagant to you," I continued, out of my own pressing desire to find clarity in a morally confusing universe, "and maybe the thirty-five dollar pair will do just fine, but then you have to figure out what you want to do with the extra sixty-five dollars." Kevin's look of embarrassment turns into an expression of sadness mixed with puzzlement, but again he is silent.

"What do you feel is worth spending money on? There's the homeless shelter you mentioned before, but you've also talked about feeling badly that you've barely painted in over a year and that your paints have dried up; what about new art materials, or that vintage car you salvaged from the junk yard and painted lemon yellow?" Apparently, I had hit upon something, for this time Kevin smiled impishly and his eyes twinkled.

"I went on a drive for the first time last Saturday and it was awesome; the flowers were blooming and I felt totally free; I left all of the junk from work behind. I think one of these weekends I'll ask my father if he'd like to take a ride; he doesn't get away much, and I think a change of scene would do him so much good." I took this response to mean that Kevin enjoyed the liberties I had taken, but was not altogether comfortable taking them all by himself. He wanted companionship. We had indulged in speculation, wandered away from the weighty problem of Mother Teresa and the limits of giving, and when I left it up to him to lead us back, move us along, or redirect us elsewhere, he moved us along and fantasized about bringing his father.

Initiating this form of dialogue was the honest response I settled for, and I cannot claim it was morally neutral or fully satisfying to either one of us. But by revealing to Kevin that we shared a common human dilemma – that I was neither a mindless hedonist nor a neutral observer and he was neither a solitary idealist nor a jungle monkey – I offered him an escape route from his paralyzing polarities, and left him the freedom to create an alternative reality. Perhaps my own confusion encouraged him to speak more openly about his contradictory feelings, because our conversation about Mother Teresa and the price of shoes eventually led us to a discussion of Kevin's gloomy father, his own threadbare attire, and his tardy arrival at our sessions, which then led us to the various meanings Kevin attached to wanting and wanting not to want.

The explicit question Kevin had raised concerning Mother Teresa's extraordinary capacity for self-sacrifice was connected to the implicit question of whether he should concern himself with his immediate feelings of coldness or his chronic feelings of frustration, or whether he should reproach himself for thinking that these very ordinary feelings matter all that much in deciding how to live. If Mother Teresa places no limits on her care for others and expresses little concern for her own material well being, what kind of a person would he have to be to come to my office (albeit late) and spend time and money focusing for one hour exclusively on himself? Should he stop "whining," swallow hard and gracefully accept his less-than-ideal life (which on face value was a lot better than his father's), or should he defend his ideals (which includes the ideal of living life creatively) as fervently as Mother Theresa defended hers? At Kevin's initiative religious and philosophical themes recurred in our conversations over the next several months, and with poetic license I recreate some of our incompletely satisfying and inconclusive experiments with meaning.

Giving, Giving In, and Giving Up

Kevin: "I was at work till 11:00 p.m. Friday night and then most of Saturday and Sunday." (Kevin reports despondently.) "It seems like I am always behind because I get distracted and can't concentrate. I never could. I feel buried, but then it's not like I would want to hang out with the guys at the bar on the week-end, looking to pick up women."

Me: "You complain that work is mindless and endless and that your relationships outside are superficial; you are bored because everybody you know just wants to talk about football or money or how to get good sex. So you drift off, space out, or sit on the sidelines like a scientist observing the wild animals in their native habitats. You've given up on most people, but you won't give up your hopes and dreams. You store them away in a locked box, buried, as you put it, for safe keeping."

Kevin: "Well, should I give them up? I try not to put a damper on the conversation when everyone around me seems to be having fun, but I can't pretend to be someone I'm not. But then, when I sit back and analyze everyone I feel like Scrooge, so I think it's probably better to make up some excuse and go home early."

Me: "So then you do end up living a secret life, pretending. Do you ever try to go deeper? Are you saying that in order connect with people you have to muzzle yourself, which of course is a contradiction in terms?

Kevin: "Do you really think anyone wants to talk about child-labor practices in Indonesia or the latest genocide when they get off work?"

Me: "I don't know. You do?"

Kevin: "I'd rather talk about that than about how the Cubs are doing."

Me: "You seem to think that you have to choose between living in the real world as a diluted version of yourself and living stranded alone on a desert island with all of your intensity and no place to put it."

Kevin: "No. Maybe it would be different somewhere else. I have very strong opinions and I'm pretty certain most people I meet don't want to hear them. Either they're completely focused on their careers or their relationships, or else they find me weird because I'm arguing with what they've been taught in Catholic school. I've been told to either grow up or lighten up and I think it's because I can be very intense. Maybe I'm a manic depressive?

Me: (Now I am silent since I refuse to take the bait.)

Kevin:"Really, I don't like to be insensitive or to be the kind of person who gets up on a soapbox and sermonizes, so I try to tone myself down. Actually, I'm told I'm a very good listener. Everyone, including my mother, my sister, and my eight-five year old grandmother, confides in me. I like to be the kind of person people can confide in."

Me: "But you also say you feel like a robot and that you get easily distracted; and when you do get excited about a new project, it never lasts, you lose interest. You've told me that you have sculptures in your basement that you started and haven't completed. Could it be that you've toned yourself down so much that you've created a life that is very dull and a you who is mindless?"
Kevin: "I'm directing a play with some kids at my church and I had what was a kind of radical interpretation of Christ's Sermon on the Mount. But there's a woman a little older than me who has been involved with the youth group for years, and she had very different ideas. I know she's very insecure, and the last thing I want to do is to get into a competition with her– the point of doing the play is not to promote my interpretation but to get everyone to work together so that the kids have a good time. So I've backed off."
Me: (An alarm goes off in my head, and though I try not respond, at least not in any obvious way, Kevin probably senses my concern.)
Kevin: "Most people don't realize it, but it takes a lot more strength to see the larger picture than to get into a petty power struggle. I probably had too much of my own ego invested in the drama group anyway."
Me: "So your ego looks big, maybe even grotesque, when you compare yourself to that woman at church who seems so insecure. But what do you mean by your ego?"
Kevin: "I felt that my interpretation was so much more interesting than hers, which is pretty arrogant of me. I don't know what other people would have thought since I restrained myself and let her take the lead, but I do know that she would have felt very uncomfortable if I had tried to convince the group to do it my way. She would have ended up in tears; I've seen it before."

Me: "But how do you feel about working on the play now?
Kevin: "I wish I hadn't made the commitment. I don't know how I'll find the time, what with all my work; but I certainly won't let them down."
Me: "So you were excited and now you're not; in fact, it's a drag. Your thoughtfulness left you feeling unenthusiastic and caged, which is a familiar feeling for you, and I wonder whether you have much left in you now to give anything real to those kids."
Kevin: "My friends don't notice, or if they do notice they don't seem to care, when they barrel over other people. It's the macho marketplace mentality, and they get a charge out of the competition; I imagine that a lot of people see me as a loser or a non-entity. I'm sure I'd be a lot happier if I could just turn a switch and let loose. I should think like a venture capitalist; I'd certainly be more successful. But I can't not notice or not care."
Me: "Well, you've described these venture capitalist-type people as jungle monkeys jockeying for positions, preening, and mindlessly going through their mating rituals; so even though you say you envy them their carefree existence, you make it look pretty ridiculous and degrading."
Kevin: "I feel guilty even thinking about people like that because when I do I'm not being sensitive at all. I feel like a hypocrite. Christ loved the prostitutes and the thieves, and didn't judge them, even though he was perfect."
Me: "So, you are not Christ. He gave without thought of what he would receive, while your love is conditional. You sound like you try desperately to model yourself after Christ and to be unselfish – without an ego – but your heart isn't in it and because of that you end up feeling either mean-spirited or mechanical.
Kevin: "Okay. So what should I do?"
Me: "What do you think?"

Kevin: "I knew you'd say that! You're the doctor."
Me: "Okay." (Hating to give advice, I was buying time trying to figure out how to get out of this corner.) "What would it be like, do you think, if you gave yourself permission to be more of what you call egotistical, to care about your feelings and preferences at least as much as you do about the feelings and preferences of others? Do you think you would be more or less good-spirited in the long run, more or less honestly generous?" (These were leading questions, to be sure, but at that point I had deliberately decided not to hide my desires for Kevin to stop hiding and squelching his desires quite so much.)
Kevin: "I'd probably be happier."
Me: "And if you were happier, would you be more or less Christ-like?"
Kevin: "Well, I'm certainly not much fun to be around now. My father said most days are grey. Are yours? Do you always enjoy your work, Dr. Block?"
Me: (Oh no, I'm thinking, another question about me.) "No, I don't, not always, but I try to enjoy it. But what does my enjoyment or your father's greyness tell you about what you should do? Do you think that somehow by joining the ranks of the grey people you are doing someone a favor? Does it qualify you as a member of the real world?"
Kevin: "Well, it makes me not a thoughtless egocentric kid anymore."
Me: "And if your days were brighter and you felt more creative, you would be?"

In renegotiating the boundaries of desire, we had to explore Kevin's beliefs about the value of suffering and sacrifice. Did he think he could give more and ultimately have more of what is worth having by taking a detour through sadness and self-abnegation? Did he imagine that his threadbare winter coat brought him closer to the truth of existence or created a barrier between him and other people? Must the fire inside be extinguished in order for him to build a bridge to the world?

Paradoxically, as Kevin's therapist I was there to help him create coherence out of confusion, and yet at the same time I was there to legitimize and join in his confusion, that is, to let him know that in being confused he is neither aberrant nor guilty. Making choices we can live with is rarely easy! Only when I can accept that there are limits to what I can offer Kevin by way of clarification, empathy, and the freedom to choose how he is going to live, can I continue to defend both of our desires to see more clearly, connect more deeply, and to push against as well as away from the edges of these limits.

Sometimes we get tangled up in our words and seduced into thinking we can solve the existential riddles through logical argument. When this happens, feelings get buried and the values we have identified become emptied of value. It is then that I cry "Uncle!" and insist on a "time out" from what has become an exercise in philosophy, a distracting language game that can be absorbing but goes nowhere. To quote Pascal, "The heart has its reasons that reason does not know." At such dead end junctures I wish to introduce variations on this theme. Indeed, when I can induce Kevin to take a temporary detour from the weightiness of existential angst through the free floating trail of our loose associations, it proves restorative and therefore meaningful.

Heroism Reconsidered

For years, quiet intensity was Kevin's most prominent distinguishing feature, but since his unconventionally conscientious adherence to traditional religious ideals was a source of self-respect as well as social awkwardness, of artistic inspiration as well as sexual inhibitions he was as reluctant as he was eager to "lighten up." He didn't want to become a two-dimensional man and float away into cyberspace. I shared his ambivalence. Kevin's sincerity, his devoutness, his weighty self-reflections prompted us to think deeply about ultimate meanings, which I liked, but it also discouraged us from living fully in the moment, from following the trail of Kevin's associations and mine, and taking pleasure in letting ourselves go, which I didn't.

Indeed, since Kevin took great pains to justify spending our time and his money on uncertain and "unproductive" activities, when I was with him I also felt a pressure to be especially productive and insightful. "Good enough" was unlikely to qualify as good enough in Kevin's book of rules, and it was all I could do to resist trying to prove that this talking cure was really worth our while. Were our sessions a microcosm of Kevin's strained relationships at work, in his church group, and in the dance bar? Most likely. Because heroism can be debilitating for the hero as well as for his admirers, its effect is paradoxical: what starts as an earnest wish for a deeper and more honest connection turns into a mechanized embrace of inauthenticity. Ironically, the tension that both of us experienced in our relationship was another one of his "gifts," a living proof which we could experience together that his way of managing desire felt less than good enough even for just the one hour.

Kevin's idealism was both a strength and a liability, in life and in therapy, for it generated hopes but then shut off the possibilities for translating them into reality. As it became clearer that Kevin's suspicious relationship to his material, "egotistical" desires was elevating as well as deflating both to him and to me, I knew what my contribution to our experiment had to be. Rather than simply retreating behind a blank screen (mimicking his father's grey colorlessness with my own) or matching Kevin's intensity in an attempt to substitute an ideal of self-fulfillment for the ideal of renunciation, I had to take the risk of exposing my uncertain relationship to wishes and desires, by qualifying my opinions and shamelessly alternating between intense focus, microscopic analysis, and unpremeditated play. Simultaneously, I had to respect and challenge the standards that Kevin aspired to, and I had to remain hopeful that we could find more inspiration with than without a measure of disillusionment.

So when Kevin allowed a twinkle to steal into his eyes, or when the corner of his lips curled devilishly as he described the antics he played at work or the disruptive remarks he made at church, I twinkled sympathetically, secure that I was not just giving into a childish temptation to act out but was actually participating in a therapeutic breakthrough. After months of grueling analysis that was supposed to enlighten us but didn't, we stumbled onto experiences that weren't supposed to but did have this serendipitous effect. Lingering on the unimportant details of daily life, such as fixing up and painting his "junkyard" car a bright yellow, toying with the unpredictable and hypothetical (what would it be like to quit his job next month and find some work with native villages in South America), we found that our spirits were restored and that the tough road ahead appeared less fearsome. What a pleasure to take a vacation from Kevin's dark "realism" and reconnoiter, not in solitary fantasy, but in another shared reality – the reality of imagination and desire.

And then one warm spring afternoon, Kevin presented me with a wire sculpture of a flower, a miniature version of the life-sized wire tree he had recently constructed and "planted" in a field adjacent to his father's farmhouse. Moved by the very personal nature of the gift, knowing from our conversations how much he cherished his creativity and how much he had doubted that other people would, I felt tremendously gratified and at the same time embarrassed. I guess he was too because then, after announcing that he had decided to go into the Peace Corps, he added casually that this would probably be our final session. He had toyed with the idea of the Peace Corps months earlier, but as far as I knew his plans were vague and his vacillations were paralyzing. It turned out, however, that without talking about it, maybe in order to not over-think it, he had taken a leap. His desires were no longer limited to the realm of fantasy, and so despite my surprise at the mix of openness and secrecy in our final hour (the personal gift, the averted eyes), I was not about to weigh us both down with deep interpretations. Kevin was preparing himself to fly away over the horizon, and I wasn't going to be the one to hold him to the standard of relentless self-reflection. That I had to do for myself, and on my own, and so I write.

The wire sculpture was a gift to me, but, as it was a daring act of self-expression, it was also a gift he gave himself. Similarly, his choice to join the Peace Corps combined his spirit for adventure and his wish to leave a personal imprint on the world with his desire to give to those who are denied choices, wishes, and adventures. Was he avoiding the competition of the marketplace and the sexual temptations of the singles scene just as he was avoiding meeting my eyes at our final session? Or had he forged a reasonable compromise, one that he could live with respectably, a compromise between selfless love and selfish desire? Whatever the interpretation, and I suspect they both are "true," as Kevin loosened himself from the grip of his idealizations he was able to take the risk of committing himself (with conditions and reservations) to a less-than-perfect sculpture, a less-than-perfect career path, and a less-than-perfect vision of what his life would look like from the perspective of tomorrow. (No mention of love or sex. Would they ever be included in his life overseas? I was wondering, and probably so was he.)

Looking back now, two years later, one voice in my head reproaches me for having allowed the therapy to end so abruptly, so unilaterally. "Everyone knows this was acting out on both your parts!" We should have taken time to analyze the meaning of his precipitous leave-taking (his pattern) as well as the relief and embarrassment we both were feeling as we said our good-byes. But another voice in my head is less certain of my missteps and more sympathetic in regard to my indulgences; it assures me that going light on the interpretations was precisely what Kevin needed at that juncture. He was flying off in the fashion that suited him and I felt he needed encouragement to do precisely that.

I speak with both voices, the critical one that presses me on to do more of the uncomfortable scrutinizing ("Don't settle for the superficial, mine the deeper meanings"), and the empathic one that is satisfied to understand some of what we have done and why. Since at the time of our parting Kevin was speaking in not just one but in both of these registers, it was apparent that our conversations had generated new versions of old meanings; and though I can easily find traces of our nervous beginnings in our poignant but awkward ending, I can also see differences and that feels good enough for now.

IN THE SHADOW OF SELF-RELIANCE

> "Man is timid and apologetic; he is no longer upright; he dares not say 'I think,' 'I am,' but quotes some saint or sage . . . It is only as a man puts off all foreign support and stands alone that I see him to be strong and to prevail. He is weaker by every recruit to his banner . . . A political victory, a rise of rents, the recovery of your sick or the return of your absent friend, or some other favorable event raises your spirits, and you think good days are preparing for you. Do not believe it. Nothing can bring you peace but yourself. Nothing can bring you peace but the triumph of principles."
>
> (Ralph Waldo Emerson, "Self-Reliance")

The Courage Not to Hope

In contrast to Kevin, Judy was always a few minutes early for her appointments, and because she was so punctual I made an extra effort to be punctual too, inadvertently mirroring her pride in being reliable and conscientious, and fueling her hope that I would be too. However, just as there was a price to pay for the "free time" Kevin gave me by being predictably late, there was a price to pay for the bonds of connection that Judy and I had come to share each Thursday afternoon as I gestured to her to come in at precisely 4:30 pm. For as soon as Judy planted her compactly rounded shape into her customary corner of my couch, she would challenge me, with a jaundiced expression in her eyes, to clear up the mess inside her head that made the mess outside feel insupportable. Sighing for no specific reason other than to acknowledge the burdensome weight of messes that we now shared (along with our reliability and conscientiousness), she would proceed to unpack a fresh supply of incriminating evidence, designed to persuade herself (and hopefully me) that the people in her life (and in life generally) were irrational, irresponsible, and unreliable, and that despite her efforts to straighten up their Big Messes, she was routinely unsuccessful, unappreciated, and unfairly marginalized.. "Most people prefer to stick their heads in the sand," she says. "Look at all the people who simply declare bankruptcy when they can't pay their credit card bills. So you'd think that by this time I'd realize that I'm the one with the problem." (Is Judy being consciously ironic or not, I wonder silently, not certain if I am understanding her implicit message.) "Why should I keep trying when it's obviously hopeless? And," she adds with a sardonic look on her face, "nobody likes the messenger of bad news; as my mother used to say it's my own fault that I am sitting home alone on Saturday night. I'd catch more flies with a little honey."

But as Judy warns me of the dangers she faces as she stands fast by her principles, trying to enlist me as her ally in her frustrating mission to find a sense of peace without compromising the truth, she neglects to mention her own aversion to facing the truth, namely the truth about her disorderly emotions which she has unsympathetically, and thus unreasonably, exiled to the dark corners of her busy life.

She would tell me, that logically she shouldn't care about things beyond her control, but it was apparent that she had always cared intensely (she suspects that she cares more than most people), despite the frustrations and the shame and her impassive expression, as variations on this theme recurred throughout our sessions. Indeed, what brought Judy to therapy were the contradictions between her unabated wish not to let external circumstances matter, and the reality that they did, between her eternal hopefulness, and her chronic disappointment in her hopes for herself as much as for the world outside.

Thus the dilemma she faced when life failed to conform to her all too reasonable expectations was complicated by its implicit moral overtones. The rhetorical questions she asked me (she wasn't actually about to rely on me or anyone else to provide her with a personal answer) were the ones she asked herself repeatedly in earnest: "How much should it matter to me or anyone else what other people think or feel or how they choose to live?" Listening silently to her insistent stream of questions to which I could provide no certain answers, I too wondered where to draw the line between too much and not enough concern for the responses of other people. Should she or should she not attempt to build a life 'without recruits,' as Emerson advises in his essay "On Self-Reliance," nourishing and supporting herself, drawing hope and strength not from human relationships which are certain to be inconstant, but from the certainty of reasoned principle? Moreover, should I? As she reached a crescendo and her voice began to falter, I joined her in her ruminative speculations about the relationship between personal integrity, courage, and hope. Is it irrational, simply wishful thinking to believe, as I and Judy sometimes do, that the basest, most destructive tendencies of human nature (laziness, selfishness, jealousy, and irrational fear) can be subjugated to conscious will? What would Freud say, given the unrecognized power of the unconscious? I consult him while Judy consults me. With her eyes glued to mine so that I cannot avoid answering her unanswerable question, she asks me if hope is a kind of grandiosity, the American Dream of the limitless frontier which Emerson was too smart to count on, and which recent history has proven to be an illusion. If this is the case then doesn't her integrity depend upon her ability not to place much hope in hope, and by extension doesn't mine?

Because Judy's questions blended personal confusion with metaphysical speculation (the emotionally charged, concrete particulars of her life being artfully camouflaged by abstract intellectual language), I was reminded of the problem I faced when Kevin confronted me with Mother Teresa and her limitless giving, and asked me personally to draw the line for him between destructive selfishness and creative self-expression, passive resignation to the less-than-good-enough and sensitive awareness of the limits of desire. How, I asked myself, should I respond to Judy? And why was she, a highly intelligent woman, asking me questions that I shouldn't answer because I couldn't possibly give her an honest answer?

Not surprisingly, these conundrums about caring and not caring, dependency and self-reliance, threatened to shake the already shaky foundation of our necessarily asymmetrical relationship. After all, every Thursday Judy was puzzled as to whether she should be driving thirty-five miles after a long day's work and paying me, an "objective" third party (whose care was purely professional and whose own personal "messes" were mostly invisible), to help her untangle her unsightly messes. Should she be wrestling with them (in perpetuity) all by herself? I imagine that on her drive to my office Judy might have asked herself (with the same impatient edge to her voice that I hear when she describes the incompetent people she has to work with) if she wasn't wasting her time talking (complaining, her dad would have said), rather than doing something more productive, such as going to the gym and firming up her flabby stomach, working in her garden, or even burrowing into the corner of her own cosy couch with a bowl of freshly popped pop corn and a thick biography of someone she admires – Eleanor Roosevelt, Winston Churchill. Or, rather than driving forty minutes back and forth and spewing more toxic fumes into the air, she could be reading a classic work of literature that has passed the test of time; she can't go wrong with Jane Austen, George Eliot, or Tolstoy.

Indeed, each evening as Judy narrated her present-day experiences and repetitiously memorialized her loss of innocence, pointing out the pitfalls of co-dependency and the uselessness of hope, we reconstructed and then deconstructed an ideal of self-reliance that had both anchored and tyrannized her since she left home twenty-five years earlier to go to college. Until she discovered a new ethical compass by which to orient herself – either in the direction of caring more about how other people thought and felt or caring less – she could neither settle into her current life nor pull up roots and create another; she could only rage against the disappointments that she documented so meticulously, and be ashamed of her disappointment, her meticulous bookkeeping, and her rages.

Of course as I relate Judy's narrative account of who she is and how she became who she is, I realize that this is how I processed it and therefore, that it is my narrative as well. As I reflect her story back to her, inevitably there are pieces of my story included and thus we build a third narrative.

The Loss of Innocence and the Birth of an Elusive Ideal

To stand firm, to exercise will power, to act in accordance with one's convictions without regard for sentimental considerations, and to purge the self of unwanted foreign influences: these are ideals that Judy aspired to as a champion of social justice, sexual equality, and individual freedom. Sandwiched between an older brother who was regarded as the family's beloved "prodigal son," and a younger sister who would forever be its adorable "baby," Judy had taken pains to construct an alternative model for herself as an independent thinker with few desires and fewer needs. (There wasn't room for yet another helpless child or nurturing breast in that over-written drama.)

Standing at attention, soldier-like, and in contrast to a mother who craved approval and lived anxiously within the shadow of her husband, Judy wished to be the arbiter of her own value. She would not tailor her opinions in order to please or appease, nor would she rely on anybody for recognition, encouragement, or forgiveness. Free from the yoke of childlike dependency, she would not feel ashamed if she had to stand conspicuously on her own, or sleep alone, or eat dinner in front of the computer. She would deliver her judgments about herself by herself, and take responsibility when she failed to meet her own rigorous standards. At least that was her plan – to live honestly and cultivate whatever garden she could within the shadows of self-reliance.

The ideal of self-reliance holds an attraction for nearly every human being, regardless of the family system in which that person develops. Having once gotten out of diapers and recognized the funny face in the mirror as none other than our own, we are all duly humbled by the realization that there is a world outside ourselves that matters very much to us but over which we have only limited control. According to psychologists, this is a turning point in emotional development, as such awareness of the self as an object in the world of other objects brings forth the capacity to experience shame. Ironically, the more we become conscious of our dependency and of how much other people affect our thoughts and feelings, the more we tend to believe in the value of autonomy and freedom, and commit ourselves to the construction and preservation of an internal, private world in which we alone define the terms of success and failure.

Any implication that we alone are responsible for our happiness is laced with contempt for those who link their sense of well-being to external factors beyond their immediate control. Thus, despite the inspirational elements we may draw from Emerson's message, it sounds simplistic as well as hubristic given what we now understand about what makes us human. Given the multiple "versions" of the self that collide within all of us, including at least one in search of "objects" to relate to, and another in search of meaning within this world but outside of ourselves, the ideal of self-reliance is inherently unstable and ambiguous.

Indeed, our very desire for self-creation, or what may fall under the rubric of "self-reliance," is subverted by our contrasting, and equally authentic, desire for belonging, affirmation, and losing ourselves in something bigger than ourselves. In his book *The Reasons of Love*, the philosopher Harry Frankfurt maintains that we are happiest when we are so absorbed in what we are doing and feeling that we forget ourselves. Our wish to remain impervious to outside influences reflects, therefore, not only our awareness of how susceptible to we are to such influences, but also how essentially pleasurable and painful that susceptibility can be. So whether psychologists refer to Eros, object relatedness, or inter-subjectivity, to narcissism, oedipal conflicts, or mirroring transferences, the very point when we realize fully that we are separate individuals is the point that we realize that other people are also individuals and that we are bound to an unpredictable and unstable world.

Judy could split apart her contradictory wishes to stand alone, to be *seen* standing alone, and to be loved and respected for not caring too much whether other people loved and respected her, but, in the end, she could not escape the contradictions As Judy and I paid homage to the allures and the dangers of self-reliance and to how, as a way of moving through life, it has limited her freedom to hold on to hope and melt away despair, to celebrate her victories and mourn her defeats, we realized how unreliable her other-worldly idealizations had proven themselves to be. Judy's fierce determination to live freely by relying exclusively on herself and her principles had not only isolated her and denied her access to the usual sorts of emotional sustenance but had left her feeling devoid of pride and laden down by self-doubt. Ironically, as an Amazon Warrior she often felt more rather than less vulnerable than the more domesticated women who chatted with each other on their lawns in the evenings, commiserating as well as discreetly bragging about their families' hectic schedules. Indeed, lately, when cleaning her clogged gutters, mowing her lumpy, mole-infested lawn, or writing a caustic e-mail to a lazy school administrator, her independence looked to her more like a shameful legacy of failure and rejection than a monument to freedom, power, and sexual equality. Why, she asked, was she the only woman on her block who didn't have anyone there to help her with the yard work. And why was she on her computer at eleven o'clock at night, the self-appointed whistle-blower who, having dared to speak the truth, would probably never get promoted. Was she being punished for some defect of character? ("You catch more flies with honey," her mother's reproaches echoed relentlessly.) Had she inadvertently unsexed herself and made herself unloveable in her calculated escape from sexual bondage?

Judy's imperviousness to social niceties and her scrupulous adherence to principle could look powerful and at times it could even feel powerful to Judy, as, for example, when the director of the social service agency in which she worked sought out her help on important hires, or when the women in her neighborhood stood in awe of her hand-constructed cedar wood deck. But these qualities, impressive as they were, were also alienating and intimidating: I could see her wearing them like a banner with which she announced to the world that, no matter what the cost, she, at least, would not take short cuts, meaning that she would not be seduced by her own or anybody else's wishful fantasies. The good-enough is *less* than good enough and don't try to convince her otherwise!

My initial response to Judy's stark vision of life was that it was honest and therefore worthy of respect, even of admiration, particularly when I compared it to the consumer-friendly versions of reality I heard from some of the other women in my practice who were un-self-consciously driven by an anxiety to please. And yet, after spending concentrated time with Judy, I came to the conclusion that her vision was not only self-defeating but also distorted and inflexible, emotionally ungenerous and therefore *dis*honest, if honesty takes into account the lives of real people. Indeed, upholding standards of excellence in matters of behavior, speech, and character left us both feeling deflated and misunderstood as she responded with a reflexive "yes but" or "no" to nearly everything I said. (What balloon would she first agree to blow up and then pop this session?)

Although Judy's principles had fortified her against the perils of feminine helplessness and childlike dependency, they had also denied her the pleasure of sharing gratitude and forgiveness, the pride of little victories and the pain of ordinary failures. They had provided her a stable criterion for sustaining hope as a solitary figure in a unreliable world, but they had also imposed on her a justification not to hope for anything but solitude, unreliability and struggle.

"Hope is the most hopeless thing of all."

> Abraham Cowley, "On Hope" (from a poetic dialogue on hope with Richard Crashaw)

Judy's secret love affair with unactualized (perhaps unactualizable) possibilities frequently left her feeling foolish and angry, judgmental and guilty when she discovered herself breathlessly running in place with nobody cheering her on, let alone running by her side. Which is why she dreamed of developing the courage not to hope. Yet, by stoking the flames of her desires rather than reconciling herself to disappointment and locating her sources of happiness exclusively within reach if not entirely within her own mind, she revved up her motor and protected herself from falling victim to boredom and indifference or middle-aged inertia, dis-eases that aren't listed in the Diagnostic Statistical Manual of mental disorders (IV) but are the sources of mindless consumerism ("retail therapy") and the infamous mid-life crisis (sexual infidelities and the "total make-over").

As her therapist, but also as another living, breathing human being who was committed to making a difference in the color, texture, and rhythm of Judy's life by relating to her in a particular way for one hour each week, I could hardly feign indifference to her wish – which sometimes sounded more like a threat – to extinguish her flames and disengage altogether from the "madding crowd." I assumed, moreover, that she wouldn't really want me to help her become as bland or dispassionate, complacent or politely unobtrusive as she claimed she wished for otherwise she would not be talking to me about it. She described her problem as one of caring too much, but I hoped that we might come up with an alternative to her dubious ideal of caring very little, which ultimately would mean dampening her hopes, compromising certain other cherished ideals, and banishing her dreams and ambitions into hiding. When I saw Judy's ashen, dead-pan expression cloud over the flashes of fire in her eyes, I would remind myself that the phoenix rises from its own ashes, but, as she was a real person and not an imaginary creature of symbolic proportions, I had to wonder whether my hopes for Judy, who on alternate Thursdays claimed that she had been burnt out by her desires, were not hopelessly naive. Was I promoting a product whose value was inflated, marketed and packaged within the popular ethos of individual self-fulfillment?

Hope is a pivotal value for everyone. When is it realizable and when is it anesthetic? In the eighteenth century, the poet Alexander Pope observed, "Hope springs eternal in the human breast." Ironically, I think of that line when I look past the cynical glint in Judy's eyes and catch a glimpse of wistful longing. But just as I am uncertain as to what to make of "eternal hope" in my position as a twenty-first century psychotherapist, the Enlightenment poet leaves room for interpretation; he does not presume to tell us whether this infinite recurrence is reasonable or not, for good or for ill, only that it propels us towards the future ("Man never is, but always to be blessed.")

"Dum spiro, spero" (while I breathe, I hope) is a Latin proverb that is somewhat less ambiguous, as it suggests that hope cannot be separated from life itself. But when Judy breathes shallowly to avoid breaking down into tears, I recall the seventeenth century poet Abraham Cowley's warning that hope is "the most hopeless thing of all," which anticipates the darkness of Freud's vision and implies that we rely too heavily on illusions to ease the heart and quiet the mind (or, in contemporary psychological terms, defend against anxiety.) Because Judy ricocheted violently between these varying perspectives, not taking the time to give either one its rightful due, her life was torn asunder by unreconciled contradictions.

"I should do what everyone else seems perfectly happy to do, which is not to care so much about all the stupidity and wastefulness in the world; that's just the way things are and I'd save myself a lot of grief if I didn't try to change it." Judy would make pronouncements such as this after offering me a blow by blow account of yet another episode of her work life in which she had banged her head up against an apparently impenetrable human wall built of incompetence and apathy. But since on such occasions she would invariably dart me a quizzical glance as I paused to contemplate how to respond to this mix of moral, pragmatic, and self-preservative imperatives, I gathered that her resolutely hopeless tone was merely a camouflage for paralyzing uncertainty.

Indeed, had Judy really been certain that the better way for her to live was to turn defeat into victory and disentangle herself from the power struggles she routinely engaged in (defending the underdog against her father's Old World prejudices, confronting her mother honestly against her staged helplessness, and her boyfriend Bill for his aimless drifting), she would have already substituted the ideal of self-reliance or its Eastern variant, Buddha-like detachment, for her romantic ideals of restoration, self-determination, and transformation, but evidently she hadn't. For when she arrived at my office, she was feeling both fatalistic and morally outraged, ashamed of her failures but proud of her battle scars. ("No peace without justice" was her mantra.) Propelled in different directions by contrary versions of the American Dream that anything is possible if you only put your mind to it, Judy flirted with one idealization after another, and then with the possibility of living without ideals of any sort, since hope proved to be as much a source of frustration as vitality.

"Hope is a four-letter word; it's my drug. I've got to let it go." Choking on her words as she made her vow of abstinence, Judy used to remind me of a bulimic, who, after recklessly gorging on a private stash of chips dipped in extra hot salsa, imagines that she can only find peace of mind by violently purging. Perhaps Judy was hoping that psychotherapy would curb her monstrous appetite for unactualized possibilities, but since that too was proving to be disappointing, she was preparing to recycle the traditional but radical solution to the problem of disappointment – stoical self reliance and the emotional cleanse.

Sometimes as I listened to Judy's diatribes, first against unfulfilled potential and then against unfounded hope, I felt as confused and helpless as Judy seemed to feel, since I could no more promise her that life would turn out to be "fair" (meaning that all potentials would be fulfilled) than I could reassure her that she could or should establish a sense of inner peace nevertheless. I questioned whether she would feel less lonely and hence more peaceful if I empathized with her grim vision of reality (which could easily spiral into hopelessness) or if I cast doubts by questioning its shadowy origins. And then I wondered, as analytically trained therapists do, what her positive or negative responses told me about the value of my therapeutic intervention. There is something wrong with therapy, I told myself, if I am just her echo and she mine, or if she always ends our sessions complimenting my insights and feeling upbeat and vindicated! Didn't we agree from the outset that the truth is often painful and that the messenger of bad news is rarely welcomed with open arms? And yet, like her, I was willing to be such a messenger, even if it made her angry and me uncomfortable.

In one emotional register, Judy's descant on hope sounded unduly somber if not downright cynical – it was inimical to an ethos of self-actualization that has been implicit in my psychotherapeutic practice. But in another, it sounded enlightened, progressive, and, in its own peculiar fashion, life affirming. As long as she experienced her hopes as an addiction, a wish-fulfilling fantasy that only clouded her vision and laid the ground for bitterness and resentment, then (in a variation of the Beatles song) I had to agree: "let it go, let it go, let it go!" And to borrow from Freud, there is no future in an illusion!

Judy's flare for the rhetorical fueled both sides of the argument, but I have to admit that it was my own inconsistencies that rendered me vulnerable, first to her disenchantment with the world and its unreliable provisions, and then to her renewed passion to transform the world so that it is more habitable and she can find sustenance in it. (Once again, I hear echoes of my bitterly pessimistic father and my naively optimistic mother.) There may indeed be no future in inflated hope, but a choreographed future, drained of purpose and authentic connections that she had conjured up as the only viable alternative promised to be just as insubstantial and considerably more lonely.

Disengagement: Defeat or Victory?

(In which I examine how difficult it is to determine when emotional detachment is a defensive avoidance of life's inevitable messiness and when it is a healthy acceptance of the limits of desire.)

As the only woman in her German immigrant family to go to college, let alone get a Master's degree and be elected to office in a professional organization, Judy was determined to do what her mother was unable to do, which was to stand up for what she wanted and believed in even if it might make other people uncomfortable and leave her standing alone out in the cold (a "hard ass bitch," a stone-faced sphinx, an evil prophetess, or, from Judy's perspective, an earnest David mistaken for a brutish Goliath).

To remain coolly detached from the world of steamy emotions, impervious to the pain of isolating rejection, was appealing to Judy. She had always wanted to be one of those slender, self-possessed women in the classic movies who wore tailored suits with narrow skirts and never had a hair out of place. (Grace Kelly was her model, maybe Katherine Hepburn, but certainly not Marilyn Monroe.)

And yet, Judy was chunky, not slender, and detachment from her desires and emotions often conjured up images of feminine submission and passive surrender – her mother's cowardly retreat from open conflict, her domesticated sister's disappearance into her suburban stupor. Indeed, hope and passionate resistance against injustice and limitation (conventional morality) was Judy's private religion even if it doubled as her personal problem. Was it her problem because it was private, pushed underground and rendered hopeless, I wondered to myself? Or was it private for safekeeping, preserved securely within the recesses of her heart so as not to be lost forever? Undiluted, uncontaminated, nonconformist, Judy was *not* consumer friendly, nor should she be according to my therapeutic values. But which interpretation should we work with on a given afternoon? Which presented Judy and me with a greater problem?

When I had met Judy three years before, she was mourning the end of a five-year relationship that was supposed to have culminated in marriage and children but had instead unraveled when Bill, on the spur of the moment, accepted a job in another city without first discussing the move with her. Bill waxed poetic whenever he spoke of his feelings for her, and even after moving three hours away continued to send her flowers every other week for no particular reason, but when it came to charting a course for their future life together this self-directed (self-absorbed) post-modern lover procrastinated, circled round exhaustively, and paid homage to her spirit of independence. "You're different from the other women I meet. You have a mind of your own and a life of your own; you don't tip toe and aren't afraid to make a few enemies which is why I fell in love with you."

Judy could not deny that she was flattered by Bill's praise and gratified that he appreciated the very qualities that often cast her apart from the other women in her small, family-oriented Michigan community. However, in the telling of her story, it was also clear that Judy had lost patience with Bill's inclination to live reactively, or, as he put it spontaneously, unattached to anything but his feelings in the moment, and with her patience she lost her enthusiasm for playing the part of chief Major General, aka Everybody's Know-It-All Mother. "Sure, I can do it all myself and make it on my own, I can even map out and coordinate future career paths for the both of us, but why should I have to? Do I want to? I am competent and responsible, I straighten up the messes so we can move forward and get stuff done, but . . ."

I inferred from the despondent look in her eyes at the conclusion of her unfinished sentence that whether or not she was successful in galvanizing the troops at her workplace or coordinating a week-end excursion with Bill, Judy found little in her life worth celebrating. For while hope inspired her passionate struggle against inertia and complacency, pushing the rock up the hill like the mythical figure Sisyphus was a lonely passion – autoerotic, sado-masochistic, and anti-climactic. Indeed, whatever the outcome, as the Solitary Struggler or the disembodied spirit of self-reliance, the spirits of Judy, the woman, sank beneath the weight of envy and failure. "I feel like I'm treading water, going nowhere fast. Sure, I've survived, and have proven myself (though no one seems to care enough to notice), but what have I accomplished if there's no love or joy? I've lived in my house for eight years now and still don't feel it's really home."

Although her tone of voice was unapologetically irritable, the expression on her face was frequently one of genuine puzzlement when she asked no one in particular, "Why do I have to be so goddamn demanding and insist that people live up to their principles? Am I a perfectionist as Bill insists, or am I simply a fighter, not willing to settle for less than what is possible and pretend that that is okay? Should I just be happy going with the flow like everyone else?" Furtively, Judy searched my face for some form of direction. Once again it was difficult to know how to respond to her gruff appeal to my professional judgment as it raised so many complex moral issues along with the usual intra-psychic ones. (Go with the flow? Be happy? Maybe. What's so bad about that picture? Conform? Dumb down? Certainly not!)

Was Judy hungry for deeper insight into her staunch refusals to compromise her noble principles and find pleasure in settling down, which would mean that I should accept her invitation to chip away at her rationalizing defenses as painful as that might be? ("Yeah, what are you so afraid of drifting into if you let yourself go with the flow?") Or was her question not a question at all but actually a plea for me to understand her unpopular but more ethically complex perspective on life and love? Did she need support and empathy rather than probing analysis as she documented her frustrating encounters with an unreliable universe?

Knowing that some therapists would respond in one way to her confusion and bitterness and others would respond in another, I was in a quandary. If I ventured an interpretation that implied that some of her misery was self-created, defensive, and therefore unnecessary, would she hear it as an accusation or a message of hope? Would my analysis of her disavowed, unconscious feelings only confirm to her that she should not rely on me anymore than anyone else for understanding or moral support, or would it have the opposite effect? After all, I argued in favor of a more classically Freudian approach, if I don't uncover some deeper meaning, or cast a fresh light on her stale repetitions, then on what basis would she have to question her dismal perspective on life and human relationships or her rigid adherence to a creed of self-reliance?

Wishing to come up with some combination of insight into the early childhood origins of her emotional and spiritual isolation, and compassion for her current experiences of frustration and disappointment, I was intent on not sacrificing the one authentic therapeutic response for the other, as I wondered whether her mournful but stolid decision to force Bill's hand, to either set a date to marry now or go their separate ways, was overly peremptory and self-defeating or justifiably demanding and self-restorative. We needed to know whether Judy's insistence that Bill make a commitment was her latest subversion of "normal" human needs for love and attachment or a defense of them. Was she trying to break loose from the bondage of an ideal of self-reliance (in which case I would want to support her) or was this move a variation on the same old mournful theme. "I always knew I shouldn't rely on anyone else and should just resume my struggle to be happy on my own." A belief in the value of self-reliance and the courage not to rely on unfruitful hope could be life affirming, but it could just as easily be truncating. Which was it this time for Judy?

Sometimes when I listened first to Judy's pointed criticisms – of Bill's slipperiness and her colleagues' laziness – and then to her self-recriminations over her obvious failure to remain sufficiently impervious, I hoped that through our conversations we would cultivate an appreciation for ambiguity, along with a greater tolerance for human frailty. "I like your sharp angles, Judy, but don't you ever want to round the edges, wander aimlessly, and just cuddle on the couch?" I free associated to myself, noting her rounded thighs, her loosely fitting blouse, and her baby fat double chin. "And how is it that we've never talked about sex or babies, or how you feel about being overweight and single when the office chatter is about husbands and children, good places to eat and the latest diets?"

But then there were other occasions when I identified more with Judy's prickly intolerance, when I even admired her bulldog-like refusal to tread more lightly with Bill, exercise more diplomacy with her colleagues, or speak euphemistically, with sensitivity to the "politically correct." Perhaps, amidst the myriad pressures to conform – get married, go to the gym, be grateful for collecting a paycheck and being able to try out a new restaurant Friday night – what she needed most from me was recognition for the loneliness of her worthy struggle to uphold her principled independence. ("Don't dull your feelings of outrage at the sorry state of human relations including Kafkaesque bureaucracies, mall culture, and Bill's inconsistent lovemaking; don't limit your aspirations to those of the suburban cul de sac or the singles culture of unattached sex; and certainly don't sell yourself short by signing onto the latest miracle diet.") If I refused on account of my principles to offer Judy hope for a 'happily ever after' as a wife and mother or a resistance fighter, couldn't I at least offer her my genuine appreciation for her insights and frustrations? "Hold onto your spirit and don't lose your bite!"

Indeed, as much as Judy appealed to me to liberate her from the lonely tower of suspicion to which she reluctantly retreated periodically to lick her wounds, she continued to imagine that the self-respect she derived from separating herself from the flock would prove, in the long run, to be ample compensation for the loss of simpler pleasures. If I too were able to imagine that one day Judy could turn her back on hopeless hope and find sufficient solace, if not vindication, in a world of self-sufficiency, I would have had a clearer sense of where she was headed in life and where we were headed in therapy. Honestly, however, I couldn't, the fantasy didn't seem real.

Thus, it was with a mix of curiosity and envy that Judy described Kerri, another social worker at the agency where she worked, who seemed better able than she to tolerate life's disappointments. "She's always cheerful, she gets along well with everybody in the building, and is clearly proud that she never takes her work home with her; she probably thinks I'm a troublemaker because after all these years I still hold people accountable – I can't stand to see children suffering because of ignorance, laziness, or cowardice, and I am very vocal about it. But then who is the one who will get an ulcer in five years or die of a heart attack banging her fist at the next team meeting?"

On that particular afternoon, after a week of receiving no e-mails from Bill, there was no question in Judy's mind as to who would end up suffering that unhappy fate. However, as soon as she began to toy with the possibility of emulating Kerri's sunny and undoubtedly more quiescent approach to life's complexities and frustrations, I could feel her start to bristle. "According to my father, I'm too damn picky, and according to my mother, I'm single at forty-three because I've never learned how to please a man. 'Why don't you bring Bill his coffee, I bet he'd like a little pampering'..." Apparently, Kerri's equanimity – her ability to "go with the flow" and bend without breaking – had evoked memories in Judy of her parents' admonitions and negative judgments, and it rankled her to think that they would enjoy Kerri's complacency and condemn her disquietude. Thus, the moment in which making love instead of war looked inviting passed quickly. Placed in the context of her personal history, it was difficult to distinguish flexibility from capitulation, peaceful accommodation from a cowardly, stereotypically feminine response to life's grueling battles. "Kerri can turn the other cheek and win the contest for the most-easy-to-get-along-with, but I will persist in my refusal to tolerate fools," is how I understood her silent stare.

Bearing witness to Judy's frustrated aspirations to love and intimacy without being blinded by love or stretched limp by connections, I was once again torn between varying perspectives as to what would be the most helpful response. After all, Judy's problem was essentially the existential dilemma that every one of us faces in one form or another. But if I simply commiserated with her about contradictions in the human condition (which I certainly could with all sincerity), how could that possibly help Judy wrest herself from her entanglements? And furthermore, how transparently confused was a psychotherapist supposed to be?

By sharing in her experience as she described it rather than directing her attention inward in search of unconscious and less rational motivations for her particular brand of unsettledness, I would be hiding my doubts about the credibility of her story. So, was I being manipulative by encouraging her to trust me as an empathic listener, hoping that she would be willing, at some point in the future, to dig deeper in and consider a more analytical perspective? Through my steady gaze and rhythmic nods, I was inviting her to rely on me as a person who understands and does not judge. But I had to ask myself whether this invitation, this provision of a temporary "shelter from the storm" (to borrow from a Bob Dylan song), would serve her well when after the hour was up she had to walk out of the office and re-enter real life? Was empathy a temporary fix I was indulging in, one that gratified both of us but was merely an easy way out?

My inner dialogue continued: Perhaps instead of calming her unsettledness by trying on her uncomfortable shoes, walking alongside her, and understanding her pain, I should be prying the old shoes off her feet, pointing out the callouses and blisters, and casting doubt upon the tightly wound logic of her narrative ("Your story is compelling but it is a distraction; your pain is self-perpetuating; try as you may to prove yourself a victim, I refuse to be misled by the obvious facts and collude in your fantasy constructions in which you are martyred to inviolable convictions.") By probing beneath the surface, in search of buried and unknown sources of her disappointment and despair, I knew I would be taking the risk of rupturing our seemingly seamless connection, and adding myself to her endless list of people who saw her as the problem and wished she would just make peace, "adjust," be nice (like everyone else in the Midwest) and settle down. And yet, wouldn't the rupture that comes from uncovering the truth be consistent with her values as well as mine?

I had no doubt that some psychoanalytically minded therapists from my New York past would reproach me were I to offer myself to Judy as a softly lighted mirror or supportive mother figure rather than as an expert guide to lead her on a grueling archeological dig. They would warn against the dangers of gratifying rather than interpreting a patient's childlike wishes for love from an idealized parent. They would remind me that the ultimate goal of treatment is attaining self-reliance and breaking free of infantile dependency relationships that cripple. Any detour that distracts us from that goal may be a seduction, and hence a form of resistance on both our parts. These classical analysts (the purists of my imagination) cannot spy on me in my office in South Bend, Indiana, but their ideals and prohibitions, engraved inside my head, challenge me to draw the lines between good pleasures and bad, between being an anchor and a resource for my patients (which every healthy adult needs) and being a life support system, an idealized paternalistic or maternalistic figure (which every healthy adult shouldn't need even if he harbors wishes for it).

Ironically, when Kevin and Judy look to me for validation and reassurance, hoping that I won't judge them as too monstrous or too crazy, now that I know their guilty secrets, they prompt me to seek outside support (if need be in memories of people whom I admire) before settling on a response that is both honest and encouraging. I, along with my New York contingency, may uphold an ideal of individual freedom and self-determination that echoes Judy's commitment to being the office whistle-blower and Kevin's resistance to following the fashionable dress-code, but I would be deceiving myself if I didn't acknowledge the shadowy inheritance of shared principles (the principle of self-reliance being one) that I have distilled from someone, somewhere, sometime.

So when Judy sneaks me a soulful glance out of the corner of her steely grey eyes, or throws a poison dart in my direction, hoping perhaps to see that even her therapist bleeds, I am more aware than ever that I rely on my "imaginary friends" and critics to help me shape my ideas, and, moreover, that I should. Within me there are faint and unarticulated memories of my childhood, my teachers, my former therapist that surround my personal fears of giving in too much or too little; they advise me on the reliability of hope and how best Judy can live with or, if need be, without it. Should I then, as certain of the "purists" suggest, deny her the help that I take freely for myself if only in the privacy of my imagination?

Self-reliance? An ideal born from a union of hope and despair. Should I try to convince Judy, the "freak of nature," the "office trouble-maker" to give it up? Well, not entirely. Relying on other people is always risky business, with hidden costs, so if I lure her out of her lonely ivory tower I must not make false promises that I know I cannot keep. As Judy's therapist I hoped to rescue hope from a premature death-in-life, yet I did not want to abandon its close relation – the courage not to.

Judy could argue eloquently first for and then against the morality of hopelessness, the dignity of self-reliance and the honesty of disillusionment, but until we addressed the proverbial elephant in the room (her quivering lip, her weight, her blunt disdain for her own and other people's "laziness," not to mention our paid-for intimacies), neither of us would be convinced that her well-reasoned arguments could tell us how she should govern her actions tomorrow or even the next hour.

She was reeling from her decision to put closure on what she had once believed to be a promising love relationship, a relationship in which she had hoped she could be a little bit "lazy," if lazy meant relying on someone else to take care of her even though she could do it for herself. And so, when she proclaimed that she would find greater happiness in detachment than in attachment, greater dignity in self-sufficiency than in the heated pursuit of "impossible dreams," it had to be understood against this backdrop. "Impossible?" Her voice catches, the prophecy unravels, and fortunately as much as unfortunately I have no crystal ball by which to predict the future, only the power of the self-fulfilling prophecy, and that is immeasurable.

Might she not discover in twenty years, around the time that she is ready to retire, that the sobering picture she had painted of reality was as much of an illusion as the romanticized dreams she had rejected as a matter of principle? Indeed, her vision of the Good Life stripped of dreams and attachments might turn out to be not only less than good enough, but less than what was realistically possible. She was only forty-three, I was tempted to remind her, and she had only just begun to consider seriously the possibility that emotional entanglements are not by definition dangerous entrapments. Should she foreclose on a possibility that had been incubating for so many years within the shadows of self-reliance? Granted, possibilities might miscarry or be stillborn; surely reality would never match her carefully preserved ideals. But why be so certain that the "good enough" is not good enough?

Although it is my bias that my hopes and fears, my ideals and prejudices, should not be imposed upon my patients, whatever choice I make – to mirror or to interpret, to provide personal support by way of sympathetic nods and frowns or to remain as neutral as is possible, offering interpretations without any sign of emotion and leaving all that up to her – is an expression of them. Thus, no less than Judy, I had within my private library opposing "books of rules" that offered me different definitions of courage, different sources of pride and joy, and different visions of the Good Life, and everything I said or did not say was bound to be a kaleidoscopic reflection of them.

The kaleidoscope turned from moment to moment and week to week, but despite the revolutions in thought and feeling something remained constant: my belief in the process of recollection and self-disclosure. Indeed, regardless of our repeated failures to find a single originating source for her unhappiness or a universal principle to guide her towards a self-fulfilling life, I had faith that Judy could draw strength from having intimate conversations about irrational feelings (which typically masquerade as rational arguments), and in the process come to realize that self-reliance was sometimes but not always the most honest or most reliable principle to live by. If this were to prove true, and my faith were to prove to be not just an illusion, then that itself would be good enough.

"The Ego is (not) Master in his own House"

Sigmund Freud, *Introductory Lectures on Psychoanalysis,* (1917)

(In which Judy resists the bondage of dependent love and finds herself imprisoned by her independence.)

A brief history of the swinging pendulum: Before Bill asked Judy her ring size and her preferences in living room furniture, before he repaired her leaky faucet and spoke of summer vacations in which they would explore the wilds of Alaska, Judy fixed her own sinks, dreamed up her own more modest vacations, and placed little value on rings or furniture or extravagances, either aesthetic or romantic. Having weaned herself at an early age from dependence on her parents' unappetizingly conditional love, Judy sought to create her own sources of nourishment and stimulation, and had managed to draw courage, if not joy, from her capacity to do and do without.

Indeed, for most of her adult life Judy had maintained that she didn't need rings, that she scarcely noticed the condition, let alone the design, of her hand-me-down furniture, and that she was fully capable of piecing together a patchwork quilt of summer vacations, conferences, and continuing education courses at a moment's notice. Rings, bedroom sets, and family trips planned well in advance were the kinds of things that her mother nagged her father about, and what the disconsolate women she knew foolishly depended upon to lift their droopy spirits.

While Judy had never explicitly identified herself as a feminist, since affiliating with any group was inimical to her notion of untrammeled autonomy, she had made a point of distinguishing herself from stereotypically feminine women such as Kerri whose self-worth seemed to hinge upon the frail props of social convention. According to Judy, these social forms offered women the mere illusion of unconditional love, and the mere promise of self-respect, and robbed them of the reality. Or at least this was Judy's memory of how she had once understood the politics of sexuality.

So, how could Bill have guessed that, five years into their relationship, Judy would be hurt and offended when he took another job, sold his house, and moved into a studio apartment three hours away, without offering to make her a firm marriage commitment? An Amazon lady warrior such as Judy was not supposed to hunger for a permanent home, let alone put pressure on a man to build it with her; nor was she supposed to rely on the institution of marriage to legitimize her rights and consolidate her future. No Sleeping Beauty lying in wait for Prince Charming to bring her back to her life, Judy should have been capable of holding on indefinitely and loving without encumbering conditions. Why, then, Bill must have asked himself, did she seem unwilling to? Was it that she had lost sight of the true source of her dignity, was the question Judy asked herself, or was it that she had developed deeper insight into how to defend it in her relationships with others?

Neither Judy nor Bill had anticipated that their intimacy would make cracks in her walls and change the way Judy thought about the character of courage. Nor did they imagine that her brush with domesticity would make her less willing and, consequently, less capable of either marching forth alone into battle or settling for a life of solitary contemplation and independent action. They couldn't have known that glimpses into Bill's secret vulnerabilities had whetted Judy's appetite for late-night confessionals, that his unpredictable highs and lows cast her sober righteousness in a darker light. Paradoxically, Bill's admiration for Judy's vinegary personality stimulated within Judy replenishing fantasies of mutuality and surrender. Whether she labeled it an addiction or a revelation, she couldn't deny that she wanted more than the life she had had.

So at the age of forty-three, the moral distinction that Judy had once drawn between respectable love that was given and taken freely, without pressure or conditions, and pathetic love that was grasping and entangling with strings attached, began to blur, and the complexion of courage changed. As her attachment to Bill intensified, her prior attitude of stoical detachment appeared to be less an honest expression of positive self-regard than a disingenuous retreat from emotional reality. The ideal of transcendence had lost its luster (a distant star of no immediate consequence), and then it did matter to her where Bill slept during the week and whether he planned to regularly share with her a morning cup of coffee. Most significantly, however, it mattered whether what mattered to her mattered to Bill or anyone else. And then came the blow . . .

Since his precipitous move to another city for a job opportunity that neither one of them anticipated, Judy had methodically boxed up Bill's pictures and papers and hauled his desk into a corner of the garage they used to share. And yet, six months later, the empty space in the bedroom that used to be strewn with Bill's excess papers was still empty, and Judy continued to respond, albeit non-committally, to Bill's unpredictable, yet not infrequent, appearances and e-mails.

Impassively, Judy reported the facts to me during our first session, and then scanned my face for a reaction. I felt as if I were being tested, but it was a peculiar kind of a test, as neither of us had access to the correct answers. No doubt she wondered what I felt she should feel and do about Bill. (Should she be more or less tolerant of his inconsistencies, his unreliability? Was the amount of love he offered good enough despite her feeling otherwise?) And then probably she questioned whether my feelings, any more than Bill's, should have an influence on hers and on her life decisions. Clearly she wanted my help orienting herself (just as she had wanted Bill's), but as she was unaccustomed to requiring help from anyone, she didn't feel comfortable wanting, let alone asking for it and then getting no definitive answer.

In Judy's experience independence had been a cure for her unhappiness, but now she was confused as to whether that was the source of her unhappiness. When she was living with Bill, her stubborn refusals to give in, slow down, and change course on a moment's notice presented barriers to intimacy. She had wanted to dismantle those barriers and despite the enormous resistance she had felt within herself, she had steadily chipped away, her eyes had been fixed on the distant horizon where Bill had beckoned encouragingly. Once Bill left, however, she wanted those so-called barriers back – her strong opinions about politics, her preferences in music, her dislike of cooking, and her week-end routines and rituals. These were what had always made

Judy Judy; they were her backbone and what distinguished her from everyone else. Without this backbone she seemed shapeless and unattractive, she was scarcely recognizable to herself. No more the "hard-assed bitch," she now was a blob. So, naturally I wondered too – about her being accommodating and then not accommodating to Bill, about her turning her gaze hopefully towards him and me and then pulling away and looking within herself for her purpose and her anchors.

I wasn't about to make a claim that the real truth about Judy had finally emerged from the recesses of her unconscious now that she acknowledged wanting a committed romantic relationship, not simply an open-ended one, or that her signature of self-reliance was nothing other than an artful self-deception. But I did want to affirm that this newly articulated experience of things mattering was the truth of how Judy felt now, and that there would be serious consequences were she to live as if it weren't.

Depressed, angry, and as much confused by the disruptiveness of her emotions as by the uncertainty of Bill's attachment, Judy could shore up her flagging defenses and renew her life-long battle against the dangers of dependency (gathering support from stoics, feminists and certain classically trained psychoanalysts who, like stowaways, I sneak into our sessions), or she could bandage her wounds and forge ahead still bloodied and wobbling (with the encouragement of romantics, other feminists, and the inter-subjective psychotherapists who quarrel with the values of the analysts), at the risk of chasing a shadow down a blind alley.

The implicit question Judy posed during her first session was deeply personal; in essence she asked me, "What should I do about my feelings for Bill?" Yet, it was also existential; in effect, "How should a person respond to emotional upheaval?" The choice she tentatively made, to seek resolution for her dilemma in an open-ended dialogue rather than in decisive action or solitary contemplation, was a foreshadowing of the form the resolution would take.

Cracks in the Walls: Tragic or Fortuitous?

Because it was out of character for Judy to ask for help, whether she was cleaning up other people's messes or sweeping out her own private chimney (to borrow a phrase from Freud's patient Anna O. who referred to his talking cure as "chimney sweeping,"), I felt privileged that every Thursday evening she granted me permission to lend her a hand. I imagine that in the early stages of therapy, paying for my help was what made it possible for Judy to even consider accepting it: as long as she could depersonalize our relationship and see it as simply an exchange of "services rendered," she did not have to run the risk of feeling dependent, indebted and, following her trail of associations, inadequate. (The "world's oldest profession," religious confessionals, and the more recent popularity of Facebook computer sex all suggest that Judy is not alone in feeling more comfortable exposing her private parts to a virtual stranger who, by definition, is detached from her "real" life.)

Thus, ironically, the myth of therapeutic neutrality, in mirroring Judy's own myth of self-reliance, encouraged her to deviate from it. And while I will never know for certain whether it was my professional anonymity or my personal responsiveness that made Judy feel safe enough to expose her felt weaknesses to me, I am certain that Judy's anxieties about becoming too dependent and hence too submissive were sufficiently contained in our relationship for her to renege on her childhood vow to make her way entirely on her own. She needed outside help if she wished to understand herself and not just plaster over the cracks in her walls. Unlike the analyst who positions himself behind the couch, I look Judy straight in the eye because I want her to see me and also to see that I see her. If we weren't face to face like that, how would she have had the opportunity to take the risk she wanted to take of admitting that she had such a need?

Such admissions did not come painlessly, however, and usually right after having exposed herself as not entirely self-contained, Judy would ingeniously divert our attention elsewhere, away from her amorphous wishes for more, toward some distant conflagration which no rational person would want any part of. Indeed, if it had not been for the fact that at some point in nearly every session Judy's eyes watered, and that whenever this happened she measured out her words carefully so that the quiver in her lips subsided rather than exploded into a full-fledged sob, she might have convinced me that the primary source of her suffering was her honesty, her willingness to "tell it like it is." ("You know that nobody can handle a woman who doesn't smile and bake cookies; people see me as a . . .")

The sentence trailed off, as her sentences frequently did when she was about to approach a sensitive subject. She smiled smugly, but only for an instance, consciously refusing to grant her adversaries a platform for their libelous attacks on her character. I saw her struggling, afraid to admit that she herself had doubts, and, moreover, that she cared whether people saw her as principled or simply bitchy. Her words had echoed her mother's words which apparently still stung when she recalled them to mind. Could she brush them off like pesky mosquitoes or would I see her flinch beneath her veneer of contempt? As she hurriedly wiped away a solitary tear, pretending that it wasn't really happening (a sort of negative hallucination), her resolve to stand firmly on inviolable principle became indistinguishable from her self-induced blindness to her own and others' emotional realities.

So, whereas Judy was more honest than most patients, when it came to accurately pointing out my every mis-step, such as a glib interpretation or a clumsy stab at empathy, she showed no visible signs of recognition or appreciation for what to me were startling moments of insight and emotional connection. Selectively attentive, seeing only the gaps and little else, she deprived herself and me of honestly earned, shared pleasures that both of us deserved to enjoy. How unfair, how incomplete and how mis-representative, but also how predictable, given her creed of self-reliance!

Nevertheless, over the course of three years, Judy rarely missed a session and I always looked forward to seeing her, despite the struggles we became entangled in when I refused to share her despair or her sardonic tone or encourage her gratuitous depreciations of all the intellectual and moral lightweights that populated the world. I wasn't about to defend the Kerris of the workplace who paper over all that isn't pleasing, or the Bills who shrug off responsibility and hope that the fates will look kindly upon them. Nor did I wish to plead forgiveness for the kind of bureaucratic laziness or passive resignation that was easy and dishonest but led to untold suffering. And yet, as we peered into the widening cracks in Judy's fortress-like walls, cracks that were not qualitatively different from the cracks in mine, we were able to rely on a shared hope of making peace with injustice, of being able to open up just enough to breathe in some fresh oxygen and breathe out some old waste products.

Because Judy could not help but realize through our conversations that I too had unrequited desires (for one thing I didn't have the answers she wanted and didn't try to hide it by disappearing or pontificating), and that I too had to make peace with the unreliability of the world, what would have previously signified her weakness and humiliation came to signify as well our human connection. My failure to sift out the ambiguities and home in on the Truth frustrated and disappointed my secret aspirations to be a therapist of extraordinary insight, but it relieved both of us of the stigma of being frustrated and disappointed. If I could publically acknowledge the incompleteness of my understanding and helpfulness, then maybe she could stop pretending to be complete unto herself.

Between us we generated a dissonance that might have been unbearable in solitary contemplation, but in that dissonance we were able to affirm certain essential truths: lived reality is highly subjective (hers was different from mine), subjectivity is inevitably unstable (she changed me and I changed her), and instability is a catalyst for an intimacy that need not be founded on blind faith. (We connected best when she was neither mindlessly submissive like her mother nor mindlessly dogmatic like her father.) The price Judy had paid for living as an apostle of self-reliance was that she could never feel at home in the world. As she began to feel at home with me, she could consider whether shaping a life apart from Life was worth her efforts.

Eschewing absolutes as a matter of principle, my moral relativism in regard to the question of how to live was tempered by the belief that if Judy were to emerge from beneath the shadow of competing idealizations (Hollywood's and Emerson's), she would find the courage to hope while preserving the freedom not to.

When Judy first arrived at my door she was already wavering in her commitment to an image of the good life that set her apart from all that was unreliable – her emotions and the world. Doomed to fail, inasmuch as success in such a life would constitute a form of self-erasure, she was also doomed to struggle. Although she wouldn't have admitted it at the time, Judy came to me with the hope of gaining access to a less shameful and hence more serene experience of herself and a home. Self-reliance, as she had translated it in her life up until then, had failed to deliver on its promise. I had confidence that if she could just let me help her acknowledge both her hopes and her disappointments she would feel more serene about how to proceed with life, with or without Bill.

Which was the greater challenge for Judy, now that marriage had receded from her horizon? To be more or less self-reliant? To struggle for more of what Bill failed to give her in the way of support and consistency or to step away from the struggle and make do with less? The answer turned out to be another riddle, for the challenge was to do all of the above and therefore neither one nor the other.

Postscript: The Courage to Hope and the Freedom Not to

One Thursday morning after I had left for the office, Judy telephoned my home to cancel that evening's appointment. After awkwardly apologizing for having mistakenly dialed the wrong number, she spoke briefly with my husband, telling him that she had to leave town unexpectedly and would call me back at some point to reschedule. I wasn't surprised by the message as I knew that her mother's health had been precarious, and that her father was not only an unreliable source of medical information but also an unsympathetic marriage partner who had grown increasingly callous over the years to his wife's anxious dependency. As Judy described it, she was alone in her refusal to accept the inevitability of her helpless and hopeless mother's decline. Therefore, by default, it had become her job, not her married younger sister's or older brother's, to plow through the ever-accumulating medical, legal, and relational debris. ("My brother never calls them and my sister doesn't see that there are any major problems; then again, first things first, she has to get the kids to soccer.")

Nevertheless, I was surprised that she had "accidentally" dialed my home rather than my work number, and was even more surprised when the weeks slipped into months before I was to hear from her again. (Both behaviors were aberrations.) Her absence forced me to rely exclusively on my own imaginings to make sense out of what happened, and this I did, but at some cost. (More proof, if I needed proof, that self-reliance, even as a therapist, is perversely undependable.)

In my imagination Judy was angry or disappointed with me; after all, the one time she had tried to reach out in a moment of crisis, breaching the invisible boundary line that divided my professional from my personal life, I was not there. Knowing Judy, I wouldn't be surprised if, while holding onto the receiver, she had felt exposed and foolish, wanting to end a conversation with my husband that she never should have started. And what's more, by discovering inadvertently that I had a husband whom I could rely on (if only to take my messages), she might have felt envious and then turned the tables and become suspicious of my therapeutic intentions. How could she trust me to be her model or to be an independent-enough woman to serve as a counterweight to her overly dependent mother? Did I resemble the infamous Kerri? And more importantly, if she stayed in therapy, would she lose her bite and begin to resemble her as well?

As the weeks slipped by and I still didn't hear from Judy, I asked myself whether she was keeping her distance because she was afraid that psychotherapy would weaken rather than strengthen her. Perhaps Judy was the bull-dog whom everyone rebelled against, but by the same token, who else could be depended upon to barrel through adversity, run interference, and uphold the law. What would happen to her, her mother, or the foster children she was advocating for on her job if she absconded, if she went with the flow? Who would take up the banner in her stead? Certainly not me or Bill.

Such interpretations of Judy's "resistance" to returning to therapy were credible; nevertheless, I knew that they could easily be projections of my own anxieties, and therefore misguided. After all, Judy's absence might mean that psychotherapy was silently "working," that within our semi-sterile "laboratory of meaning" she had reconstituted the strength that Bill's departure had shaken. Maybe now, after having relied on me in small doses for an extended period of time, she was able to wean herself from my weekly support. Self reliance can be a virtue not merely a defense! Indeed, her "failure" to contact me might be a hopeful sign that she was now able to manage her family's conflicts without becoming overwhelmed or hardening her heart as her father tended to do in the face of emotional upheaval. Perhaps, in contrast to her brother and sister, who avoided their parents' messes by simply moving on with their lives, Judy had struck a balance between caring too much and not enough.

But why the radical break with therapy? Why cut off such an intimate connection so precipitously? Having been relieved of her paralyzing indecision with regard to Bill, did Judy assume that our connection should dissolve unnoticed, as stitches do after an operation? Now that she was "healed" and had survived the most dangerous of storms, did she figure that she should resume being as self-reliant as ever, that a petulant bull dog was the only alternative to a tail-wagging, people-pleasing cocker spaniel? There is no end to the fantasies about people's motivations that one can weave when there is no living person there to talk with. Some are beautiful, others are perverse, but they are all fantasies nonetheless. I needed contact with outside reality to untangle the mess accumulating inside my head.

When Judy called my office to make an appointment, four months after the mistaken call to my home, I could hardly contain my excitement. And as I listened the next week to her version of her temporary disappearance, I was relieved to hear more confirmation of my hopes than my worst fears.

Slowly wiping away the tears that spilled from the corners of her eyes (which she did not try to hide as she had in the past), Judy began by describing how her efforts to organize her mother's medical treatment had brought some minor successes but mostly resistance and frustration. Judy's father and sister were passive and her mother spoke of wills and death. And when Judy tried to galvanize the family in the direction of recovery, her sister nodded vaguely but disappeared, her father accused her of meddling ("Leave it to the doctors,") and her mother pleaded ignorance ("I don't know if there is anything that can really help"). All very predictable, she assured me, as she caught the troubled look in my eyes.

But Judy's narration didn't end with the usual exhortations against cowardice, dishonesty, and failed potential, and her tone was uncharacteristically lacking in sarcasm. On the contrary, as Judy led me through the familiar familial maze, she acknowledged her sadness and frustration at her mother's condition, located her impotence within the irrational family system she was trying to negotiate, and memorialized the ways in which hope had come to be classified in her lexicon as a "four letter word." Having emerged from this maze, she described how, dizzied and defeated, she was aware that she could see little purpose in rearming herself and storming back in. And yet paradoxically, because she no longer felt she had to remain impervious to all obstacles and subsist on the intangibles in her own mind, she felt a lot more hopeful. She was freer than she had ever imagined herself to be when she was a devotee of the creed of self-reliance. Facing the truth of her own desires, limitations, and disappointments, which she had refused to face in her less-than-honest commitment to abstract principle, gave her the hope of finding inner peace despite the desires and limitations of her family and the medical establishment, despite the unreasonable injustices of the world.

"I had organized a summer trip to California last winter – a conference with a week extra for vacationing on my own. With all my mother's plans in a state of utter confusion I was just about ready to cancel. But a girlfriend said I owed it to myself to get away, and for some reason this time I decided that I needed it, that I was not going to attempt to not need it, and I took off. Driving down the coast, with the mountains on one side of me and the open sea on the other, I felt a tremendous burden slip off my shoulders; it was magical, like I'd finally come home."

I asked Judy what made this adventure into the unknown feel like coming home, and she replied, "The freedom to be myself. It was as if the person who is the struggler stepped aside and someone more powerful moved in." Self-reliance, I thought, but a softer version; inside *this* self there was a blend of something new. One month later, back to her usual life, the same old contradictions remain: Bill still sends flowers and e-mails but fails to mention the ring he put on hold a year ago at the local jewelers, and her supervisor still asks for her advice but fails to give her credit or follow through on what needs to be done. What has changed, however, is that Judy feels differently about unpredictability, disappointed dreams, and frustrated desires. "It used to be that everywhere I went I found struggles. I dreaded them but at the same time I felt I couldn't avoid taking them on whatever the actual loss or gain. Now I can give up struggling when there's no point to it, when it's the outcome that matters. And now that outcome includes how I feel too, which, to be honest, does not always have to be unbearably disappointed."

I was confused. Had the Amazon woman-cum-social critic lost her fire or given up on her principles? Had she become a pacifist by default, a pragmatist, a conciliator, another version of Kerri? Any of these labels might have fit, but none did justice to her subjective experience of victory in the face of disappointment. The Struggler was gone, but she had not lost her standards. The outcomes still mattered: what could that mean? In order for Judy to feel "at home" driving down the coast in California, or responding to Bill's unreliable displays of affection, or her boss's inconsistent responses to her opinions, she had to grant herself the freedom to hope along with the freedom not to. Not caring about external reality was no more an attractive option than caring too much, but, luckily, she discovered that she didn't have to make that choice. Freed from an ideal she could never hope to meet, Judy could live courageously and without shame (and even hopefully), knowing that she had some freedom to choose how to care and what to care for, but no freedom to choose not to care at all.

My eyes began to fill with tears, and I confess that this time it was I who was trying to hide them. Wasn't this what psychoanalytic therapy was all about? Ordinary unhappiness (life's frustrations and our personal disappointments) had taken the place of neurotic misery (the unproductive maneuverings by which we trick ourselves into feeling purposeful). But Judy was, nonetheless, back in my office and feeling increasingly at home on my couch, so what now?

As the hour drew to a close, Judy confessed that there was no necessity for her to come back. Hesitating and uncharacteristically awkward, she wanted to know, however, if she should come, could come, even if she didn't need me to ward off an impending crisis? What parameters should a self-respecting individual adhere to, if she likes the challenge of a good hard struggle but doesn't identify herself as The Struggler on principle? Beyond the limits of budget (which are often more elastic and more subjective than commonly acknowledged), I insisted that she devise her own guidelines. I would not declare that the therapy was completely finished or our relationship was of no further value to her. She smiled at my refusal to make her decision for her, and set another appointment for two weeks later. Sensing that she was relieved that it was her decision to come back, knowing that I was relieved that she had softened enough to decide to make that decision, I wondered what that blend of softness and decisiveness meant and what would lie ahead.

POETIC JUSTICE: METAPHORS OF SUFFERING AND FORGIVENESS

" I believe that human beings are the only source of justification but that this source is not sufficient. . . . We live with insufficient sources to justify our ethics and morality."

Avishai Margalit, *The Ethics of Memory* (2002)

Metabolizing Suffering

"Men hate themselves and blame themselves on God"
(Henry Weinfield, "Fables from the Dark Ages")

"I remember on the first day of kindergarten, all the kids sat on the floor in a circle and the teacher asked us to call out our names. When my turn came around, I said 'Bastard. ' I thought that was my name because "bastard" was what my mother had always called me. The teacher looked at me funny – I remember the expression on her face like it was yesterday – and she told me that my name was *Julius.* I didn't know what to think or say. Who was I supposed to believe, my mother or this strange white woman? I felt stupid and embarrassed."

Julius paused, his eyes were burning with quiet intensity as he cast me (another white woman), a meaningful look, and then continued. "In the fourth grade there was a group of kids who called me Jun the Bum." (Jun was short for Junior, I was to learn later, and paradoxically, Julius "the bastard" was named after his father). "My clothes were dirty and full of holes, and maybe they knew that at night my mother ran numbers. I was embarrassed then too but I never let on. I put cardboard in my shoes when the soles wore down and hoped that nobody could tell the difference. When I was ten I got a job at the Puerto Rican grocery store on the corner and made my own money; I kept it hidden in a safe in my closet after my mother refused to give me back the forty dollars I gave her to hold onto. Pretty soon everyone in the neighborhood knew Jun' was the one to go to for pizza and candy. When my sister got pregnant – she was just fifteen – I'd go out and buy her diapers. At fourteen I opened up my own bank account. My mother found the bank book and saw that I had about a thousand dollars. She told me I had to start paying rent. My sisters didn't pay rent, so I refused. That was the beginning. The next year I opened up another account. She never had any bank accounts of her own, she always paid the bills with money orders that I'd buy for her down the street, with crumbled up single dollar bills and a handful of loose change, and here I had two. I feel I should love her, she gave birth to me, but I can't forgive her for what she did; it's not just the beatings and her cursing me, but that she never showed me care."

Silence followed this rapid stream of words and images. Once the tension had drained from his powerful body Julius appeared smaller and sadder as he leaned back from the edge of the couch and fiddled aimlessly with the corner of a pillow. Indeed, before my very eyes Julius seemed to be dissolving, and instead of seeing an adult version of that unself-consciously resourceful boy who figured as the brave protagonist of Julius' childhood story, I saw a self-consciously defeated man who held little faith in the value of such stories. As Julius' eyes misted over, I recalled how earlier in the session he had compared his depression to a wave: "I don't know when it will come or why, but when it does, I go under and feel helpless and ashamed."

Julius' mood had changed dramatically as what was beginning to be a coherent narrative fragmented into painfully disjointed memories before it ended abruptly, without a sense of closure. Just as he seemed to be gaining momentum and sharpening his focus, he fogged up, lost hope, and with it the mysterious pleasure he had been deriving from revisiting his pain by telling his stories. At the time, I was unprepared for the downward slide that followed on the heels of his reflective mood and our shared intimacy, but now I understand, even if I can't always predict when it will happen. Words confer a reality on what are otherwise diffuse and unsubstantiated feelings, and Julius explained to me, that this can be both good *and* bad. "Sometimes I don't want to come here and talk, because once I say that I'm depressed or feel violent, that I hate my mother or care about what the white people think when I walk into a restaurant, it makes it real." And so, whether Julius unpacks his memories from childhood (memories that are over-saturated with unprocessed feelings), or speaks of his girlfriend's unfaithfulness, his brother's death from AIDS, his father's mental collapse, or his supervisor's duplicities, he puts himself at risk.

As he shifts his body to the edge of the couch, drawing me in closer while he leaps with lightning speed from one story fragment to another, my heart beats faster. I see Julius wrestling with a pain that he can neither catalogue and file away nor evacuate, and I know that the outcome is uncertain. Since I am not merely a disinterested observer but an active participant in this match, the space between us becomes electrified, and the therapy hour is over too fast (though not fast enough, as the circuitry is in danger of overloading.)

The anguish of "the wave" has a different quality altogether from the turmoil I bear witness to most of the time. It is suffering stripped of meaning and of partnership, suffering without a context or a future. It is mindless, "oceanic," nihilistic, suicidal. Under its sway, Julius' speech becomes halting, my responses become opaque, and we both lose definition as we become anonymous bystanders groping clumsily, missing connections, waiting for the hour to come to its end. Either way, however, with meaning or without it, there is no way for Julius to avoid suffering of one form or another. As he rarely misses his twice weekly appointments, and has discontinued taking medication that helps take the edge off his anger and sadness but does not help him understand them, I assume that reflects a preference.

Questions regarding the meaning of suffering have always been central to humanity not only because they are connected to universal religious dualities such as Good and Evil, Free Will and Determinism, Spirit and Flesh, Judgment and Mercy, but because psychologically, random suffering, that is, suffering that is unpredictable and serves no end, may be the most difficult to stomach. Not only does it violate our belief in a just and orderly world and deny us a coherent target for our anger, but it denudes us of our individuality as we are cast as anonymous casualties of impersonal, irrational forces.

Because we want so desperately to discover (or some might say create) a logic if not a redeeming purpose for our pain, we construct narratives through which we locate its origins, assign responsibility and/or blame for its occurrence, and, most importantly, point ourselves in a direction where we can sustain hope for the future. Psychologists refer to the "Just World Hypothesis," according to which people adopt ideas and attitudes that preserve the belief in a just world. One ramification of the Just World Hypothesis is "blaming the victim." If people are to blame for their misfortunes, that is, if they bring them on themselves, then all is fair, and the belief in a just and orderly world is maintained.

In the Book of Job the problems of suffering and justice are considered in all of their ambiguity. At the beginning of the story, Job is singled out by God as a righteous man whose good fortune is consistent with his good character. And yet, precisely because he is both virtuous and fortunate, generous and blessed, he is chosen to become the victim of various mental and physical afflictions (not unlike the Jewish people, from whom God expects more because they are His chosen people).

In an effort to make sense out of this unanticipated and unjustified turn of events, Job's friends come up with reasons and justifications for the disasters that have befallen him, and offer practical prescriptions for what he needs to do next to secure his future. Since it is taken as a given that the God of the Jewish people is one God and that He is all-good and all-powerful, it is only logical to conclude that Job must have wronged Him in some fashion or another. His friends argue that Job's insistence on his integrity is misguided, and moreover self-destructive. In good faith, they advise him not to defend his innocence, but to assume his rightful burden of guilt.

Although this interpretation provides a simple solution to the ethical puzzle posed by the story, and in the process holds out the hope for future reconciliation and forgiveness, the text makes clear that this interpretation is wrong, and not the one that God himself offers. Indeed, as the book draws to a close, without any immediate sign of respite for Job's suffering, Job is enjoined by his Creator *not* to listen to his friends, whose formulaic analyses fail to appreciate the unfathomable and the mysterious.

To be sure, there are always reasons for suffering, but its relationship to virtue is neither predictable nor transparent. Instead of blaming himself or cursing God (as Job's wife suggests that he do), one can interpret the story as encouraging us to tolerate the ambiguities and contradictions of existence, and accept with dignity, and a minimum of rancor, the limitations of our knowledge. Job suffered, but he was not guilty, and yet the story suggests that there is coherence in the universe, though its meaning is often hidden.

If this is the case, and our conscious experience is just one tiny fragment of existence, then we are free to forgive ourselves and God, and to wrest ourselves free from the clutches of the unforgivable. Or at least, this is what I would argue as I try to apply the story of Job's suffering to the suffering of my patients. Particularly when working with couples, I am struck by how paralyzing those clutches are. Paradoxically, we do and do not wish to forgive ourselves and those we love. Indeed, when we are feeling hurt, it is infinitely more difficult to forgive but not forget, than to dig the claws in deeper as we gather supporting evidence of deeds or intentions that are unforgivable. And yet, by not forgiving, we deprive ourselves of the greatest of life's pleasures: the chance to love and be loved, and to move freely through time, albeit, with scars and wrinkles.

Because the resolution to the problem of suffering offered by the Book of Job requires us not only to acknowledge the partiality of our vision but also to suspend indefinitely our desire for clarity, it is unstable outside of a religious or quasi-religious system of meaning. Compensations must be made for unjustifiable suffering, and a measure of free will must be folded into an intricate plan of self-transformation, if not spiritual transcendence. But how?

Scientific methodologies and evolutionary theories, ten-step recovery programs, and psychoanalysis, erotic and artistic sublimations are among the approaches by which we attempt to metabolize suffering even if we cannot eliminate it at its source. Depending on the language we are fluent in, we see suffering as a medical riddle or a neuro-physiological malfunctioning, the return of the repressed or a prophetic warning, a mark of personal integrity or submission, a shameful social stigma or the battle scar of a hero. The French Romantic poet Charles Baudelaire composed "Les Fleurs du Mal," a book that can be translated either as "Flowers of Evil," or "Flowers of Suffering," which suggests that moral ambiguities are built into the language.

The Freudian Unconscious, which includes a virtual menagerie of invisible and powerful forces battling for hegemony, provides yet another vocabulary: suffering (at least the kind that is the proper subject of analysis) is not simply a passive experience that we endure but an active "compromise formation" that we invent to shield us from a still more disturbing reality. Subjective feelings of unhappiness are just the proverbial tip of the iceberg, which surfaces when we express, expel, and repudiate our Oedipal longings and fears, our unconscionable cannibalistic and oceanic fantasies. Without reference to God or Satan, or to the troublesome doctrine of Original Sin, psychoanalytic dogma reassures us that our failures and miseries are not arbitrary but symptomatic, "parapraxes" governed by the pleasure principle or some superordinate principle that lies beyond.

By transforming suffering into a metaphor we can manipulate, a diagnosis we can treat, we transform ourselves. No longer blind receptacles of unprocessed and unwanted feelings, we reclaim a measure of power over our psyches and establish points of connection to the universe.

"I try to see it as a gift . . . something I can learn from. . . . If Tom hadn't left me I might never have realized that I can manage on my own."

"You are strongest at the places where you were broken."

"I have to believe that whatever happens is supposed to happen."

"I wonder if I don't deserve the back problems I've had for the last ten years because after Lenny died, I never mourned properly. I pretended to go on with my life, but actually I still don't feel whole."

"I haven't had children, I've lived for myself, so at fifty-nine, now that I'm tenured with a house and a retirement plan, I figure it's payback time."

"As soon as I have any money I *have* to get rid of it; somehow no matter how much I earn I'm always overdrawn, I live pay check to pay check."

"I'm coming down with the flu and yet I forced myself to go running; if I don't run I know I'll be irritable with the kids; somehow it's all very punitive."

"I used to think I threw up because I binged, but now I think that sometimes I binge so I can throw up, as crazy as that sounds . . . I 'm ashamed of throwing up but it is also a tremendous relief, like the slate being wiped clean."

It is commonplace for me to hear echoes of religious themes from clients who would not readily identify themselves as "believers." Paradoxically, because they are not "religious" in the conventional sense, they want me to adjudicate their unacknowledged obsessions with the morality of how they have lived and how they are living, but at the same time, they want to believe that I do not make moral judgments and that psychotherapy, unlike a religion, is "value-free." If I were to translate their desires into the language of Freud, I would say that they want me to distribute justice fairly among the id, the ego, and the superego – that is, not to deliver judgments that are based solely on the morality of the superego.

This doubleness, this thirst for judgment coupled with an anxiety about being judged unwisely and unfairly, is to be expected, however. People come for psychotherapy because they have suffered a collapse of meaning such that institutional as well as personal metaphors of suffering and forgiveness no longer do justice to their daily experience. Pleasure as much as pain is often indigestible and unmetabolized, and so that experience itself cannot be reliably trusted. Reason too is an unreliable helpmate as it has been bowdlerized by its fraudulent look-alike, rationalization, or what philosopher Harrry Frankfurt describes in refreshingly blunt language as "bullshit."

Truth? Authenticity? Passion? Reason? Old fashioned words that are difficult to believe in. Suicide bombers are passionate, as are the bombers of abortion clinics; news anchors talk of "spin," not of facts; and political leaders *appear* on television talk shows and perform as just ordinary folk. While the ethical and emotional limbo in which we seem to live presents itself as a "virtual reality" that offers the allure of indeterminancy, giving us a smorgasbord of choices, it becomes *in*sufferable because there is "no peace without justice" or the illusion of it (among peoples or within the psyche).

As a psychotherapist, I not only bear witness, but also act as midwife or, if you will, collaborator in what constitutes a personal "truth and reconciliation" project. Indeed, I am actively recruited to make the unintelligible not only intelligible but also palatable, to make naive art out of life's raw materials. But if I've explicitly signed on to fill in the gaps in meaning and restore some semblance of balance by helping my patients construct a scaffolding upon which to build a life, this does not occur without ambivalence on both sides of the couch. Sometimes I fear that I am too ready an accomplice in my clients' efforts to draw conclusions that paper over discontinuities between "then" and "now," or contradictions between the self that identifies with "I" and the self that identifies with "Me." Words are the medium we work with, but words are never pure of unconscious allusions to prior conversations, of inaudible sense experiences or invisible memories encoded in the body. We would like to believe that we understand each other, but we speak in different dialects in an echo chamber where though we mean what we say honestly, we may not be capable of knowing what we mean. In other words, what feels truthful and coherent at one moment in time to one individual, may have only an oblique relationship to a shared understanding of truth.

One week my patient Sophie's suffering represents a measure of her insight, generosity, and self-determination, while the next week it represents a symptom of her guilt, insatiability, and self-delusion. "I suffer because my appetite is voracious and I want so much," poses one set of problems; "I suffer because I am highly sensitive," poses another; while "I suffer because I demand so little and accede to anything I'm offered," poses yet another. Often we lack the confidence to risk positing objective criteria by which to privilege one metaphor of suffering over another, and so we waver between opposing interpretations.

Sophie's restlessness, her chronic state of disequilibrium, her ruthless assaults on "the way things are," embitter her, constricting her imagination in addition to jeopardizing her physical well-being; and yet, by Sophie's own accounting, these are the very qualities that constitute her value and inspire her to acts of selflessness, creativity, and courage. As long as she can have a smoke she can delay other forms of gratification indefinitely! What then is the goal of treatment today? And wherein lies the hope for long-term cure in the future?

Managed care bureaucrats demand objectives and goals, specific dates for termination of treatment, and behavioral measures of success and failure. But subjectively speaking, a good psychotherapy session is one in which this wavering between opposing interpretations temporarily ceases, and, unpredictably, without premeditation or coercion, a coherent picture crystallizes out of the dense tangle of words and images. Although nothing has actually changed the familiar "facts" appear different – Sophie's baleful look and faded orange jeans, the gold medallion not quite hidden beneath Julius' crisply ironed tee-shirt, Judy's sour remarks and unapologetic double chin – combine idiomatically and make perfect sense.

Like the poet who transforms pain into pleasure by selecting and arranging language beautifully, my patient and I have momentarily transformed a monotonous and paralyzing experience of suffering into a metaphor of hope. Inspired by our accomplishment, we grant ourselves permission to postpone indefinitely all of the unfinished business, all the "remainders" of life that invariably come creeping in the door unsolicited next session.

"How should my life continue now that we've exposed the twisted roots, now that we have touched the splintered branches which are the latticework of my unhappiness? How much instability, disharmony, and chance occurrence *should* I open myself up to in the future? How should I forge a new relationship with the once forgotten past? Ironically, just as we begin to bask in the pleasure that comes with having attained a sense of "clarity," ethical questions emerge from the shadows and disrupt our complacency.

I enjoy sharing metaphors, and I relish becoming more fluent in a person's language of fears and desires, but when it comes to settling these conundrums I stammer, I disappoint, I claim no expertise. Such determinations of should or should not lie beyond all principles of psychology. They are the opportunities we all wish for and dread, opportunities for each of us to express a preference, to exercise free will to its limits. Can we pass them up? What are the alternatives?

Forgiveness as an Inoculation Against Humiliation

> To suffer woes which Hope thinks infinite;
> To forgive wrongs darker than Death or Night;
> To defy Power which seems Omnipotent;
> To love, and bear; to hope till Hope creates
> From its own wreck the thing it contemplates;
> Neither to change nor falter nor repent:
> This, like thy glory, Titan! is to be
> Good, great and joyous, beautiful and free;
> This is alone Life, Joy, Empire, and Victory.
> (Percy Bysshe Shelley, *Prometheus Unbound* IV)

Perhaps it had something to do with Julius' Prome- thean capacity for suffering and forgiveness, but as usual the threatening "wave" passed over us, and upon surfacing Julius picked up his childhood stories right where he left off.

"Then in high school I started playing football. My mother said I couldn't run fast because my fat-ass head was too heavy. But I trained every afternoon till it got dark, and by the end of ninth grade I was scoring more runs than anyone else on the team. I couldn't really believe the numbers I ran, but I acted like I did, and after winning a game I'd run off the field singing out, 'Here comes Jun' the Bomb. 'By the time I graduated and went into the Air Force, I was a kind of celebrity in my neighborhood. . . . My mother used to curse me, saying that I thought I was better than my raising. But the other mothers would point to me and say to their daughters, 'Marry a man like Jun'. Most of their sons were either in jail or strung out on heroin."

As he sat on my couch recounting his story, it was painfully clear to me that, at least on this day and on most of the days that had immediately preceded it, Julius didn't feel better than "Bastard," the boy his mother had raised, despite his mother's accusations to the contrary and his hard-earned reputation as the neighborhood "celebrity." His high "numbers" (on the football field, among marriageable black women, and in the "white" company's management rankings) felt no more legitimate to him than the "numbers" his mother ran, under cover of night, on borrowed credit. "I'm not myself," he lamented persuasively. But if that was the case, who was he? And how reliable was this oral history?

Silence in the courtroom! Make way for the defense attorney's "expert witness." If only Julius's mother had been right and Julius had thought (or could now think) that he was better than his "betters," better than his "raising." Perhaps then he would be "himself," which would mean that he would be somebody quite different from the unhappy man who was ashamed to tell me his story. He would be a person who had suffered no permanent, life-threatening injuries to diagnose and tally up, whose vivid memories of the welts from assorted electrical cord beatings, though they have long since disappeared, would be reminders of past injustices rather than cues to re-enact the crimes again. If Julius could see himself, *feel* himself as healed (not simply sealed over and leaking), then he would not have to hate his mother for making him hate himself by branding him a bastard; then he could forgive his childish gullibility, his gentle father's disappearances, even his mother's rages, and shut down the kangaroo court and move into the future. Was this a foolish rescue fantasy that lay beyond the realm of possibility? Was forgiveness the proper goal of psychotherapy?

After having endured the "unforgivable" (a woman too brutal to be called mother, a father too removed to provide protection for his son) Julius had weaned himself of his childish fantasies of escape or vengeance and had become an avid believer in the power of forgiveness. Forgiveness offered him a sense of mastery over his feelings, if not his fate, while at the same time promising to secure a permanent residency in another world of his own making, a world of unconditional love and acceptance. For if he could forgive what could not be forgotten or ignored, then it wouldn't matter all that much what other people did or failed to do, and he would not have to burn up with rage, shrivel up with shame, or prostrate himself before God or the powers-that-be (the White Man) to be free from the stigma of abandonment and injustice. Poetic justice was an ever-present possibility which he could indelibly inscribe in his life. He didn't need his love for Superman (an embarrassingly childish memory in a man of forty five); all that he needed was self-discipline, imagination, and a universalizing vision.

Indeed, since early adolescence, Julius had sustained himself by a quasi-religious belief in the power of his own mind, an amalgam of faith and reason. Consciously refusing to believe that there was anything in this world that could break his spirit or subvert his mission, Julius turned the other cheek without even feeling the slap, made excuses for everyone but himself, and scaled the craggy pyramids – the military, the social, and the corporate ladders neither of his parents ever hoped to climb. Heedless of the personal injuries he incurred along the way, he developed a resilience affirming that he was a free and self-created man and that suffering was as much his fuel as it was his enemy. Amen.

"A lot of black people are quick to shout "racism"; they used to tell me I was blind if I didn't see things the way they did. But it's not that I didn't see what they saw; I know a lot of people are prejudiced – Susie's step-father wouldn't come for Christmas dinner if he knew I was going to be there. It's that I had always tried to understand where the other person was coming from, whether he was white or black. I didn't want to just react . . . I liked to think of myself as bigger than that, and since I was bigger, I had a choice. I didn't want to be angry and confrontational like my mother; I never drank like my father did on week-ends; I wanted to figure out how to make things better. I usually did."

By the time I met Julius, however, shortly after he had been passed over for promotion to regional manager in his firm, being "bigger" felt smaller, more like a special pleading than an expression of free choice. Poetic justice, once an inoculation against humiliation, had become a euphemism for self-deception – empty words, smoke and mirrors. "When they said that my productivity didn't translate into upper management leadership qualities, and that what they read about me on paper didn't match the office's performance this past quarter, I felt stupid."

Unable to swallow the "injustice" that his superiors called "honest feedback" and his friends called racist politics, Julius loosened his grip over long-forgotten memories from childhood that he had, up until this point, successfully held at bay. As past and present images and sensations melded together to form one vibrating mass, Julius felt as if he were a little kid again, squirming and speechless, stripped naked with his mother's foot on his neck. The humiliation was public, irrevocable, and defining; worse yet, it was uncannily familiar. ("Bastard, your father has a sixth grade education. . . . he doesn't send money, he never wanted you.")

Julius' ability to digest, from a very early age, an extra large portion of life's pain and frustration had once been proof that he was a man with a mind and not just a bundle of raging impulses. But meanings can shift as unexpectedly and dramatically as Job's fortunes, and once they did, this ability came to represent a pathetic rationalization of the irrational, a strategy devised by a coward to hide from the ugly truth. Julius' experience of degradation before the board members of his "parent" company was the dreaded exposure, the punishment he felt he deserved for trying to blot out his history. Or at least this was one edition of his newly revised life story.

"Tony, my regional manager, used to give me all the accounts that were on the verge of failing, and though he never said it directly, I understood that he depended on me to turn them around, even if it meant playing with some of the numbers. Everyone stretched the rules, and if we didn't we wouldn't be competitive. My own production was always way up there, but if I was going to be what they called a team player, I needed to be willing to cover for everyone and not just think of myself. I'd work eighty hour weeks to get a job done. Nothing was impossible; the whole office counted on me. I liked to joke around: 'Here comes the king Julius Caesar' (a new edition of the high school football hero's moniker 'Jun' the Bomb?). Friends couldn't understand why I didn't ask for a fancier office and a larger bonus, or at least to not work around the holidays, but to tell you the truth I really didn't care about those things. I was bigger than that. Now I'm pissed."

As long as Julius could trust that his ideas were not simply solitary fantasies but indelible connections to a world of shared experiences, he could balance the imaginary scales of justice imaginatively inside his head. (Hence his credo "Words make things real," cuts both ways.) But when this connection between thought and action was severed, when Tony manipulated words and failed to support Julius' promotion, the injury was the equivalent of a religious crisis – a crisis of faith in the Father and of faith in reason.

His superiors had used the phrase "weak leadership qualities," so apparently Julius' deliberately polished language (one time his sister told him that he spoke as if he were educated at Harvard) and his detailed statistical analyses of production held little weight; the graphs he put on power point may just as well have been childish scribbles. His numbers had "exceeded expectations," and his staff were unwavering in their devotion, but the company executives brought in from corporate headquarters had their doubts. Something didn't add up, they said (there was that deal last February that turned out to be a disaster), as they proceeded to challenge the relevance and authenticity of the written records. Was it because they had failed to see that Julius was the brains behind their "favorite son" Tony, or because Julius had failed to see that he had cast himself as Tony's fool, his faithful *nigger,* handicapped in being groomed from birth to save faces and hide feelings?

When a white female candidate from a larger West Coast office with lower numbers was chosen for the position over Julius, his friends shouted "racism," but Julius didn't know what to think or even what he wanted to think. Tony held out his hand and avoided his eyes, and stammered: "The timing was bad; last year they had to settle a suit over sexual harassment; move on man, let it go, try again next year." Who can know for sure what all of the facts were, I think to myself, as Julius ruminates week after week about the "facts," and, just as Tony did with him, avoids my eyes and his feelings.

Guilty for having massaged the truth at Tony's behest to play the white man's white collar corporate game, Julius "the bum" had returned with a vengeance, and Julius the (Super)man in the well tailored suit was exposed and defenseless. For apparently, despite his out-of-ghetto experience and education, Julius had misunderstood how he was viewed by upper management and what qualifications were necessary to get promoted. How, then, could he be certain as to how else he had miscalculated, and what he had overlooked, or misconstrued?

Years before, when Julius' black friends (he had only just a few) had pointed to the metaphorical glass ceiling in the corporation, he had not seen it but had instead seen past it – at the time he had told himself that these friends were shortsighted and relied on excuses, whereas his vision was broader and he could rely on himself. But now he was left wondering: he was the one who was unemployed, collecting disability, screening phone calls, and considering a lawsuit.

Julius had overestimated his power to understand and control, to balance out the forces of irrationality and destruction (inside and outside), and to turn his back upon the past. His boss' self-serving political maneuvers, his girlfriend Susie's "sexual addictions," his father's week-end drinking binges, the ethnic jokes circulating around the cafeteria, were intimations he should have heeded but had overlooked (forgiven) on principle. The power of forgiveness may have been no more legitimate than the super-hero powers of Jun' the Bum.

Julius' kindergarten experience of confusion and embarrassment, of wanting a name but not the one he was given, was repeating itself. He was taken by surprise, and yet because it was so hauntingly familiar it was as if it were all predestined. The kindergarten circle foreshadowed everything in Julius' life, and everything in Julius' life became its natural extension. The repressed had returned with a vengeance. Unable to de-legitimize his illegitimacy by forgiving those smaller people who were so clumsy as to tread on his soul, Julius now was at a loss as to how he should inoculate himself against humiliation.

As Julius' universalizing vision fractured into pieces, he was left to sift through a motley collection of particular instances of unforgettable suffering. Which is how memories of his mother's curses, his father's muted presence, and the safe where he used to hide his money were reissued as prophetic warnings, sacred texts of uncertain practical value to guide him through his current life.

Ghostly echoes from the past, which for years were scarcely audible, now accompany Julius wherever he goes. They harangue him so that he cannot sleep at night or even concentrate on the golf course. They challenge his every decision, claiming to defend his honor against insidious assaults, making it impossible for him to look for work, or commit himself to another girlfriend, or sleep in his bed instead of on the basement couch in front of the television. As their thundering voices howl for justice, he slavishly collects new evidence for them to examine. Under the lens of an old microscope (smudged with his mother's fingerprints), kindness appears as weakness and mercy appears as complicity. He wants judgment for the perpetrators as well as for their unsuspecting, overly gullible victims, but what is admissible as evidence, and who can he trust to deliver the verdict and arrive at a fair sentence?

"I never liked to see myself get angry; I'm not an angry person. I remember when I was ten my mother beat me with an electric cord for something I didn't even do. But I discovered then that I didn't have to feel the pain, that even with her foot on my neck I had a choice. But now I'm explosive – I feel violent – and then there are these waves of sadness that come over me and I just want to hide . . . I feel weak, I'm not myself."

A conquering hero turned psychotherapy patient, an executive of a multi-national corporation certified by the federal government as mentally disabled, Julius defends himself not as Job defended himself: "I have not sinned, look at the record," but as one who is guilty for being both a victim of cold-blooded calculation and a calculating imposter: "I sucked it up and lost my self; I told myself I didn't need to feel pain and now I can't turn off these violent feelings." Vomiting "sweet" forgiveness that unpredictably had turned rancid in his stomach, he feeds gluttonously on bitter reminiscences that parasitically feed on him.

Frequently when I'm with Julius, I feel an urgent need to say something but find myself hesitating, stumbling for words; he holds words sacred, chooses them carefully, and is always sensitive to my mistranslations. So my head shakes involuntarily, in sympathy, filling the silence. "Why are you shaking your head? Don't shake your head, I don't want pity," he says hungrily, and I understand his dilemma; pity magnifies his pain and weakens his resolve to transcend it, but what is the alternative? I couldn't betray my feelings by remaining steely-eyed and still expect him not to betray his, and yet I do not want him to feel pitied in the way he understands pity. It *is* a pity to me that Julius feels weak and confused and wants to hide, but I do not see him as pitiful. Can he experience the difference? I too am confused and do not know why that white woman with lower numbers was chosen for the promotion over him, but I do not doubt that whatever the reasons for the company's decision, Julius is not simply an empty suit, an Uncle Tom, or an identity thief, even though he is not the super-hero he performed for appreciative audiences. Can he stop doubting?

On good days Julius agrees with me about the pity and the confusion, at least he does in theory. But on the days when he cannot forgive himself for being himself, for being the Bastard child who "made it" in spite of his upbringing, he cannot decide whether he should fold his laundry as he used to or let it just sit, shovel his neighbor's sidewalk or just take care of his own, allow his new girlfriend pay for a Caribbean vacation or tell her to bring back the tee shirt that she borrowed last month without first asking.

As Julius reconsiders the meaning of suffering, the honesty of his avowed detachment from the pain of his experiences, and the value of poetic forms of justice, he wonders if it wasn't his idealism, his determination to transform suffering rather than to let it transform him, that ended up leaving him vulnerable to humiliation, exploitation, and betrayal. I wonder too. Would I be guilty of "blaming the victim" in thinking that Julius might have won more respect, recognition, and loyalty from Tony and from Susie, his faithless girlfriend, if he had been less forgiving, less judicious, less stoical? Had Julius inadvertently masterminded his own unhappiness and choreographed a life of humiliation when he systematically set out to inoculate himself against one? What would Freud say? And what about the Equal Employment Opportunities Commission which would, a few months from now, be adjudicating Julius' law suit?

"What if" questions are dangerous when Julius becomes mired in regrets about a past that can't be known, much less altered, but when they open him up to the possibility that he can create a future, not simply stumble upon one, he is more equal to the power of "the wave" of depression. His statement, "I question everything" is a statement expressive of both of hope and terror. I am continually moved by the nakedness of Julius' confessions, and excited as he virtually writes my chapter for me. I rush home to my computer each week with new adjectives to modify old subjects. But for Julius this is not an intellectual exercise or a poetic epiphany. His existential crisis can be paralyzing; it robs him of real time, and he is pulled back under the wave, holding his breath. Each session Job's problem hovers at the edges: how *should* Julius create a future from the wreckage, and, for that matter, how should I?

Selflessness as aFoundation for Forgiveness

> "I offered up my innocence and got repaid with scorn"
> (Bob Dylan, *Shelter From the Storm*)

> "To Err is Human, to Forgive Divine."
> (Alexander Pope)

"Who am I?" Julius asks at age forty-four, brushing away the tears that collect in the corners of his eyes as if they were malarial mosquitoes. Unless his memory is playing tricks with him, which is the unresolvable question that keeps him up at night, Julius used to know precisely who he was and what he believed in, or that is what he told himself (words make things real?). Indeed, his unwavering commitment to a set of personal ethical principles was his most defining characteristic, one that generated a constant stream of admiration and envy. A bear-like man whose bulk seemed to contain ever-replenishing sources of gentleness, hopefulness, and wisdom, Julius was once known for filling whatever spaces he entered. He was the embodiment of benevolent authority, and people flocked to him.

What happened to Julius' steady pulse, that mono-maniacal life force from which spawned hope in the place of envy? And how can Julius, the man who periodically dissolves beneath a wave of depression, reconstitute the shelter he once provided for himself and others? Did Julius' heart just stop pumping because of an undetected defect, a congenital abnormality caused by a deficiency in his mother's love? Or was Julius ambushed by his own immune system, by years of accumulated anger he turned inwards against himself? Did the powerful Julius of beloved memory ever actually exist, or was he merely a synthetic composite of diverse fantasies (his own and other people's), predestined from the inception to decompose?

Each school of psychoanalysis has its own vocabulary and its own explanation of depression. Self-psychology refers to a basic deficit in the structure of the self owing to a failure of empathy within formative relationships. In order to develop a sense of a coherent self we need our feelings to be mirrored and we need to feel contained within an environment that can hold us. Classic Freudian theory describes depression as anger turned inward, though later Freud posits the existence of a death instinct which pulls us backwards, away from life and love, and is in constant struggle with Eros. Object relations theory might understand Julius' self-loathing and hopelessness in terms of the internalization of bad objects: a conflict that was originally outside has been transferred inside, which would account for why Julius hates, fears, and identifies with his mother as well as with "Jun' the Bum."

"I raised myself on television and when I wasn't practicing my football after school I would secretly study the way the lawyers on all the courtroom shows spoke and moved their bodies; I created myself using these TV people as my models. . . . I'm not real." Julius' eyes well up with tears which means, I hope, that he is no more persuaded of his non-existence than I am.

Incredulously, Julius would recall how, as a child he had submitted, without protest, to his mother's beatings. "'Get over here Bastard. Lie down. ' I still feel her foot on my neck. But then I told myself, I don't have to feel the pain." At fifteen, however, something snapped, a lightbulb went on, another went out, and quite literally, there was no going back. (Though, as Julius discovered twenty-five years later, there was no going forward either, as every path he took circled round the sharpened edges of the past, and was littered with memories of violence and submission.) And yet, on that occasion, when his step-father Nathan tried to hold him down for his mother's assault, Julius became suddenly aware that he was stronger than Nathan, and that Nathan's authority was as illegitimate as the Bastard's. So, for once, without considering the consequences or looking at, what he would later call, "the bigger picture," Julius responded violently and with emotion. Stunned upon seeing the blood streaming down Nathan's face, and feeling the surge of rage exploding from within himself, Julius fled from the home that was never a home, hid out, and proceeded to scour the surrounding neighborhood in search of his long lost father. Powerful in his rage, Julius felt powerless at the prospect of becoming the mirror image of his mother.

Julius' father had virtually disappeared from Julius' life when he was five years old, but he had, nonetheless, remained a benevolent, if invisible, presence in his life. Indeed, Julius was fiercely loyal to his unsubstantiated father, whose modest dignity and quiet resignation had always served as a counterpoint to his mother's angry posturings. After reuniting with this phantom figure, Julius turned his back on "Jun' the Bastard" who doubled as "Jun the Bum" (forever guilty until proven innocent), and attempted to establish a new legitimate identity without the imprint of his mother's hand or foot. With conscious planning and blind persistence Julius wrested himself free of his suffering self and inaugurated, with words and deeds, a respectable, soulful alternative to a life of humiliation and obscurity.

An Olympian long distance runner for a father handicapped by a fifth-grade education, an archetype of masculinity for his sisters, his children, and their mothers, a personal guide for those endangered by an impersonal work place, "Julius the bomb" shattered the mirror his mother had held up to him. Indeed, everyday he would produce and deliver a fresh supply of evidence to contradict the libelous stories that she had told about his character. Her damning prophecies had lost all claim on legitimacy; or at least those were the terms of the bargain he had struck with himself.

Through scrupulous self-examination, and unforgiving judgment, Julius knew that he "counted" because he held himself accountable. He knew that he was "bigger" not because he could bloody Nathan's face, but because he held himself to a higher standard. Anger and embarrassment, humiliation and revenge were not part of his working vocabulary, and the self that suffered by itself and for itself to no avail was banned from consciousness. With good deeds and a daring leap of faith in the power of his dreams, Julius delivered within the secluded courtroom of his mind a just verdict for himself. In that courtroom,, there were no "bums," or "bastards," or lethal suicide "bombs."

Meanwhile "real" life ran a parallel course. "For seven years Susie lied to me about having sex with other men. She'd deny it when I confronted her – remember how I told you about the time I found the condoms in her wallet – but then she'd break down crying hysterically, begging me to forgive her – she said it was like an addiction, that she was trying to stop herself but couldn't. I'd forgive her every time because I could understand how insecure she was feeling. I liked to think that I was not reactive, but the kind of person who could see the larger picture. Sometimes I think that frustrated Susie even more; she told me she felt less than me because I never got angry or upset, I never lost control . . . " Julius' voice lowered, his sentence trailed off, and he avoided my eyes. We were both uncomfortable with the idea that the power of forgiveness, that he had cultivated so assiduously, could have had a debilitating effect on "the forgiven." Had Julius, inadvertently, contributed to his own demise? How perverse; how unjust! Was his calming response to Susie's emotional outbursts an echo of his submissive response to his mother's foot on his neck?

Susie used to blame Julius for her sexual infidelities, claiming that his unflappable demeanor made her feel flighty, his tendency to analyze rather than react made her feel shallow, and that his broad shoulders and generous spirit (ever ready to stop the car and help the person standing on the side of the road with the flat tire) made her feel selfish and insignificant. But now, after eight years of stalwartly forgiving Susie her weaknesses, Julius had broken down and was crying "Enough! You have wronged me, but you are right. I acted too big, so big that I lost sight of my self and now am nothing."

Selflessness and neediness have blended together and the blend looks more pathetic than powerful, more self-aggrandizing than empathic. Loving or enabling? Forgiving or self-deceiving? Julius' moral compass cannot stop spinning. Who was he to think that he could be bigger than his suffering, that he could transcend the violent emotional storms that were raging all around him? His father's homespun, pacifist philosophy couldn't protect Julius from his mother, Julius' brother from AIDS, or his father from alcoholic binges and, most recently, a psychotic depression. What made Julius think that he was better than his "raising?" "'Forgive your trespassers . . . ' To what purpose? Appeasement never works when you are dealing with terrorists, Dr. Block, and how are you supposed to tell the difference when they're wearing civilian clothes?"

Ironically, the more Julius secures his borders, hunkers down into his basement, and screens his phone calls rather than rushing to the rescue, the more insecure he feels. "Now I feel out of control because I can't forgive Susie, because I don't even want to forgive her, and feel angry and callous. I'm suspicious of everybody, and I can't get her or Tony or my mother out of my mind. They are all the same now. I don't trust women, I can't trust myself to get another job. I'm not normal."

Julius is not certain why his supervisor Tony failed to recommend him for a promotion, any more than he is certain as to why Susie cheated on him continually or why his father, who left him to fend for himself at the age of five, never fully recovered from his youngest son's death. However, what is far more disturbing to Julius than his confusion about Tony or Susie or his father is his uncertainty about what he should feel about himself – the self he remembers he was and the various permutations of the self he has become.

Julius says that he will not be able to live with himself if he forgets himself again, which may be why he keeps re-visiting his painful memories, forever adding in more details and shades of color. However, and this is the paradox, if he does not forget himself and his history he may not be able to live with himself or step back into life as the man he could be and thinks he should be today. "Do I think too much, Dr. Block? Sometimes I wish I could turn off my feelings like I used to be able to do. Was I better off then? The one compliment my mother paid me was that I was so tough I could walk barefoot on glass."

Shouldn't I have anticipated that somewhere down the line Julius would ask the unanswerable questions? Better off? Too much thinking? Yes and no. Since this was year number four of our relationship, I felt no obligation to be inscrutable and allowed myself the liberty of smiling sadly by way of reply. I was confident that we could share the sadness (and the bittersweet humor) because he trusted that the sadness was hopeful and the joke was not on him. "What's the look?" he asked, though at that moment, when we were able to smile sadly together, words felt superfluous. "Look at the business I'm in, I have my prejudices and you know that encouraging you to walk barefoot on glass is not one of them."

I believe I make an honest living from the talking cure. (If I didn't, I couldn't continue to practice). And yet, in all honesty, after our sad smiles had faded, the riddle of Julius' suffering and of how to relieve him of it remained unsolved: self reflection is "good," feelings are human, but if too much of either one is not enough for Julius to forgive the past and create a future, not even enough for Julius to go out and look for work, what is? What, aside from insight, is the basis for therapeutic change? Is it the relationship of trust, which we have created incrementally over so many years, that will generate something new? "I am most real in this room," he tells me repeatedly. "I love you, Dr. Block. Does that make you uncomfortable?" It doesn't and it does, as the realness that stimulates his loving feelings is not yet fully translatable to the world outside and that is the point of psychotherapy isn't it?

The Fruits of Disillusionment

> "I fall into bad faith if I take one or both of the two dishonest positions about reality: If I pretend either to be free in a world without facts or to be a fact in a world without freedom."
>
> Hans W. Cohn, *Existential Thought and Therapeutic Practice* (1997)

January, 2003. At the prodding of friends and the encouragement of former co-workers Julius decided to file a discrimination suit against his employer. "It's not about the money or even the promotion; I don't know if I would have wanted the extra responsibilities anyway; it's about honesty and justice." But even after the Equal Employment Opportunities Commission had examined his documentation and determined that his case was credible and worth their while to pursue, Julius remained ambivalent.

Corporate headquarters had their story and their team of high-priced lawyers, so who was going to believe his? He could say "Look at my numbers, and at the accounts I was given to work with. They could say, "We evaluate everyone equally, and there are gaps in his resume. The numbers are high but they don't add up to leadership qualities; he needs some fine tuning, maybe in another few years." Who could know for certain what was fact and what was fiction, who was seeing Julius clearly and who was prejudiced? Promotions, public recognition, and company politics never meant all that much to Julius in the past, so why should they now? Was it their lies that was unforgivable or was there a truth in their analysis that was too painful to absorb?

Disabled complicated matters further. Julius wasn't himself, so how could he defend the legitimacy of his feelings and perceptions? He was filled with anger at his mother, he felt like a fool to have stayed with Susie, and for over a year he had been avoiding a visit to his father, who scarcely left his house anymore and responded minimally on the telephone. What right did he have, an unforgivably pathetic individual, to hold the company responsible for his depression and anxiety, his overwhelming sense of injustice? Was he a victim of racism? It certainly looked like that, but if only it were that simple. His head was swirling, and after an hour of balancing judgment against counter-judgment, so was mine. "How do we get out of this circle? How do we stop the kaleidoscope from spinning out of control?"

The Equal Employment Opportunities Commission case was settled out of court. Julius' lawyers assured him that the compensation was fair, given the evidence and the precedents, and life went on. Not surprisingly, Julius did not find psychic resolution in the legal system, and fantasies of suicide and revenge continued to plague him. He found himself driving by Tony's house in the middle of the night plagued by the idea that Tony was probably sleeping peacefully when Julius could not. He broke off contact with Susie, but continually thought about what she might be doing, who she might be sleeping with, and dreaded some chance encounter on the street. "I don't want her to see me the way I am now," he would say. "Justice" didn't compensate for the unforgiving self that had established residency in Julius' body.

March, 2003. "When I left for the Air Force I promised myself that I would never go back home. I do go back but I don't feel I really belong, not at my sisters' or at my father's. I watch how I speak; people say I speak white, now the guys on the golf course say I sound like I come from Harvard. So I'm very aware not to use certain words. I don't want anyone to feel lesser, uncomfortable. When I see my sisters on holidays we always end up talking about our childhood, they speak as if it was a wonderful time. They don't remember what I do. They say my mother loved me, that she would brag to other people about how I'd made it on my own. That pisses me. She always told me I owed her cause her beatings made me strong, but she's gone now ten years from cancer and I still can't forgive her; I hate to even call her my mother. I don't want to be thinking about her, I never used to think about the past, but now I can't stop thinking about it. May she burn in peace."

For an instance, our eyes locked together in an uneasy embrace as Julius tried to gauge my response and I tried to understand his. Would I recoil in horror at his unrepentant callousness, his self-consuming anger, or, worse yet, would I draw him deeper into the mire of helplessness and self-pity? How, after more than four years, was psychotherapy supposed to restore a sense of human decency when talking kept dredging up memories from which sprang hateful feelings? How was Julius supposed to find an honest substitute for the sometimes angry, sometimes anguished, rhetoric of homelessness that was the spoken dialect of his true home? "Jun' the bum," "Jun' the celebrity," and "Jun the ticking bomb" are voices in the chorus that Julius brings with him to our sessions, but the "Jun' of unknown future possibilities" has not found a language through which to speak.

Each week Julius brought in fresh memories, and each week during our first three years they spilled out with mounting intensity. As he anticipated the hour drawing to a close and, still unfinished and unsettled, steeled himself to leave my office, I asked myself whether I was the sorcerer in the famous fairy tale or the sorcerer's apprentice, and whether Julius' compulsion to remember was fruitless and destructive or creative and restorative.

But then, repression was not a choice, by definition, it never is, so what were the alternatives? The iron curtain that had once securely separated Julius' past from his present-day experience had parted (otherwise Julius would not be seated across from me hugging a pillow to his chest, straining to hold back his tears), but for how long and to what end? Since Julius couldn't will himself to forgive or forget now that he felt overwhelmingly compelled to judge and remember, he was faced with an ethical as well as a psychological dilemma: what should he make of his memories and how could he best live, with the pain, or numbed and distracted, without it?

The talking cure takes diffuse feelings of shame, pride, hope, and confusion and translates them into grammatical sentences. It offers meaning but at considerable risk. As Julius retrieved, dated, catalogued, and embellished upon lost details of past grievances, he faced the danger of spiraling endlessly through a tunnel containing holographically vivid accounts of his origin. When periodically Julius says that he needs to take a break from his therapy ("I want to talk but I want to put the past behind me"), I do not try to dissuade him. Sometimes I have had my doubts as to whether he and I should continue to converse with ghosts who have no eyes or ears and are incapable of dialogue. Must we, for the sake of peace, resurrect the iron curtain (or some facsimile) that will effectively drown out the angry voices and cement over the demeaning images, so that Julius can live with injustice and dignity once more? But when I think such thoughts I feel like a traitor to my profession. With memory there is always loss and disillusionment, always premonitions of a future in which one is linked to the past and not entirely determined nor entirely free, but without memory there is no substantial self because such a self must exist in time. Isn't that worse?

"I don't want to be seen as more capable, as the black guy who doesn't speak like the ghetto, the exception to the rule. I don't trust compliments. My lawyers call me articulate. I don't like that. I was more prepared than they were at the deposition, but that's the way I've always been and I don't want to be that way anymore. For awhile I was volunteering at my daughter's school, and then a few weeks ago they asked if they could interview me for some television show about black fathers in the community – the principal said I'd be the perfect person. I wouldn't do it, I felt manipulated, and I haven't been back since. It's like that everywhere. As soon as a woman tells me that I'm so thoughtful, that she's never met anyone like me before, I want to back off. I don't return her phone calls, I'm suspicious. I think she doesn't really know me; what does she want? I count the change in the grocery store before I leave, and the other day I wouldn't let an old black lady cut in front of me on line. I'm ashamed of myself; I'm ashamed to be sitting here talking to you week after week, though I feel I have to in order to get better, and I'm ashamed that I am feeling so ashamed."

Now that Julius is disillusioned with his selflessness, thoughtfulness, and all the other variations on being "bigger," we worry whether he won't disappear from sight entirely as he pursues a minimalist, forgotten-about self. He could drift off under what he calls the depression and lose the threads of his narrative, or else he could ball them up so tightly inside – like the money he hid in a safe, in a closet with a padlock – that even he could never untangle them again. Thus far, our fears have proved unfounded.

The waves pass, and there is Julius, not just his shadow, gripping the threads in his hand, choosing his words precisely and still believing in their creative power to sculpt if not eliminate his destructive feelings.

"Today there isn't the sadness. I vacuumed, I did my laundry, and when I leave here I'm going to go to the gym. I'm embarrassed to tell you – these are such small things – but to me they are tremendous. People used to say my house was immaculate, and I used to plan everything a month in advance; I even wrote into my daily planner the free time hours I was going to spend with Susie. It irritated her; she said I was anal. I don't trust living by those rules anymore, so I'm trying not to and am constantly checking myself to make sure that what I do is something I want to do, not for Susie or because I want to be a certain kind of person. But I actually like having my socks folded up neatly in the drawer according to color, so when I did it this morning, that was big."

It is big, far bigger than what it may sound like to other people who don't know Julius as I do. And then there is more. Julius places his hand gently on a hand-painted bowl that lies on an end table holding my business cards. "This plate is yours; it's personal and it matters to you; I respect that. I want to feel like the things I have are mine and that they matter to me. My walls are bare, you have pictures all over your walls and they express who you are. I have hundreds of photos in boxes in the closet. I bought a poster of Tiger Woods three years ago that I still haven't hung up. I want to put up pictures, maybe buy some new posters; I'm not sure yet what to put up and what I want to throw away; until I know I don't do anything."

March 1, 2004. Innocent or guilty, a victim of racism and corporate politics or a product of his own idealistic (some might say deluded) thinking? On occasion, I still find myself entangled in the obsessive ruminations that have devoured Julius' mind and prevented him from working and sleeping for over four years. "What happened to the Julius who once lived harmoniously and generously with eloquent words and magnanimous actions?" When I circle around in this tunnel, hungry for a definitive answer, my appetite remains unsated. Like Julius, I too can feel incapable and immobilized.

But something has been changing lately in my mood and in Julius'. The jury is hung and we have shifted our focus. Themes of justice and forgiveness continue to echo from the margins of our conversations, but they are no longer deafening; oddly enough, they seem almost irrelevant to the mundane tasks at hand. The theme of disillusionment and what forms of life can survive afterwards has taken their place. Regardless of whether what happened to Julius' is just or unjust, the result of a flaw of his, of the world he lives in or, what is most likely, a mixture of both, he has been profoundly disappointed, and for once in his life, it is his subjective experience that matters, his taste in photographs or prints, his preference for neatness or clutter, his desire to forgive or not forgive, that will bring personal meaning into his home.

On some days, Julius' disappointment is directed outward, toward his girlfriend, his former supervisor, his mother, and his father, along with a compendium of other unreliable people who have been semi-permanent fixtures in his life. On other days, his disappointment is directed inward, toward himself, his inability to be spontaneous, and his propensity for selflessness and sacrifice. The problem of forgiveness remains, but it is folded into the problem of who and what and how much to trust and what he should do with his indestructible need to care. This problem is not of the past or about somebody else, but for the present and future and about Julius. After trying to orbit above it, Julius has re-entered his body, a body that takes pleasure in little things and that has a previously uncharted capacity for suffering.

When Julius was four years old, his ten-year old sister told him that with his Superman cape he would be able to fly. He believed her ("I was so gullible") and jumped off the second floor terrace and broke his ankle. She also told him that if he repeated to himself the words "it doesn't hurt" he wouldn't feel the pain when their mother beat him. He believed her then too, and though she cried when their mother beat her, he was proud that he did not. "Did I feel it? I don't know, but I did feel stronger."

Can Julius forgive himself for turning his desires into dreams and then putting too much faith in their reality? Can he forgive life for disabusing him of his illusions, and trust that life without illusion has something of value to offer? The Superman story is a standard family joke, but on New Year's gatherings the stories about the beatings are never mentioned, and nobody talks about his brother's death or his father's hallucinatory collapse. Embarrassment and pride, hope and despair, all are present in Julius' experience of suffering. "So, Doctor Block, I mean Joyce, what is the truth about me and what have I made up? Since I was a little boy I was always afraid I'd end up homeless. I feel I can be myself in this office, but the minute I step outside . . . I've wanted to belong, but everything I've belonged to, that I created, has turned out to be shit."

For Julius to have believed that he could be free of his history, that he could cancel out his classmates' racist taunts, his mother's random ravings, his father's mysterious disappearances, by pre-meditated acts of will was an illusion. But for Julius to believe that he is nothing but his history, a poor facsimile of a person, a celluloid character, is also an illusion. Disabused of the illusions of omnipotence and insubstantiality, Julius feels naked and ungainly, he holes up, throws on some old clothes (purposefully at random), and calls out to me, "What's next?" Regularly, Julius gently touches the hand-painted china bowl I brought from New York fifteen years ago. It is our secret code. The bowl is a metaphor for my taste and my freedom to have my taste despite its fragility. That's all Julius wants to get from our conversations; that alone would be poetic justice.

March 18, 2004; Postscript: "I'm embarrassed to look you in the eyes sometimes, but I want to, and I want to tell you about this link bracelet I got a couple of weeks ago. It has my birth-stone and the birth-stones of both my kids. One link has a picture of a golf ball, because golf is my game now, and there are the letters for Jun'. I never used to want anyone to know I was a junior outside of my family. It reminded me of Jun' the bum. But now I feel my history is me; it's not that I'm proud of it, or that it's the only thing that's real, but I nearly lost myself and I don't want to lose myself again. Having this bracelet and telling you about it is enormous for me; it's like saying my name is mine and whatever it means I want to stand by, I don't want to change it or make myself disappear."

Our eyes link; years of unshed tears (mine and his) quiver at their edges. Today there isn't danger of a flooding. The drops that spill are our living poetry, and they are water for the fruits of disillusionment.

IN PURSUIT OF HAPPINESS: THE PLEASURE PRINCIPLE AND BEYOND

Inalienable Rights and Wishful Fantasies

Most people come to psychotherapy in pursuit of a happier life, and, despite my wish to be a stalwart seeker of the unvarnished Truth, in the tradition of Freud, and *not* one of those "touchy-feely," "New Age" psychotherapists, I would be lying if I denied that I am their ally. Indeed, when patients express ambivalence about the "selfishness" and "childishness" of their hedonic aims ("With all the *real* misery in the world, how can I be so self-indulgent?"), I raise my eyebrows and tilt my head. "You are not crazy, infantile, sinful, or presumptuous to want happiness" is the implicit message I send encoded through my body. But I quake inside, and purposely do not commit myself to speech since I know neither the cost nor the yield of such ambitions, let alone the source of their fulfillment.

Moreover, what does happiness have to do with talking about wishes (abstract or particular), and what does talking about wishes have to do with growing up and living fully (which must mean living honestly, with eyes wide open), when so often our most enduring wishes are "pre-historic," contradictory, untranslatable, and in reality may never be fulfilled? (In a letter that the psychoanalyst Adam Phillips quotes, Freud defines happiness as "the belated fulfillment of pre-historic wishes.")

The pleasure that comes from huddling together with a benevolent parental figure, spilling forth and mopping up guilty secrets, paying tribute to "unthought" histories of unforgettable and unrealizable desires, may be all I have to offer my patients. (I make allusion here to Christopher Bollas' idea of the "unthought known" as being those inchoate experiences that follow us everywhere in our lives, that are as much us as anything, but that we have never articulated in words or thought about consciously.) And though this socially sanctioned deviant activity may seem a luxury and not a "medical necessity" to most people of the world who cannot afford it, when our time is up and life proceeds as usual (there are the tissues; we'll see each other again next Monday at five thirty; someone else is waiting), neither of us will be happy unless we feel that something useful has come from a retreat from normal reality, that something of enduring value, which we can take back with us (a souvenir) to help us in our project to become participant-citizens of the world beyond, has been gained. Is it a sense of meaning and purposefulness that we hope to distill from the amalgam of emotions we have undammed, or the freedom from having to always make good sense, by distilling and defending our meaning and purpose?

In a secluded therapeutic space, within the confines of a fifty-minute hour, no apologies are necessary when it comes to wishful fantasies or repugnant wishes – unconditional acceptance reigns supreme. However, *Caveat emptor* (let the buyer beware); the safety net of transference love extends only so far! After catching glimpses of a happiness that arises from just being open to unfiltered experience, a happiness that is accidental and unexplainable, that seeks no information as to origins or purpose, the moment passes, and one of us is bound to grow restless: to seek out explanations and purpose, and try to minimize the risks of accidental occurrences that defy explanation. Like my thirteen-year old daughter Vera, who, after having satisfied her appetite for "dress up," digs herself out from beneath the piles of old clothes in the basement so that she can get down to writing an essay about the use of propaganda in George Orwell's *Animal Farm*, we too feel the need to get "real," take aim, and sharpen our focus. Free association, unconditional acceptance, being without concern for doing, and miraculously we feel sufficient, and feeling sufficient, happy (purged of shame and guilt), but only for so long. While Freud's original "hydraulic" model of the mind conceived of pleasure as tension reduction, even he was not prepared to say that the state of quiescence was equivalent to happiness, given the complex interplay among our conflicting desires. We have wishes that go beyond the elimination of suffering; we want more than the absence of anxiety that is an intimation of death.

In psychotherapy, as in the rest of life, the foundations of sufficiency are unstable and shift according to the context. Outside the cradle of a near-perfect relationship with an archetypal mother or an idealized therapist we become conscious of what we lack and what is lacking, and well we should. Skeptics by nature, because it is our nature to experience and to reflect on our experience, we require material evidence in support of our unproven claims. "Sufficient? To whom and for what?"

Indeed, as soon as we recognize our faces in the mirror, which comes at a point in development when we are increasingly independent and mobile, grandiose fantasies of omnipotence are shattered as we discover that we are objects in a world of other subjects. With the potential to feel small and insignificant shadowing the potential to feel big and proud, we begin to devise intricate systems of weights and measurements, build hierarchies, set goals, and scale imaginary pyramids, straining to fill the gaps with *something more.* In theory we may be reconciled to the fact that perfection is unattainable, but in practice, we insist on making progress toward that uncertain end. Not coincidentally, Abraham Maslow's famous hierarchy of needs is depicted in the form of a pyramid, with self-actualization and transcendent peak experiences being at the pinnacle of human desire. Thus, after our basic needs for love and security are satisfied, we need not reference God or an afterlife to explain our spiritual yearnings.

And so, when a patient wants to know what she is supposed to do with all of her irrational feelings, the sad, angry, and shameful feelings that make her *un*happy, she is challenging me to defend the utility of our all-too-successful "fishing expedition," in which we dive recklessly into a dense whirlpool of emotions, without any certainty about what we might want to retrieve or whether on close examination the water-logged artifacts beneath the surface are actually worth retrieving anyway. I dread the question because, in the form in which it is posed, there is no answer that can satisfy: she may not be able to do anything about sadness and anger, limits and loss, about wanting what cannot be had, and I certainly cannot make her bad feelings disappear. I had hoped that understanding, mixing empathy with insight, would be sufficient, but on alternate weeks it isn't. At times, connecting the dots and gazing at the sketchy picture that emerges, a picture that is unfinished and will never be completed, is not progress enough! Not for Julius or any of my patients who fear that they will be forever trapped within the imaginary boundaries of that picture, painfully aware that they are simply repeating their histories. "Now that I know how I got here, now that I realize I'm not to blame, how do I get over my anger, how do I get rid of the sadness, how can I stop willing what cannot be willed so I can move on?" These are the questions I hear as sub-texts when my patients express their helplessness in the face of feelings. They hammer at me and make me anxious. Willing what cannot be willed is what existentialist psychologists claim is the basis for anxiety. I would have them not feel what they feel, and so my anxiety is a mirror of theirs.

Speechless, and forced to face my insufficiency as well as my patient's, I shrug my shoulders and once again quake inside. I have fallen off the pedestal to which I had been precariously elevated the previous week when we were soaring on the crest of an emotional epiphany, and my powerlessness has been exposed. I'm tempted to say in our defense, "There is nothing to *do* aside from what we are already doing," but I am equally tempted to do something, or at the very least appear to do something more. Maybe I should relax my rules, which are relics of my psychoanalytic training, and at least offer reassurance in the form of a loving look, a hopeful prediction, or an authoritative, paternalistic suggestion. (Maybe if I were smarter I'd have the answer, or if I were fuzzier or more secure or less "anal" I wouldn't care about being so rigorously truthful and would just give her one anyway.) "Have you thought again about doing volunteer work or taking that pastel water color class?" "You are so impatient and harsh with yourself." "Here, borrow my rose-tinted glasses." What harm is there in being an optimist, a comforting mirror, a surrogate parent who gives assurance that she understands even when she doesn't entirely?

Torn between doing too much or too little, visualizing inner peace or acknowledging the inevitability of life's frustrations, I sometimes feel as disappointed and confused as the patient who comes to me with the hope of discovering her one true self and in that discovery finding happiness, but instead discovers that the true self is inconstant and that happiness is having faith in its endless pursuit.

"What Does (Wo) Man Want?"

> "Enough is left unexplained to justify the hypothesis of a compulsion to repeat – something that seems more primitive, more elementary, more instinctual than the pleasure principle which it overrides."
> Sigmund Freud, *Beyond the Pleasure Principle* (1920)

Freud is famous for questioning the stories we tell ourselves about ourselves and what we want, and for insisting, that despite our conscious intentions, sexual pleasure is what drives us, as a species and as individuals: it is our purpose dressed up as Purpose. Ironically, however, Freud is infamous for questioning the certainty of his own propositions when he poses the question "What does woman want?" and admits that the answer remained an enigma, even to him. But because such a question implies that Woman is especially mysterious, and that her aims and hers alone fall beyond the normal and the knowable, that is beyond the scope of scientific inquiry, he begs the larger question of what any person actually wants when a given reality is inevitably wanting but pleasure is, at best, an unsustainable source of satisfaction, and, at worst, a regressive step backwards down a path towards un-self-consciousness, repetition, and destructive fantasy. What diverse purposes propel us to reach beyond the pleasure principle, in the hope of vanquishing anxiety, compensating for what we are missing, and creating happiness out of incompleteness, disharmony, and disillusionment?

Grappling with the contradictions between his theory of desire and his observations of life inside and outside of clinical practice, Freud postulated, in his later writings, an instinct toward death, *thanatos,* which translates into a drive to return to an earlier, inorganic state in which there is no delineated self: a womb-like existence, if not nothingness, "dust to dust." Since pleasure had always been formulated as tension reduction, pleasure and death were, paradoxically, inter-related (partners in crime), though life and death still remained at odds with one another. Thus, within this psychoanalytic formulation, we are constituted in such a way that not only do we want what we cannot have, but we also want to *not* want. The battle that ensues is as inevitable as it is interminable as analysis turns out to be.

To my knowledge, Freud doesn't speak frequently of happiness (a concept better suited to philosophy than science) but mainly of pleasure and, neurotic as well as ordinary, unhappiness. But my patients speak of happiness all the time (they rarely mention "pleasure"), even though neither of us can define it and it is nowhere to be found. Whether they are religious in the conventional sense or amateur poets living metaphorically, each imagines his own version of a Golden Age that may be located somewhere in the past or future – a Nirvana where he is no longer in slavish bondage to false desire, or a paradise where desires are fulfilled and in harmony with the world. Indeed, despite the fact that happiness eludes them in the here and now, the pursuit of happiness is an ever present purpose that assumes many disguises. An "inalienable right" written into the American constitution, even the most disillusioned assume that they should believe in it (otherwise why pursue it), if they ever want to feel "normal" and "wholesome," like full fledged members of the human community. Moreover, what besides the prospect of "happiness" (a secularized version of salvation) could justify the time and money spent on psychotherapy, or compensate me for my unconditional acceptance and them for their indeterminate pain?

And yet, whether they are true believers in the American dream or die-hard sceptics, religious conservatives or secular post-modernists, Republicans or Democrats, they intuit that happiness is no more synonymous with intelligence or virtuousness than it is with physical beauty, wealth, or popularity – if only what made us happy were so logical and predictable, how much simpler our lives would be!

And if I had any doubts, my patient Izzy provides us both with corroborating evidence: "Andrew Jackson ran for president out of spitefulness, not because he actually wanted to, and Abraham Lincoln suffered from depression; every month there is a new biography out about some famous person who was either tormented or psychopathic; Rousseau abandoned his wife and children, Jung slept with his patients, and look at Van Gogh, he cut off his ear."

It is with a hungry expression on his face, that Izzy, an intractably anxious and depressed sixty-five year old man, informs of me of the dire "news," and rapidly scans my face to see if I can come up with a logical interpretation. (He hasn't found one from the rabbis he consults or from the Wayne Dyer books that he quotes, or from rifling through the dog-eared pages of the legal pad of notes he scribbles during sessions). The historical truths are counterintuitive, the romances are tawdry, and this is both confusing and consoling to him. "If so many of the men I admire were imbalanced, immoral, and unhappy despite their genius, good fortunes, and extraordinary achievements, what are my chances, and why should I expect to feel otherwise?" In the dark and plaintive look he casts my way I detect a gleam of vindication.

He's off the hook (maybe he should give up his dubious quest; maybe happiness is over-rated and unessential to living the Good Life after all?), but not for long. Scarcely skipping a beat, Izzy veers off, in hot pursuit of another hook and lures me onto one of his usual tangents, in the context of which he monotonously recounts his extraordinary successes in business and the stock market and his unjustifiable failures to be helped by a variety of financial and medical "experts" (present company included). "But we've gone there before, haven't we?" I interject, betraying my own bias in favor of my mother's unflagging faith in humanity as opposed to Izzy's and my father's, unflagging skepticism. "We've circled back and round again and to what purpose?"

"Addicted to negativity," is how I described Izzy once to himself and, surprisingly enough, he did not argue with my off-the-cuff diagnosis. Perhaps, he draws from his dispirited calculations microscopic drops of pleasure which stream into his veins where they inevitably coagulate into pools of resentment that a cabinet full of anti-depressant and anti-anxiety medications cannot dispel. We would be hard put to find anything that resembles happiness sloughing around in the quagmire Izzy routinely pulls us into. Nonetheless, there seems to be a method to Izzy's madness, what analysts used to call "a secondary gain." His tendency to go off on tangents and his negativity serve a purpose even if his aim is skewed. By graphing his unprofitable investments against his levels of serotonin Izzy circumvents his intractable enemy – irrationality – and provides himself (though not his therapist) with a stimulating (masturbatory) distraction. By shooting out the details of his history like bullets in the night, Izzy fires himself up until his eyes glaze over, and if I can't get a word in edgewise I suspect that this is his wish, if not his conscious intention. The talking cure has been transformed into solipsistic blather, and with me as captive audience Izzy slips into a stupor, while I slip behind the mask of professional neutrality and hide my frustration. But again, not for long!

Distractions are not sufficiently distracting, as the alternately stimulating and numbing effects of endless computations cannot adequately substitute for the happiness that Izzy doggedly pursues but cannot visualize much less grab hold of. Indeed, he defeats himself by the very strenuousness of his efforts. Happiness is not real happiness if he has to work so hard and measure so carefully to prove himself worthy. And yet, once I have interrupted the ricocheting bullets that spill from his mouth and disintegrate on impact, how can Izzy move from feeling bad, which means unloved, unloving, and unloveable (for no good reason) to that condition which everyone refers to but no one can define? If all his hard work doesn't pay off, but leaves him feeling more depleted than ever, what will?

Philosophers and economists, historians and social scientists are all beginning to draw the same, counterintuitive, conclusions: happiness bears no reliable relationship to anything one can measure objectively (which explains why Izzy's meticulous calculations don't compute, and why his felt losses always outweigh his perceived gains.) But if happiness is beyond the rational and justifiable – a matter of chance or destiny, of unfathomable and eradicable early childhood experiences, or of good and not so good genes – what basis (other than divine intervention) do we have for hope?

Of all the sad, angry, disappointed, and confused people I see, the most hopeful are the ones who continue to have faith in a form of happiness that transcends the laws of practical reason and contingent circumstance, but that has something to do with living fully in the present, expressing a "true self," feeling loving as well as loveable, "warts and all," and finding a modicum of inner peace. How all that abstract language translates into lived time is perversely mysterious however, since being true to oneself often appears to be antithetical to feeling loving or loveable or preserving the peace inside or out there in the real world. ("Honestly, my work is unsatisfying, the office politics are a fact of life but idiotic, and after twenty years of marriage sex is at best routine and at worst a chore; I know I shouldn't depend on my job or my wife to make me happy, but the truth of the matter is that I don't know who I am apart from my work or my relationships. Where do I go to discover *me* at fifty-two, and how do I know whether the real me is someone I would even like?")

Mother Teresa-like selflessness? Promethean quests? Buddha-like acceptance? Does happiness come from fighting for a dream and reaching beyond the limits of perceived reality, or from refusing to strive so hard or care so much or live for a dream of what could be, as a matter of principle? What ingredients are necessary and which combinations prove insufficient?

Which brings me to what Vera teasingly calls my "addiction" to writing. Unsuccessfully, I try to hide my "habit" from my family, but even on vacation I often bring along a hard copy of my chapter-in-progress, and when I think no one is looking, I periodically read it over, cross out an awkward sentence, record a serendipitous encounter, and scribble illegible revisions in the margins. I sneak in a quick fix – five minutes rallying my troops and doing battle in my private world – is all I need to maintain my equanimity, all I require to feel that vital surge which, for some ungodly reason, seems necessary to my well being.

How do I make sense of this peculiar compulsion of mine, which does nobody any harm but defies ordinary logic (after all the "troops" can wait and whatever victory I score is solely in my head)? Apparently, I am not content to drift along contentedly, uninterrupted by a purpose to punctuate the slippery passage of time. Unconditional love, serendipitous encounters, un-choreographed conversations are pleasures in abundance on vacations (which is why I love them), but I confess to having other appetites that such abundant fare fails to satisfy!

A capacity for love and work is the closest Freud comes to a definition of sanity (the goal of psychoanalysis), which means that a marriage between the Pleasure Principle and the work ethic may be the closest we come to happiness after all. It explains my "addiction," and why back home I feel the need to affix my free-floating impressions from the day to words, usually in the late afternoon, after I have seen patients or done my week-end errands, before I begin my familial – comfortably familiar – evening rituals. I am too old to play dress-up like my thirteen-year old daughter Vera, who seems intent on extending her childhood into adolescence, does. But in this transitional in-between space where I write I have the chance to play psychotherapist, a serious game, but a game nonetheless, in which I am free of the responsibilities and constraints that come when I am actually face to face with another living person doing psychotherapy. As a writer I can try out different roles and masquerade as different characters; I can be ruthless in my pursuit of insight, figuratively bare my breast and make impassioned speeches, and then retract it all by pressing "delete." Most significantly, I can shape a version of reality that satisfies my desire to make sense as well as my desire not to or at least not to have to.

Thus, embodied in this activity of writing about my work with patients I encounter what seems to me to be the essential paradox concerning the nature of happiness: We want to feel purposeful, creative, and self-determining, and are uneasy if we feel that we are bouncing along aimlessly, in limbo, without a sense of purpose, and yet we also want to be free of purpose, to surrender control over ourselves (sexually and otherwise), and to love and be loved unconditionally (and hence irrationally) just because we are who we are. ("Don't look to me to solve the Middle East crisis or even untangle the mess inside my head or yours; I'd like to let someone else run the universe for a change! I'd rather be . . ." fill in the blank.)

I can't count the number of times I have heard a patient protest that he wishes he could just *be* rather than *do*, and then, no sooner have these words spilled from his mouth, question what in fact he *is* apart from his actions in the world. Thus, in one sentence he reproaches himself for not being as creative and productive as he might be ("I have a vision and don't live into it"), while in the next he bemoans the fact that he lives as a commodity, to be weighed and traded on the marketplace of human relationships. ("People care about me because of what I do – how I am of service to them – not for who I am.")

Time and again Sophie, a woman who never stops producing even if it is clever dinner time conversation among friends, asks me, "Is this keeping of accounts, this paying off debts and accumulating of credit, what everybody does constantly all the time?" I would like to scream, "No! That's your Faustian bargain," until she somersaults ahead of me and I reflexively flip-flop backwards. "Sometimes I fantasize about going off to a Buddhist monastery somewhere in the hills of Tibet, or being confined to a bed in a hospital where I am forced by kindly nurses in starched white uniforms to eat three balanced meals a day and follow an elderly male doctor's orders." And if those possibilities sound too remote, too disgustingly infantile and passive even in fantasy, then maybe she could go on the Internet and find herself a good-natured, good-enough mate, and become like one of those white haired ladies in the supermarket whose husbands patiently push their shopping carts, pacing close beside them, consulting and suggesting before choosing together this week's flavor of ice cream.

I can barely suppress a smile when I hear Sophie's old-age fantasies, and neither can she. This romance of the Simple Life could never sustain a woman like Sophie for very long (and we hedge our bets as to whether it could sustain any form of life that claims to be human). It is a peaceful life in which there is neither the expectation nor the desire to be distinctive, or make the world a better place, or create a work of art that will be remembered past tomorrow; it stands for pleasure, but only if pleasure is simply tension reduction, the loss of ego, and ultimately death.

Sophie becomes restless doing what she calls "maintenance work" (but shouldn't she, shouldn't we?), though to her this means that she has no patience for shopping or ice cream, small talk or yoga, not even for what she describes as "fruitless" dancing which produces indescribable pleasure but nothing more. Having narrowly escaped living life underwater ("I was supposed to marry a druggist," she says with an ironic smile), her loves are not going to be flirtations that go nowhere, but passions that go beyond the everyday everywhere. Life without pain, strain, and labor, is life without purpose (a "circus" is how she described it on one occasion). Thus, in the blink of an eye her dream of Nirvana turns into a nightmare in which she would be a joke, not the clever joker, a ghost of the druggist's wife who has unwittingly fallen into a coma.

Passive versus active, being versus doing, the life of the body versus the life of the mind, the feminine versus the masculine principle: call it what you like; this tension between opposing perspectives and associated desires to control and to surrender up control assumes a myriad of forms. We have no choice but to live honestly or dishonestly with the oppositions between being "awake or in a kind of stupor" (as the Israeli writer Amos Oz poses it in his memoir *A Tale of Love and Darkness*), which is why the Good Life has become the good-enough life after Freud. The only question that remains to haunt us perpetually is, how?

"Unpurposeful" Pleasures?

> I would dwell with thee,
> Merry grasshopper,
> Thou art so glad and free,
> And as light as air;
> (Alfred Lord Tennyson, "The Grasshopper")

"For awhile in the late 70's I folk danced . . . I never mentioned it to you before? I'm surprised because it was a core experience for me at the time . . . completely fruitless, when I stop to think about it now, but I loved it." Speaking off the record, Sophie frames her wistful recollection in an ironic smile ('Dare she eat a peach' and have the juice dribble down her chin or dance off the analytic couch for the sheer fun of it?). Why not temper the bitterness of straight irony? I wonder. What is the danger in being earnestly nostalgic?

"Maybe I'm what you'd call a 'Plain Jane. ' I don't have any advanced degrees, and I don't care if we have a Mercedes in the driveway. It doesn't bother me if the house is messy or the laundry piles up until the week-end; and if I want to stay up and read my book past midnight and sleep till nine or ten in the morning, why should it matter to you?" Genevieve scarcely looks at her husband, who is sitting at the other end of the couch with his eyes shut and a sardonic expression on his face, though she is clearly waiting for a response. When he fails to reply and yawns visibly, she turns to me in frustration: "I know Lee's always judging me. Whenever we go to one of his colleagues' houses for dinner he comes home singing the praises of all the other wives who are doctors or lawyers and also gourmet cooks, and then he starts thinking of new ways to improve the business, new plans to renovate the basement and landscape the garden." Exasperated by her husband's silence, which she interprets as implicit criticism, she raises her voice: "I take care of the children, and I prepare a healthy meal every evening, so why can't he just accept me the way I am?"

Impassioned speeches in unidentifiable foreign accents are punctuated by mysterious silences and then peels of laughter which reverberate upwards through the vents in our basement where my thirteen-year old daughter Vera and her friends have been playing "old fashioned dress up" for hours. Yes, unlike their more sophisticated classmates, they still *play*, though I imagine they won't be doing this too much longer. Surprisingly, at this point I do not detect even a hint of uneasiness when I hold up the mirror, so to speak, and call what they do together "play." But, to be honest, the word has a different meaning for me from the one that they intend: it turns their unpurposeful, that is, unpremeditated and unproductive, pleasure into something childish and insignificant when *they* know that what they are doing is all-absorbing and therefore unquestionably significant to them if to no one else. Perhaps I alone feel the ironic twist within my smile. And yet, I'm on their side, and, if pressed, would rally to their defense. Their quirky rituals and improvisations, their feigned flare-ups of temper and unscripted squealings, their stubborn obliviousness to the world of means and ends, are no less important to living the good enough life than practicing the piano; their unreproducible "poetry in motion" is no less essential to the development of good character than studying for tomorrow's science test, debating the pros and cons of capital punishment, or learning the accents in iambic pentameter. I know many people who would agree with me that the over-scheduled child is the unhealthy child, and today's over-achiever will be tomorrow's psychiatric patient. This doesn't solve the problem of measuring, however: what is too much scheduling or too much ambition, and what is too little or just enough?

But even if this post-Freudian or, if you prefer Piagetian analysis were to succeed in justifying to the skeptics what Vera and her friends are doing un-self-consciously without any need for justification, it would fail to pay homage to the blissfully irrational elements in their experience, and hence misses the point. Delighted with just being and with expressing that being freely, they have no concern for measuring its value in some larger scheme of things, no anxiety about missed opportunities, no intimations of future losses or hidden gains. Theirs is a pleasure that is immediate, random, and innocent of purpose (Sophie called it "fruitless"), so why must I spoil it by insisting that their play has a loftier purpose after all? Is that what neurotic adults need in order to expiate their guilt, deny their mortality, and feel worthwhile, some end or meaning reaching beyond the horizon, some *otherness* to wrestle with, like Jacob's angel on the ladder up to heaven?

Vera's comfort with what I have called unpurposeful activity is foreign to my adult, quasi-rational way of living in the world, and since memory is a compilation of stories designed to be coherent, it is impossible for me to remember being quite so un-self-conscious, even as a child. And yet, if I weren't nostalgic for an earlier time when I too was more like Tennyson's grasshopper, or if I didn't wish to return to a simpler state of being, before self-consciousness, before the Fall from paradise, Vera's "purposeless" spinning would probably not be so inviting, so enviable, so irritating, and so contagious. It would not seem so unrealistic and yet at the same time so incontrovertibly natural and honest, at the very essence of a life that is free of what Ecclesiastes calls "Vanity." (Once again, I quote Ecclesiastes, but in this instance I read the biblical text not as an echo of the death instinct, which circles us back to our origins –from dust to dust – but as a call to embrace the transient pleasures of existence and aim for whatever happiness we can.)

Indeed, on those occasions when I permit myself to cast aside my adult responsibilities and open up to being fully present in the moment with my daughter, we slip into an earthly paradise where it doesn't occur to me to worry about the purposelessness of repetition or about my purpose in life or anybody else's. There is pleasure but no obvious usefulness to reading *Alice in Wonderland* together aloud for the umpteenth time (or watching re-runs of Seinfeld, or collecting beach glass and sand dollars, fragrant eucalyptus buttons and heart-shaped chestnuts), and, if there is some use, we truly do not care. Miraculously, abstract questions such as, "Why are we doing this *again*, should we be doing something more productive in our free time together?" and "Where exactly are we headed?" sound hollow – these questions are the waste of time, not our apparently purposeless activity. Thirstily, I drink in this version of what is of real value in life and what is counterfeit, as if it were mother's milk and I were a hungry baby. And I think: "If only Julius and Judy, Kevin and Izzy, Sophie and Genevieve's husband Lee could join me and Vera on this comfy couch and drink, without guilt or shame or paranoia, from the abundant breast. If only they could feel so confident and yet so unambitious, so uncalculated and yet so unambivalently entitled to feed until fully sated!"

And yet, as I translate these diffuse feelings into words and read them aloud to myself, I am relieved to be alone in my secluded space upstairs, secure in the knowledge that nobody is peering over my shoulder. For I can hear my husband's accusations and imagine my older daughter's grimaces were they to catch me in the act: "Your argument for authenticity is superficial; its sentimentality is dishonest; the analogies you draw between living fully and 'nursing until sated' are nauseating; the thinking is purposely fuzzy."

Embarrassed and confused, I would be hard put to defend my naive and undignified position or deny that the predictably unpredictable screeches and pregnant silences that burst into the living room are not only endearing but also tedious and distracting. They make it difficult for me, my older daughter Saralena, and my husband Henry to focus on what we are reading as we sit beside each other (each in our own designated spot on the milk-free couch), and we do want to focus, we want to make progress – we feel sharper and more substantial when we visualize a target, take careful measurements of our distance from it, and then aim.

Saralena expresses our collective ambivalence by looking up from her book and rolling her eyes as if to say: "Does Vera live on some other planet?" But Henry, my more ambitious "other half," cannot restrain himself from taking charge and delivering certain judgements: "Has she finished her homework? Isn't it time for them to clean up the mess they've made? When's dinner?" The Mad Tea Party going on downstairs, in which the same dishes circulate around the table endlessly and no one cares about table manners, personal space, calendar time, or making sense, is not his idea of happiness!

I'm caught in the middle of the triangle (between the superego, the ego, and the id), a position I am all too familiar with in my family and with my patients. But the evening quarrel that is perennially simmering in our collective consciousness is not simply between my blissfully innocent daughter Vera and those culture warriors in my living room who are seriously committed to progress and purposefulness, but between colliding versions of the good life, the sane life, and the happy life and contradictory aims within everyone, myself included. I do not wish to waste time (or potential) any more or less than Henry or Saralena or Vera, but just how that wish plays out in practical reality, and what it has to do with the Pleasure Principle and man's search for meaning is a psychological conundrum that I fear (and hope) will never be resolved in favor of one talking head or the other. I confront it in various disguises every hour with every patient, and ironically, it is this confrontation that provides me with a constant stream of purpose that breaks my fall as I hurtle down one rabbit hole after another, in pursuit of happiness and the recovery of lost time.

A few years back I returned to reading Proust's *In Search of Lost Time* (or otherwise translated as *Remembrance of Things Past*), and occasionally, on mornings after I had dropped Vera off at school and I had a free hour or two before beginning to see patients, I would indulge myself. What a joy to follow the twists and turns of his endless sentences and end up back in his nineteenth century drawing room ten minutes later where nothing has changed, psychoanalysis has not been invented, there is no war raging in Iraq, and there is no live person twisting and turning, freely associating or being stuck and unable to let go. I savor these moments, thrilled that in late middle age I am willing and able to give myself the gift I couldn't when I was younger and more driven by purpose. But is there a purpose in this purposeless activity? Should I feel a little guilty? Should I be using my time more productively in service of someone or something?

Faith in Purpose and Purpose in Faith: Happiness is (Not) Living "Fully in the Present"

This past New Year's Eve one of my dearest friends presented the book *The End of Faith* to all those gathered around her dinner table, but to my mind the gift was only testimony that, for better or for worse, there is no end to faith in the foreseeable future! Indeed, the heated controversy that absorbed us until the clock struck twelve and we put aside all controversies, foiled her explicit purpose to innoculate us against untested hopes, unfounded loyalties, unwieldy emotions, and primitive superstitions. Only *faithful* friends, I pointed out, could disagree so violently as to the meaning of faith, let alone the value of living with or without it, and still enjoy each other's company, respect each other's intelligence, and trust in each other's good will. Only faithful friends could overlook the angry flare-ups, the logical lapses, and the faulty connections that disrupted the evening's otherwise harmonious relations.

Faith, trust, hope, "transference": I ask you, Peter, as our representative scientist at the table (he's a fervent anti-Freudian who shares with Freud an irrationally intense distaste for religious yearnings), "Would we really want to strip ourselves of all our unreasonableness, our sustaining but unverifiable faith in Life's (if not God's or Science's) hidden purposes? Would we want to have next New Year's Eve without our customary high-pitched battles over psychoanalysis, the mind versus the brain, the Orthodox Jews, and "popular" culture, battles that can never be contained, much less resolved, and must be continually revisited so that we can tap into those dense pools of feeling that none of us ever fully understand? Would our ironically good-natured predictions and resolutions for the future year be sufficient to fill our bellies once dessert had been eaten and the table cleared if each of us didn't also have these un-ironic (crazy) passions that we commit to secretly (on good faith) once the festivities are over?"

When I first set out to write these reflections on faith, purposefulness, and purposelessness, it was April 23, 2006, and a book entitled *The Purpose-Driven Life* had been on the *New York Times* Best Seller list for169 weeks. While I don't share its religious perspective, and reflexively recoil from any "one size fits all" formulation of happiness, I understood its ecumenical appeal. Christian as well as Jewish patients had mentioned the book to me, and I gathered from the anxious looks they cast in my direction in response to my purposefully impassive expression that their sense of feeling empty of purpose was at least as disturbing as feeling guilty of harboring some wayward purpose. Would that account for the intractability of irrational self-loathing, I wondered, filing away my heretical idea for when I was next stymied by a case of relentless self-reproach? I empathize with the dilemma of having to choose between insignificance and guilt, as if those were the only choices we have, and would like to offer another option that includes the right measure of both: the freedom of purposelessness and the hopefulness of purpose.

As a species, we are obsessed with imagined worlds, with seeing patterns in the skies or in the leaves of tea, hoping for revelation or even an apocalypse. Anything might be preferable to nothingness. Indeed, after suffering some personal disappointment or medical crisis, many of my patients insist that they believe that "everything happens for a reason." In the face of such certain pronouncements, I become instantly uncomfortable, though I share the wish for certainty as well as the suspicion that so-called accidents and misfortunes are not without hidden meanings or secret motives. "Julius, what do you think about being late today?" "Steve, just now you said 'misogynist' and corrected yourself; you meant to say 'misanthrope.' What is that about?" But the idea that *everything* happens for a reason implies something different, doesn't it? Whose reason? Is this simply reassurance? As a therapist I cannot engage in these debates about the design of the universe; I can only ask what the person before me believes that reason is and go from there.

Sometimes I believe that we hallucinate meaning out of a neurotic wish to escape a chaotic reality, but other times I believe that we create it through our unquenchable thirst to understand and transform reality to better suit our needs. In either case, however, the wish to find and express a true but hidden self, however much this may be a worn out cliche from the self-actualization movement of the 1970's, resonates deeply with people's experience. As a therapist I find that even the most cynical people are thirsty for reality, as opposed to mere performance, and confess to it in the privacy of my office.

We can analyze images, observe and manipulate behavior, and decode the human genome, but our heartfelt beliefs about the existence of an unactualized, unobservable self remain unaltered, precisely because they are untestable and unconscious.

When traditional religious frames have failed the test of faith and historical truths have failed the test of reason, many people turn to psychotherapy to give a coherent form to their lives. Psychology and the multi-million dollar self-help industry feeds and is fed on an implicit faith in the meaningfulness of human life here on this earth, the value of freedom and personal growth, and the ideal of human potential. Another illusion? Perhaps. I laugh to myself, recalling the New Year's Eve dinner conversation with Jane and Peter, my family, and Jane's eighty-five year old mother Clara, who was a socialist in the 1940's when she shared a sense of hopefulness and faith with a group of very sophisticated New York intellectuals. Disappointed dreams. Yes, we would all agree to that. The end of faith? Not likely.

In his late writings, Freud described what he saw as the essential psychic battle which takes place between Eros and Thanatos, the instincts towards life and death. Love (which is blind) and the love of truth (which is not) forge an uneasy alliance, but ultimately they join forces in the guerilla war we wage against our deadening compulsion to turn inward, look backward, and repeat. Kevin's exercises in religious asceticism, Judy's vitriolic diatribes against the inertia of the educational bureaucracy, and Julius' microscopic analyses of yesterday's golf game are their expressions of Eros wrestling with Thanatos, while Freud's unrelenting desire "to amount to something" by uncovering psychological truths that stubbornly resist being uncovered is his. (Apparently, in an angry outburst, Freud's father had once said that he, Freud, would never amount to anything!)

The itch to stretch beyond what was and is, and to transfer wishes and hopes onto what is not and may never be, unites the self-appointed spokesman for the Unconscious with the celebrity "bastard" from the South side of Chicago. And, ironically, for both men, as for each of us, faith (of a certain sort) is the source of happiness and unhappiness, insight and blindness. In the case of Julius, faith in an imagined future kept him sane (if by sane we mean at home in the world), but it also betrayed him and drove him down into his basement, his last refuge from a heartlessly unfaithful reality.

Indeed, Julius is a perfect example to bring up at Jane's New Year's Eve dinner conversation about the end(s) of faith and faith's sacred and illicit purposes. Because he is unemployed he is depressed and anxious, but also depressed and anxious because he is unemployed, I often wish I were a healer of broken faith (if not a faith healer) and that with a perfectly crafted interpretation or an understanding gaze I could resuscitate his faltering belief in humanity (in life beyond the cruelty of the pleasure principle wedded to the death instinct) and restore him to his reason. "It is precisely because he shares your suspicion of all faith-based initiatives, Jane, that he is in danger of isolating himself from this world, foreclosing on the next, and losing his grasp on his own mind." Without faith to sustain him, Julius demands tangible proof that whatever purposes he commits himself to are and will be worthy of his love and effort; but there is no such proof, and, moreover, there cannot be!

As Julius rifles through a mountainous rubble of misfortune, remembering and narrating every last detail of his ancient and recent history to me, he volleys backward and forward between hope and disappointment, balancing on the edge and just narrowly escaping the abyss. As a little boy of ten he would literally rifle through the garbage cans at night searching furtively in the refuse for something he could use or sell. (Which strikes me as a perfect metaphor for the "bastard" self that appears worthless but can be mined for hidden value.) The work was dirty and the tough kids in the neighborhood shunned him and called him "Jun' the Bum," but he kept the faith, managed to collect a few bottles, and escape the house that never felt like home.

"I made myself not care, I saved my own money, and then they all came to me when they wanted a slice of pizza. And the truth is that nine times out of ten I was happy to give it to them. After I came back from the Air Force, I was a kind of celebrity – all the mothers whom I grew up around pointed me out as the man they wanted their daughters to marry. I go back now and most of the guys I went to school with are either dead, in prison, or on drugs."

An undeniable success story: the poor black kid whose mother beat him, beats the odds and pulls himself up by his bootstraps. But at the point when I began to see Julius he had begun to question the authenticity of the story's happy ending. What did he actually come away with from rifling through the garbage? When he was ten, on the streets of Chicago, it had seemed worthwhile, and in the Air Force at nineteen the sacrifices demanded of him were not too great. At forty-four, however, in the backrooms of the corporation . . .? He thought he was like teflon and that nothing would stick, but perhaps he was wrong and his mother was right; maybe she knew and he was just "full of shit," as she said. This is the fate of the "bastard child" who has the audacity to think that he can take a short cut through the back alleyways and hope to lose track of his roots, or so goes the latest revision of his story.

"I thought I was the bigger person, that I felt good about myself and depended on no one, but did all that sculpting and polishing, all that 'self-talk' and 'self-improvement,' all that telling myself 'I'm strong and can take anything,' make me more legitimate or less? I made myself up, so I am not a real person." Is Julius right? Should we trust his experience of being an imposter? Is the successful businessman, exemplary father, dependable friend, and selfless partner just a counterfeit of Julius the "stupid" kid who was caught with crumbs on his face after stealing cookies from his mother's cookie jar? After the beating, he consoled himself by pretending to be Superman and plotting his escape. But what should he do now when it looks like there is no exit?

His sisters laugh when they recount the story at Christmas. "You really thought that you could fly, and when mom came after you with the electric cord we had to stop you from jumping out the window." But Julius doesn't find his childish fantasies amusing, nor do I. How should he measure the value of his unflagging purposefulness, or gauge when his optimism was merely a cover for despair? Julius could turn out to be an American icon, or a tragically deluded pawn of history. He has been on disability for depression for over six years now, but is that because he was blinded by his faith and failed to protect himself sufficiently from grim realities, or because he has become blinded by the black hole that is left by its absence?

"I never used to see people in terms of black and white; I thought I could see beyond the stereotypes; but now I'm constantly aware of color and of how people see me. I used to be accused of being an "Oreo cookie," black on the outside but white in the middle; it bothered me then but it bothers me more now. It's like when my mother would say, 'I made you what you are, bastard, and don't act above your raising'." Which is the true version of the man whose closets used to be impeccably neat, whose performance ratings were "superior," and whose bills were (but now rarely are) paid before due? The version he created in front of the television that is fit for Hollywood or his mother's?

A leap of faith is a leap beyond the rational, but that may be the most reasonable approach to living in this unreasonable world. Otherwise Julius' life threatens to be emptied out of meaning, and he of the will to create new meaning – the will to get back to work, play golf, or even do his laundry. Julius is visibly embarrassed and apologizes for attaching so much importance to his laundry and his golf game, but I honor his motives and see myself in Julius. What besides my desire to feel deliberative, creative and purposeful would prompt me to get out from under the warm blankets and be at my computer at eight o'clock on a frigid Sunday morning, hammering out and refining my thoughts about happiness and pleasure, faith and purpose?

And yet, here is the paradox: as a person whose business is not only to help people understand themselves but also to help them become happier through this uncomfortable and haphazard process of understanding, I have found that some of the happiest times, times of emotional epiphany, are those in which my patients have given themselves permission to have faith in no identifiable purpose. (One man recently told me of the unparalleled and unanticipated ecstasy he felt listening to a Bach cantata and I immediately knew just what he meant.) Ordinarily driven by the need to be productive and masterful, creative and fulfilled, they yearn to *just be,* to fall unmindfully into life or love, to not have to write a beautiful poem or lead the women's group on campus or care one way or another about the significance of wrinkled laundry. They fondly recall those precious, forbidden, and fleeting moments when the idea of doing something "meaningful" never entered their heads. They may have been dancing with abandon to Middle Eastern music, sitting around a dinner table conversing with old friends, or sharing inconsequential memories of distant times, happy and unhappy. Absorbed and un-self-conscious, they felt sufficient and complete. Those times when their faith in the "good enough" is a given are the times when love and life need no reasons at all.

Thus, the nagging desire for purposefulness and the undefinable purpose of unpurposeful pleasure can pull us in opposite directions. In psychotherapy we veer off onto one path during any given hour only to get lost and weave our way back onto the other, as we work to become both more and less self-conscious, to rely both more and less on a foundation of faith.

"Love and Work," and "Optimal Levels of Frustration"

> "The more one aims at pleasure the more his aim is missed. The very pursuit of happiness is what thwarts it. . . . Only to the extent to which man fulfills a meaning out there in the world, does he fulfill himself. If he sets out to actualize himself rather than fulfill a meaning, self-actualization immediately loses its justification."
>
> Viktor E. Frankl, *The Will to Meaning* (1969)

For Freud the healthy life includes the capacity for love and work; one without the other is symptomatic of unresolved, frustrated desire and an augury of future problems. Self psychologists have suggested, however, that many problems do not stem from childhood experiences of frustration per se, but from the absence of an empathic response to that frustration. And, as Freud would argue in his *Introductory Lectures,* gratification of desire is not always the optimal response on the part of either a parent or a therapist. Indeed, for healthy development to proceed, the patient and child need to experience a certain amount of disappointment and disillusionment in order to be able to function more or less independently in the world. So, once more the question arises, what is too much frustration or gratification, postponement or sublimation, and what is a good enough amount of each?

In the middle of a Passover *seder*, after the Four Questions had been answered, first ritualistically and then extemporaneously, according to our Reconstructionist tradition, I was drawn into a conversation with David, the son of a dear family friend, about his future career choices and his desire to fall head over heels in love. Against the backdrop of the Bible story of Moses leading the Jews out from slavery, David raised questions about his tradition's customary way of being, which he sometimes experiences as neurotic compulsions. As we were waiting to mix the sweet with the bitter, the charoses with the horseradish, as is prescribed in the *Haggadah*, he described what turns out to be his own version of our communal ethical dilemma, one having to do, at least in my mind, with the mixing of the sweet with the bitter facts of life. Call it perfectionism or personal integrity, superego morality or honest self-criticism, once David becomes aware of some insufficiency within himself, be it physical or intellectual, emotional or moral, he cannot ignore it or feel comfortable in his awareness of it. Challenged to improve upon himself, he will not surrender up his will (anymore than he would voluntarily stop breathing); he cannot humbly accept his limitations.

Twenty-five years old, single, and a Ph.D. candidate at Harvard, his questions are self-consciously spiritual as much as they are pragmatic; they are questions about love and work, complacency and serenity; mediocrity and excellence; they are about keeping the Sabbath, both literally and figuratively, as he wrestles with the demons (inside and outside) that betray its quiet and mysteriously un-pragmatic purpose. In other words, David is restless, but, what's more, has not yet decided whether resting is good or bad for him or for the world at large. Does he really want to rest or only feel that he should? "I don't like my competitiveness and how I always feel driven toward reaching some goal. I'm sure the sudden panic I felt at one point last year and my being somewhat of a hypochondriac is connected to it; but honestly, if there were a button I could push that would make my anxiety and ambitiousness go away, I don't think I'd push it; maybe I'd be a nicer, more easy-going, type of guy, I'd have time to read just for pleasure, but I wouldn't feel like me, and what then?" Since I adore David, just as he is and as I have always known him to be, it would be difficult to argue in favor of pushing that button.

Leery about the dangers of untempered ambition, anxious about the pressure experienced by the over-scheduled, high achieving child, as a testament to the unconditionality of parental love we proclaim, "We just want you to be happy." But it's half truth, half lie, and so we believe our words (our earnest *dayenus*) only half the time. (In the Passover service there is a song that expresses thankfulness for all of God's blessings during the exodus from slavery. After identifying each blessing bestowed upon the Hebrew people, there is the refrain *Dayenu,* which means, "It would have been enough," and indicates that God's gifts have been abundant and we are fortunate.

We want the happiness that comes with the freedom to "just be" without concern for what that being accomplishes, but we also want more – for our children, and by extension, from ourselves. And shouldn't we? Isn't that what makes us human, that interminable "wanting more," from our children and for ourselves?

I have to remind myself that this tug of war between the grateful *Dayenus* and the fiery songs of freedom and protest I remember from my sixties era adolescence is normal, even healthy, when I catch myself feeling impatient with my still-so-innocent child Vera, who sometimes seems too content to push ambition aside, curl up with an old book she's read numerous times before, or play old fashioned dress-up with her next door neighbor friends. Sure, like every good parent I just want her to be happy, but like every "good enough" parent, I do not want just *her* to be happy, (nor do I want her to be *just* happy as a "contented cow" or narcissistic monster are happy, oblivious to the passage of time, the finiteness of life, and the larger world around them). I suspect that there is a point at which unpurposeful pleasure becomes a breeding ground for future unhappiness, a point at which unconditional love (which is what every one of my patients claims to need) would be enough to drive a person crazy, when it would thwart Vera's desire for independence and the pleasure that comes from having fought a good fight. But where does that point lie? If I were David or David's therapist, or, for that matter, his mother, when, if ever, would I want to push that magic button?

Last week Sophie spoke nostalgically about the "fruitless" pleasure she got from Middle Eastern dancing, and wished that I would grant her permission to wrest herself free of her compulsive productivity – her unrelenting desire to make the world a better place. But this week she eyes my empathic responses with suspicion. Parodying the fantasies of old age she wove the week before, which included ritualized visits to the supermarket with a doting husband by her side, she gestures dramatically how they make her gag. ("Get the pacifier out of my mouth! It is choking me! ") With the war in Iraq raging and the victims of hurricane Katrina still homeless, did I suppose she was actually serious about the banal pleasures of domesticity, of sharing a favorite flavor of ice cream, of surrendering up to the natural cycle of life and its end? Then she chides me: "You seem happy. Do you think I should take a yoga class? What's your secret?" Her question, which I interpret as containing a mixture of envy, hunger, and blame, may boil down to: "Am I just fucked up or are you and your kind just living in La-La land?" It gives me pause. I wouldn't be writing about Sophie if she weren't straining so much against the tide, if she were one of those sweet little old ladies who have found happiness in just being present in the moment. Threaded into Sophie's unhappiness lies her purpose, her happiness, and indirectly mine. Were she to unravel the threads, what pattern would she weave to recapture our imagination? Who would she be, how would she care enough, and what would we be passionately pursuing together?

Getting on and off Track and "Wasting Time"

> "A slow sort of country! said the Queen. 'Now *here* you see, it takes all the running *you* can do, to keep in the same place. If you want to get somewhere else, you must run at least twice as fast as that!'"
>
> (Lewis Carroll, *Alice Through the Looking Glass*)

"I'm sorry I've been jumping around all over the place today." Gabe hesitated by the door, searching my face for reassurance. The hour, which started out ploddingly, with an excessive amount of stops and starts on both of our parts, had taken off in the final twenty-five minutes, leaving us hanging, suspended on a limb, catching our breath. This is not unusual in psychotherapy

– risks are taken and exciting things seem to happen just when time is nearly up and we can bow out gracefully, with all our necessary defenses more or less intact. Exhilarated but also relieved that I would not be expected to keep up these mental gymnastics much longer, I was disturbed by Gabe's half-hearted apology. Why reintroduce the solemn tone, the dragging of feet, the abject smile? A moment ago we were enjoying our "jumping around," our chasing each other like kids on a jungle gym. True, we had violated the usual codes of adult conversation, but in the moment it hadn't crossed either of our minds that this haphazardness was a waste of time; to the contrary, we were grateful to have no specific destination driving us. Having fun by giving his imagination free rein was an act of courage for Gabe, and I was along for the ride.

But before I could respond, Gabe added another element to the mix of emotions that were beginning to percolate within me. "I figure you are always able to pull it together." "Uh oh," I thought, as I cautiously returned his gaze and felt my uneasiness growing. I wanted to reassure him (and myself) that it was perfectly okay, indeed desirable to "get off track," but I didn't want to dismiss his (and my) opposing wish to get back on eventually. Purposelessness was okay, he seemed to be emphasizing, as long as ultimately it had a purpose, and as long as I, his therapist, would, at some point in the future, reveal to him the "method to our madness."

My sentiments precisely! Indeed, this is the only way I am able to justify indulging in the simple pleasures of "just being" with a patient, without regard for doing something evidently productive, something that I could document for the purposes of the Managed Care establishment. I draw on my early training for support: regression can be in "the service of the ego," dreams are the "royal road to the Unconscious," and play is the means by which children (and adults) make the world habitable. Purposefully lacking a pre-conceived agenda, I could defend my professional integrity by identifying the purpose served by letting go and following (without a map) the tangled trails of free association and memory.

All of that being said, Gabe's life story is a nagging reminder that overriding concern with purposefulness can be both a blessing and a curse. Eight years before he began to see me he had "straightened out" and turned his life around. He had stopped smoking "way too much" grass, hanging out with "losers" who were purposelessly going nowhere, and married the one person left in his life who continued to have faith in him. Officially diagnosed as "ADD" and put on medication, he began to make lists of all the things he wanted to accomplish each day and checked them off religiously. Unsolicited, new items appeared on his "to do" list every morning, and since the list is never-ending, he is never without an end, never at loose ends, and almost always in focus. (Ironically, given his sense of purpose, he frequently describes himself and his life passively: "With parenting comes responsibilities; there is no room in my schedule" – which makes me wonder, "Who's directing the show?")

Clearly, I am not alone in my wondering. "Why can't I spend an hour without working so hard?" he asks as he leans forward on the edge of the couch, working exceedingly hard to organize his thoughts and make full use of every therapeutic minute. Sitting three feet across from him, it is impossible not to feel the pressure. "I want to be conscious of how my behavior impacts others; I don't want to be the kind of guy I was before I met Kirsten, but . . . " He trails off and cannot finish the sentence. Taking a detour turns out to be helpful, however, as Gabe informs me that in his other life he made it a conscious choice not to care. "I was not ashamed about playing my music till 2:00 AM, smoking grass, and living on very little money. In fact, I was in your face." Thus, he was aimless on principle (a contradiction in terms, if there ever was one). And yet, in refusing to spend time living unhappily and abstractedly imagining the future, he scattered his attention and lived indiscriminately, "fully in the present."

Looking back with embarrassment at what he describes as his over-extended adolescence, Gabe is proud to say that now he wants to be responsible and to plot out where he is going carefully. How other people think and feel matters to him tremendously, and, moreover, he believes that it should. So why is Gabe, the prototypical Prodigal Son, coming to see me at his father's urging ("You're doing great but you don't seem happy")? Why, eight years after his celebrated epiphany? Because he's logging onto pornographic web sites and feels he can't stop himself. Again the passivity in his voice, expressing an experience of aimlessness: "It isn't who I am and it goes against everything I believe in." But then he hesitates: "I'm more in control of my life since I met Kirsten, but I feel I've lost *me*." On track, moving ahead, and wasting time!

Gabe has swung from one extreme to another, from a life without concern for productivity or purpose to a life without regard for unproductive pleasures. Which is why he has become "symptomatic," and carelessly leaves out a disc of downloaded pornography on his computer for his wife to discover, jeopardizing his most cherished relationship and testing the unconditionality of her love. As much oppressed by too much purpose as he was by too little, he needs to find a middle ground, the "golden mean," philosophy's equivalent to psychological integration.

But what is that "middle ground" that "normal," "healthy" people are supposed to inhabit, and that appears to Gabe and Sophie even more remote than all their other unattainable ideals? Beyond the sermons and the cliches, beyond the serenity prayer to which everyone, even my radical, politically activist sister, aspires, who decides what amount of purposefulness in a given day (or a given life) is excessive and dehumanizing and what amount is creative and inspiring? Who determines when unpurposeful pleasure serves a purpose and life's purpose and when it is an ornamental screen for wasting time?

Small Talk

Who decides? We do all the time. Susan is a psychologist who works in the office next door to mine. Over the years we have become friends, though we rarely see each other outside the building. Sometimes I can hear her familiar laugh through the wall we share in common, and then I wonder about our differences as therapists and women. How much direction would she offer a depressed patient such as Izzy, who asks me for some "pearls of wisdom," or Julius, who laments that he finds none? And how would she respond to David's ambivalence about his ambitiousness? Would Susan interpret the *Dayenus* around the Passover table as traditional expressions of gratitude and praise, or would she understand them as David's parents do, as healthy expressions of a desire for still more. I like Susan's sense of humor, and admire her modesty, uncompetitiveness, pensiveness, and patience; I have no doubts about her personal or professional integrity and her commitment to her patients. But she likes ocean cruises, and I find them nightmarish, so I would never plan to go with her on vacation, and imagine that the feeling is mutual. Both of us are very conscious of wasted energy and wasted time and how they translate into wasted potential and unnecessary unhappiness. But we are forever hashing out just what "waste" looks like and what unsuspected purposes it serves or betrays.

Over the past eighteen years we have tried to set aside at least one hour every couple of weeks to talk, but since both of our schedules vary from day to day and week to week, and both of us cherish our freedom as much as our shared vocation, we leave open the time as well as the agenda. That means that what we end up talking about on a given afternoon serves as a kind of joint Rorschach test. Sometimes one of us will bring up a particularly difficult session with a patient, which forces us to examine why we are stuck, blinded, and unable to move forward. (This feels virtuous and risky, and like any exercise it usually hurts.) But there are other times when we talk about husbands, children, friends, or politics, or even indulge in the forbidden: "idle gossip." "What's going on with . . .?" Curiosity drives us more than a wish to arrive at deeper understanding.

On one occasion, when Susan informed me with a big grin on her face that she had only a couple of patients scheduled that day, was planning to take Fridays off on a regular basis, and was tickled at the prospect of having more free time to "play," I was irritated and felt more judgmental than I like to be toward someone I am fond of and admire. Children "play," I thought, as I tried to hide my mean-spiritedness by mirroring her unself-conscious spontaneous grin. Had she forgotten that we are of the generation of women who want to work, indeed are happy to have found meaningful work: powerful women who do not need to envy penises (contrary to Freud's anatomical determinism) or live vicariously through others? Doesn't Susan feel the same obligation that I do not to fritter away time "playing?" Doesn't she take herself seriously? She does, I know this without a doubt, but apparently not by the measure I was used to using. But then who's got it right?

"'Well, I haven't made any progress this week. I didn't get to the boxes in the basement and I could kick myself because once again I didn't follow up on a stock that I knew would be a terrific investment – I'm not talking about pennies I just lost thousands of dollars. I can't depend on my broker – he doesn't keep track of anything, and I've stopped taking those new pills my psychiatrist gave me because they affected my prostate; I'm stuck." (After more than a year of similar openings, Izzzy's meaning is obvious and the details are redundant: he, his psychiatrist, and his broker are all less than useless, and what's more, yesterday's news is just a foreshadowing of tomorrow's.) With a left hook to his therapist, but without skipping a beat, Izzy returned to where he had been cut off the last session, expressing bitterness and disappointment with himself and the way he was conducting his life, and by extension bitterness and disappointment with me and the way I was conducting our therapy: life was racing past him and he was standing still, if not falling backwards examining the lint in his navel.

When we parted the previous session he had made what therapists call a doorknob plea for some "last minute pearls of wisdom" (not exactly a hot stock tip but something equivalent – a mantra he could recite that would drown out the self-deprecating voices that waited impatiently down the hall for him to finish. ("What a waste of time and money!" they cackle). But once again I had no pearls of wisdom to offer, and felt then, as I did now, what he feels repeatedly: guilty as charged. As long as the unpacked boxes in the basement were his measure of failure, and success and happiness lay buried within them, there was no more purpose in my denying an inadequacy that he was more than willing to share with me and all the other "experts" than there was purpose in my denying our mutual failure to make any "progress" that his ruler might measure.

"Pearls of wisdom?" I don't think so! More like "pearls before swine," I free associate silently in my defensiveness. After weeks of trying and failing to penetrate Izzy's wall of negativity, I cannot help but be frustrated with his contradictory desires to be happy and to prove that he is fated not to be, as all the ordinary forms of human pleasure are mysteriously indigestible for him (as no doubt would be those pearls he hankers for).

On the outside I make every effort to appear unruffled by his unrealistic demands for an easy cure for problems he insists are either completely unique to him or else intractably human nature. After all, as his therapist I am supposed to be empathic, not judgmental. And yet, I wonder whether my duplicity (the blank screen that shields him from my visceral reactions) is a betrayal of my belief in the value of uncovering the truth and facing rather than hiding disturbing realities. His insatiability is a drain on our relationship, and I suspect it chokes the life out of many others, so shouldn't he be made aware of the damage he is doing? "You're baiting me and it's a set-up for failure."

For years Izzy had been devouring massive quantities of advice, grazing the Internet, the self-help shelves at Barnes and Noble, the audio-visuals in the library for Eastern- and Western-style sages, only to regurgitate it all on my office rug undigested. Consequently, I was not about to waste time adding more confetti to his paper trail or naively plotting how not to waste his. So, while I was left wrestling with how I could possibly inspire him to engage in life, or at the very least engage in psychotherapy, when his touch seemed to turn every piece of gold to shit, I was resolved not to compete with Izzy or the self-help sages when it came to inspirational bullet points. "Sorry, no magic wand, no psycho-babble bullshit, no pearls of wisdom. I am not King Midas who can turn everything, even your shit, to gold."

"My life is shit, I am shit, and I hate the fact that I need somebody to change my shitty diaper!" This is how, after nearly a year of weekly sessions, I translate Izzy's constant stream of complaints, which ranged from his granddaughter's failure to send him a thank you note for his generous birthday present, to his body's failure to tolerate medication, to my failure to be the idealized transference figure he had hoped he would find, someone who could make him feel that he was indispensable, that he had a purpose, but also that he did not have to have one.

And yet, as "shitty" as we often both felt after our sessions, neither I nor Izzy was ready to end our pursuit of happiness (our defense of life or what Freud called Eros). I, for one, refused to surrender up the body to that wooden Queen of Hearts in Alice's Looking Glass who, masquerading as progress insisted that he run twice as fast as normal people do, without regard for whether he gasps for breath and remains stuck in the same old rut going nowhere.

Diagnosis? That's easy, though in case I hadn't figured it out, Izzy, who wasn't foolish enough to let himself depend on anybody, had thoroughly researched it on his own. Helplessness and hopelessness with somatic symptoms are benchmarks of anxiety and depression, and, he tells me with an added twist, it runs in his family. But the origins of this dis-ease and its prognosis? Not so fast, Wayne Dyer, Dr. Phil, Victor . . . "What's his name? That psychiatrist who was in the camps and wrote about man's need for meaning." Questions having to do with past causes and future possibilities are more obscure and lie beyond the scope of the Diagnostic Statistical Manual, which classifies everything, predicts very little, and by design explains nothing.

Social isolation, a rancorous divorce, loss of purpose, a chemical imbalance – these are the obvious reasons that have been volleyed back and forth innumerable times. But what if Izzy's threatened interminable unhappiness is beyond the reach of reason and ungoverned by those principles of pleasure or reality that are straightforward and predictable? What then? Unconscious guilt for prehistoric fears and wishes (crimes of the heart) that he cannot remember but will not forget? Anger turned inward, which may be better than naked aggression if he doesn't wish to alienate everyone forever? The death instinct? "The return of the repressed?" I sift through my memories of texts I've read and experiences I've had because I can't let go of our hope for progress, and can't understand why a history of purposeless unhappiness has to repeat itself, as if that repetition had a purpose and a life all of its own.

Flashback. After "accidentally on purpose" getting his first girlfriend pregnant the very first time he had sex at twenty-one, Izzy had gone from being a drifter (a "dirty Jew" was what the neighborhood kids had called him), a boy without religious connections or family traditions he could speak of, to becoming a devoted husband, an actively observant member of a Conservative Jewish community, and the most faithful of a clan of sons-in-law. Which is how it came to pass that for nearly forty years, Izzy ran "twice as fast "just to keep up with everyone else (or at least it looked that way to him), with the hope that he could out-run his heritage: he collected degrees, conscientiously kept careful track of his wife's family traditions, built up a sizeable portfolio of investments, and learned Yiddish along with biblical Hebrew. He had found his purpose, had cut his teeth on it; and yet, from what he intimates, it didn't make him happy. This was still surprising to Izzy years later, but not to me, as even his language betrayed the purposelessness of his sense of purpose. When he described the way he drove himself and lauded himself for his unswerving diligence and focus, he spoke as a stock broker might of strategies, risks, and investments. His purpose was an *it* and, even in the best of times, he was alienated from it. "You can't gaze at happiness from a distance or think about it as an abstract principle, you have to feel it," I wanted to say, but knew that too was an abstraction and of no practical help. Indeed, wedded to his abstract principles, Izzy envied those more fortunate than himself who seemed to feel entitled to be less principled and more alive, to drift from time to time and enjoy their lives without reference to a driving purpose. Echoes of Judy.

So at sixty-five, Izzy's eyes wandered off track, away from his book of rules (his private Torah), and once again, "accidentally on purpose," he drifted into an affair (with a *shiksa,* no less), and slipped out from under the thumb of his self-consciously, purpose-driven existence. In nowhere land is where I found him, however, "stuck," making no "progress," and wasting time. "Dr. Block, I have my yellow-lined writing pad ready, give me some homework, something to sink my teeth in. I've been hungry for as long as I can remember, but what I eat ends up making me sick, and now I am afraid to eat anything at all." This is what I imagine Izzy would say if he could put his feelings into words, but he can't and instead waits for my instructions. I don't instruct and so I disappoint him, as others in his life always have. I can empathize, wade through the detritus with him, and search for ancient relics that are occupying too much space in his mental life. He seems to be filled with poisonous memories and experiences, but I fear he wants detoxification rather than therapy, purgation rather than integration.

Is he happier unmarried than when he was married to his capricious Queen of Hearts? Is he less stressed retired and living off the sizable income from his investments than when he was running a wholesale textile business and managing his wife's medical treatments for Crohn's disease complicated by depression? He can't decide; memory is also capricious. Alone and thoroughly disenchanted with the woman whose unstinting love was supposed to have made him happy, Izzy remembers the good times, now gone forever, when he had faith, worked seventy hours a week to earn his blessings, and was in his ascendency. What does he have now when he walks in my door but concrete evidence of his decline and the burns he still suffers from his domestic inferno. Neither work nor love, purpose nor purposelessness, have managed to absolve him of his guilt or provide him with a sense that his life has meaning. Hence his paralysis and our stalemate in therapy.

So how should I respond to Izzy, or anyone for that matter, who urgently wishes to be loved without conditions, as a person, not simply an instrument, and yet only values himself when he serves a purpose that extends beyond his self and his personal pleasures? Self-fulfillment has no meaning apart from his usefulness to others, he claims (and in this the rabbis may back him up). So how is he to feel when he bought his granddaughter a car for her sixteenth birthday and she didn't send him even a thank-you note? Ashamed at his desire for recognition? Bitter at her apparent indifference? Lost at his loss of ambition to earn more money, make a killing in the stock market, and outsmart all of the so-called experts?

But when I offer empathy and forgiveness for the floundering and lonely self that has repeatedly failed to sort through the boxes in his basement, and then encourage him to pursue his childhood dreams to take an art class or an exploratory trip out West, he eyes me warily and pellets me with reasons not to do any of these things. What value is there in "play," he implies as he fiddles nervously with his pen and prepares to jot down pointers on his yellow note pad? His *shiksa* girlfriend smokes and eats too much and ignores her doctor's warnings; her unschooled devotion and unconditional love may have felt good when he was married, but it lured him away from the things that really mattered to him for more than forty years – his hard-earned degrees, his standing in the community, and his successful business ventures. These achievements are not important to her; she is happy just to have him around. Will I do the same?

Though I can get irritated by Izzy's resistance to the empathy I offer in place of judgment or concrete advice, I take heed. As long as the records dating back to 1983 from his business are still in the basement rather than in the dumpster, his financial portfolio isn't maximizing growth because he isn't following the market the way he used to, and he has not committed himself to either one of his two part-time girlfriends, he wants progress and has no time to waste on acceptance or understanding. How can I blame him? Life as it stands, stuck as he is, is not good enough! Not for him, not for me.

No doubt Izzy fears that too much understanding and acceptance can be debilitating, even emasculating; it will let him off the hook, and then what is left to prevent his purpose-driven life from completely unraveling? What assurance can I give him that if he's "off the hook" he won't slide backwards, that a regression would do a disservice to his ego, not to mention his superego?"

(Heinz Hartmann was the first of the psychoanalytic ego psychologists that referred to "regression in the service of the ego" to explain how a patient's regression within therapy ultimately facilitated his developmental progression. Essentially, the idea is that in order to move forward, first the patient must dismantle his defenses and re-encounter and even re-experience early childhood fears and wishes.)

"Faster, faster," shouts the Queen; "your time to dawdle is running out." And so, ironically, when it comes down to it, the first and the last thing Izzy wants from me or anybody else is a sample-sized, time-share portion of unconditional love! Better the critical mother/wife/in-laws whose painful barbs and interminable desires got him off his *tuchas,* than the undemanding father/*shiksa* girlfriend whose desires were modest and whose love was blind to the less-than-good-enough?

I never did find a satisfactory response to Izzy's wish to create a happy future from the remains of his disappointments. We both suffered at his failure to make "progress," but I couldn't be enthused by his imagined path to happiness (a thank you card from the grand-daughter, a different psychiatrist, a condo in Florida, or a woman without any medical issues), and he had no faith in mine. "I can't concentrate and I need someone to help me set goals; I need positive self-statements, for nobody else can make me happy. Thank you for your time, and don't take this personally, but I'm going to try cognitive behavioral therapy." Was I disappointed that Izzy fired me after I had spent so much time outside of sessions, in the pool while I was doing my laps, thinking about how to unstick him? Honestly, I was and I wasn't. We hadn't made progress, not the kind that could register on his scoreboard or on mine, and so what was the purpose of repetitive failure?

It's more than six years now since Izzy has figured in my conversations with Susan as "my most difficult patient." (Though, when I've seen him in the synagogue on high holidays, and he casts me a furtive glance before saying "Doctor Joyce" to me in greeting and introducing me to his daughter, I wonder if his difficulty was an "inter-subjective" dynamic between the two of us that cleared away once we had ceased our tug of war.) I don't know if he has unpacked his boxes, or if he feels less paralyzed, or, most significantly, if he has faith in the possibility of having a good enough life with a good enough group of people with whom he can share it. The track we were on together just went round in circles, so I imagine that we are both relieved to have gotten off. I'm on another track, however, still trying to figure out the meaning of our impasse. I may never see him in my office again or arrive at a satisfying understanding of Izzy's intractable unhappiness, but for some peculiar reason (a matter of stubborn faith, no doubt), because I have kept trying to understand what happened, I don't feel altogether unsuccessful or that I have wasted our time. I wish the same for Izzy.

Postscript

Julius hates to cry, and finds it embarrassing to speak about the past. Getting back to work, feeling productive, and being "normal" (like everybody else) is what he wants above all. And yet, he says that because he is able to speak and cry openly with me, about his mother, about his unproductive and irrational feelings, he feels "real," "whole," "like everybody else." "Giddy" and "euphoric," "weak" and "embarrassed"– these are the words he uses to describe his unpremeditated experiences. After ten years of working together, we both realize that this emotional unpacking and repackaging cannot bring a happy resolution to his dilemmas. But it has heightened his awareness of unspeakable wishes and disappointments, of loves that have turned to hate, and of the purposes of shutting down and disappearing and the forbidding pleasures of opening up and being seen. When that unpurposeful, often painful, heightening of awareness happens during a session without his planning for it, it is strangely reassuring. Julius hasn't found "sanity" or "happiness," as he had hoped to when playing Superman, but since we are engaged in their pursuit, his faith in the legitimacy of his desires for some unknowable purpose is restored, and that may be good enough.

We want happiness, but maybe we have to settle for the freedom to pursue happiness, which means acknowledging that our uniquely human capacity to be happy *and* unhappy with ourselves and with the way things are is a strength, not a weakness. (Is this what it means to have hope without shame? To be only human but not inhumane?) Ironically, once we feel committed to an endless pursuit of an unknowable good, we may feel incomplete, but at the same time sufficiently whole, relieved of the unreasonable obligations to be other than who we are or to want to become nothing more. Ceasing to pretend to know more or less than what we know about ourselves and the world we live in may be what it means to be "sane," given the insane nature of existence and the uncertain existence of God. This riding the waves of contradiction brings us pain and pleasure (ordinary unhappiness and happiness), but at the same time it satisfies our irrational ambitions to reach beyond both. The unpurposeful poking and prodding, sinking and soaring, unraveling and weaving together, which is the work and play of psychotherapy, has a purpose after all.

MY BROTHER'S KEEPER

"With bitter irony he watched that gallery of faces undisturbed by any worry, those foreheads innocent of any idea. . . . My father separated himself more and more from that world of lightheartedness and escaped into the hard discipline of total dedication . . . Before we could understand what was happening, he shook himself violently, buzzed, and rose in flight before our eyes, transformed into a monstrous, hairy, steel blue horsefly, furiously circling and knocking blindly against the walls of the shop."

Bruno Schulz, "Dead Season," *Sanatorium Under the Sign of the Hourglass*(1937)

Prometheus on the Couch: Bound and Unbound

"The other faculty in my department have no problem saying they won't teach our core courses, so I always do it. I understand; naturally, the senior faculty prefer to teach courses that are directly related to their particular research interests, and the younger ones need to worry about tenure. They're all thinking of their own careers and what excites them the most, but I feel we have a responsibility to all of our students. Of course, I would also love to create a course that reflects my individual area of work, and actually many of my advanced students have asked me to. But if I did, then the incoming students wouldn't be getting the foundation I know they need, and I care about that, even if no one else seems to."

Steve was talking about work, but I was reminded of his frustrated lament last month about the new lights on the city bridge:"One got broken shortly after it was installed, and either nobody noticed or else nobody cared enough to do anything about it. Finally, I couldn't take it anymore and found the right number to call and the person in charge of city lights, and in a couple of days it was fixed. Simple, but why didn't anyone else care enough to make the call? Why did the people in charge of the lights need me to alert them to their basic responsibilities?"

Yes, why did they? I wondered. And why didn't I notice, I thought, with a twinge of guilt but mostly amusement at my equanimity concerning the inefficiency of local city officials. Just as Steve did, I also drove across that bridge every day to and from work, but somehow it hadn't mattered very much to me if one of the new lights was already broken, and to be honest I was relieved that it hadn't mattered. I was relieved that, unlike Steve, I set my mind free to wander and think about other more personally gratifying things – what to make for dinner, how well I felt my last session went, or my next trip to New York. Was I self-absorbed? Maybe, but not always; certainly not when I am wading uncertainly through the conscious and unconscious experiences of my patients. Was I an ostrich sticking her head in the sand? I would have hated to see myself in that way, though I only rarely read the local newspaper, not wishing to add more clutter to my head or my house. I would have preferred to describe myself as more lighthearted than he, which I could attribute to a handy filtering mechanism that I had unconsciously set in place in emulation of my optimistic, good-natured mother. Moreover, in contrast to

Steve, I operated under the assumption that sometimes it is, not only permissible, but actually commendable to let certain things slip by and not be constantly on the watch.

But Steve assumed nothing of the kind and cared deeply about this matter of the broken lights because it represented ("Don't you see?") a broad category of foundations crumbling for want of thoughtfulness and care. Ironically, one of the reasons he was coming to see me was that he cared deeply and wanted to continue to care deeply, but suspected that caring so deeply was literally driving him mad (he was prone to tightness in his chest, spasms in his back, and too frequently when he was driving curses spilled from his mouth uncontrollably). After straightening up this matter of lights with the city officials, he knew that some other mess would undoubtedly appear as soon as he turned the next corner and that once again he would feel trapped by his over-abundant sense of responsibility.

Although I do not presume to be a measure of what is normal, I naturally compare Steve's responses to my own and ask myself why things such as bridge lights carry such symbolic weight for him but not for me. Although he is the designated patient and I am the therapist, I resist dismissing his unsettledness as purely neurotic. That would not only be patronizing but mindlessly reductive. However, Steve was admittedly feeling debilitated and trapped and was coming to me for some form of relief and release. Thus, as his therapist, I needed to understand his experience of frustration and disillusionment, but also question the logic of his conclusions, interpret the symbolism of his meanings, and turn his misery inside out in the hope of releasing him from it. However, from an ethical perspective, I had to consider who needed more analysis, he or I. Is it honestly possible for anyone to care too much for the welfare of the community?

Committed as Steve was to being his "brother's keeper" and a "keeper of the fire," a phrase from a film he saw which resonated deeply enough for him to quote it, he wanted nothing less than the best for all of humanity, now and in the future. Which meant that, for him, everything mattered and nothing deserved a response of "whatever." Indeed, he argued persuasively that there were more than enough things in life that could not be controlled – natural disasters, disease, death, to name just the most obvious – so it was outrageous that opportunities which were within our grasp are lost because of carelessness, stupidity, or selfishness. Ironically, this was the very same distinction – between necessary and unnecessary forms of unhappiness – that Freud made when he acknowledged that psychoanalysis could only eliminate neurotic forms of misery but not the ordinary varieties, and this would have to be good enough for us even if it isn't! But while in principle Freud, Steve and I were all in agreement, in practice Steve and I discovered that such distinctions were not self-evident and were, moreover, unstable over time and place. How were we to determine which misery was self-generated, and hence neurotic, and which was not? Would Steve and I ever agree?

I wondered on occasion whether Steve was a slave to his blinding principles (Freud's superego) or I was just assuming a perspective on morality that was currently politically correct and popular within the self-help circuit, but disingenuous and self-serving. Had he lost sight of the bigger picture or had I? All these are unanswerable questions in the abstract. So I had to ask myself, as well as him, what would be lost or gained if he were to allow his gaze to drift elsewhere when next he found himself driving past a broken light? "Don't let it bother you, turn on the radio, enjoy the ride," I silently implored him. "Sure, you care, and your fellow citizens benefit because you care; there is no denying it. But as your fellow citizen and your therapist, I have to question, do you care too deeply?"

If you asked his secretary, for whom he has been an advocate and confidant during tearful evening phone conversations, I suspect that she would not say he cared too deeply. And the foreign visitors to the university, for whom he went out of his way to secure special meal plans to accommodate their dietary restrictions, have certainly benefitted, whether they know it or not, from the extent of his care. (Clearly, the staff at Food Services were as negligent in their duties as the public service employees responsible for the bridge lights.)

Moreover, I doubt that Steve's wife would wish him to be less conscientious about shoveling the snow, pulling up the weeds in their carefully tended garden, or repairing the cracks in their living room ceiling. And because he has been diligent when it comes to limiting his time away from the family to strictly work (no extemporaneous excursions to museums or remote cathedrals when he goes abroad; no delays on his return home to partake in unanticipated, post-conference festivities with friends or colleagues), she and their young son have been well cared for. This has been foundational, the domestic equivalent of the "core curriculum," and unlike many driven people he has been consistent in his commitment to upholding all the foundations not just those in his professional life. Thus, if being neither careless nor carefree has interfered with Steve getting a restful night's sleep, teaching classes that are his particular passion, or spending money on contractors for work that he can do himself, albeit laboriously during his free time on week-ends, so be it. And yet . . .

A child of the 60's from a midwestern, working class Catholic family, Steve brought to the stage of his present life a dissonant chorus of voices, each representing an amalgam of religious and cultural values: the legacies of the civil rights and anti-Vietnam War movements were interwoven with his family's work ethic and father's unheralded military heroism during World War II. The sexual revolution, feminism, and the explosion of knowledge in science and technology were foundational elements in his belief in progress, but so was his anxiety about the dangers of unbridled power. (For Steve, the so-called human potential movement had always seemed a double-edged sword.)

And while God did not figure in his current world view (his existence being at best uncertain, and, even so, highly disappointing), the story of the Good Samaritan could have been included (unofficially) in his "core curriculum." Indeed, Steve's fierce allegiance to the underprivileged and unspoken for is the one unifying thread binding together the disparate strands of his personal history. As is told in the parable, most people rush past or trample over the stranger on the side of the road in their individual quests for self-fulfillment, but Steve has refused to or else he simply cannot. So, if Steve was burdened and embittered by an inordinate amount of care for his fellow man who is, apparently, inclined to care very little, he was also horrified at the potential destructiveness of lightening his burden. An unbearable lightness would be far worse than too much gravity, he warned me, sensing that I was prompting him to consider what could turn out to be a reckless change of heart. "But are those extremes the only choices?" I asked, sensing that my question was too abstract, a filler, that was unconnected with his visceral experience.

When on the rare occasion Steve recalled fond memories of the past, playing baseball all summer as a kid, hiking for days with groups of friends in the wilderness as a graduate student, or marching in protest against the Vietnam War or unfair labor practices, I was struck by how the mix of values which now appeared irreconcilable, had once coalesced harmoniously. Steve was nostalgic for the days when individual egos were not so massive and he was relatively free of care, but also for a time when everybody he knew cared intensely about all of the essentials of life: work and play, science and love, building a tightly knit community and enjoying the openness of the wild. Caring for one's neighbor was not an impediment to growth but an ingredient of it, or at least this was the sweet flavor he tasted in his memory.

I listened to the stories, and I too was momentarily uplifted as I recalled the freedom I had had as an unmarried student (not in the New England woods but in Greenwich Village), as well as the freedom protest songs I sang around campfires in the wilderness of upstate New York in 1966:"Every man's a slave until his brothers are free;" "Tear down the walls." I could feel my heart beat louder, as the chorus thundered out the refrain, and had to catch myself from getting carried away with my nostalgic memories and nodding too vigorously in support of Steve's disheartening analysis of contemporary life. Fortunately or unfortunately, we had returned to that.

We had been speaking of the lights on the bridge and of the inconsiderateness of drivers who routinely cut him off in their rush to get somewhere fast, but all of a sudden our conversation had turned existential and the stakes were well beyond the dangers, aesthetics, or ethics of a broken light bulb or of sloppy thinking in a department meeting or four-way intersection. "The culture of narcissism" was on the stand and the verdict was clear. A society that mistook speed for progress, quantity for quality, and encouraged the individual to pursue his desires without regard for his fellow man, was an empty culture that not only endangered what Steve held dear to his heart but its very own existence.

I found Steve's arguments, like my patient Judy's, as to why he could not just relax and be happy, frustratingly logical; they were not only idealistic, but also rational and conservative in the literal sense of the word, somewhat like the arguments for clean energy as a hedge against global warming and the destruction of life on this planet. Yet, despite how gratifying it might have been to commiserate with Steve about the pervasiveness of selfish ambition, and to validate his ambition to be a responsible "keeper of the fire" and keeper of his brothers, I knew I had to pull us back to all the irrational stuff that brought Steve to my office: the internal contradictions that had turned his perspective on endangered creativity inside out. (Echoes of my sessions with both Judy and Kevin came back to me when I realized that we could easily spend an hour absorbed in political, ethical, and sociological analyses and lose track of the intractable problems of daily living that Steve wanted help untangling.)

I shared many of Steve's feelings and some, though not all, of his social history, but this was one of those occasions in therapy when too much empathy for a patient's conscious experience would be distracting rather than helpful. Were I to see the world exclusively through his eyes, I would be missing something essential about him that he himself was out of touch with, something internal that he had turned away from. Indeed, in order to actually care well for Steve, I needed to intermittently tune out or turn upside down his all-too-logical stories, which justified his anger and despair, yet failed to do justice to his complexity. I was convinced that, proud as he was to be a man who attacked problems rather than avoiding them, he was camouflaging certain problems within others and suffering from emotional neglect.

Steve would have never characterized himself as a man who was neglectful of anything, certainly not of anybody's emotional well-being. However, he admitted that he suffered from debilitating migraines, had aversions to routine medical examinations that bordered on the superstitious, and wasted endless hours at airports owing to a disproportionate fear of missing his connections. His airline connections were what he had been referring to during that session, but a few minutes after he had left, still exasperated and befuddled at his own "crazy" compulsions, I realized that, unconsciously, it was his connection to his students and family, to humanity as a whole, that was the foundation he feared was in constant jeopardy of disintegration.

Why? I recalled his mother's episodic depression, his father's wartime traumas and subsequent suicide thirty years afterwards, and the vow Steve had made to himself in college that he would not to allow opportunities to slip through his fingers. No wasted potentials, was his mantra, and, as with any mantra, it had to be repeated endlessly. Which brought us to what troubled Steve most of all, which was his disproportionate and misdirected anger. It was irrational in its proportions, but, worse yet, it was perversely self-destructive: anger, and the guilt that followed closely at its heels, fractured the very connections he had devoted his life to building and conserving, threatening to put cracks in his foundational principles.

"The other day I was actually cursing out loud at the driver in front of me. He couldn't hear through the window, but I worry whether the poor lady who is the clerk at the 7/11 where I get my morning coffee picked up on how impatient I was with her this morning; this is not the way I want to be."

Although, Steve assured me, he usually managed to contain his anger, he could not hide it from himself, and it felt explosive and corrosive. Aha, I thought, this may explain why he dreaded his yearly routine medical examination. What might a conscientious doctor uncover that Steve would rather not know? What clogged artery was the anatomical analogue of his clogged feelings? Would an inflamed organ betray the shameful and guilty reactions he secretly harbored against his fellow citizens? Ironically, he had good reason to worry about doctors, particularly my kind, as he had a chest full of unacknowledged trouble stored within his large, but not infinitely elastic, frame.

Steve is an attractive, broad-chested man who played football in college, but he told me during one of our earlier sessions that he felt too big for the congregation of his family's church, and that, unlike his young son, who is frequently bursting with confidence and enthusiasm, he couldn't remember when he last felt proud of himself or excited about life. "I feel uncomfortable when I am praised or even thanked, and I notice how quickly I turn myself to the next hurdle as soon as I have succeeded in getting over one. I've never even felt comfortable in the clothes I wear."

"Mostly even," is how he described his recent moods, and when I raised my eyes, betraying a hint of concern, he told me that he could count on one hand the number of times over the past several years that he felt at peace with himself and the world. Happy? Excited for the future? He looked sadly puzzled as he considered these experiences, as if they were intriguing foreign objects I had offered for his examination. Steve shackles himself and then feels shackled, I thought, and I was reminded of the myth of Prometheus. The titan hero, man's benefactor, was chained to a rock for stealing fire from the gods and, not unlike Steve, strained against his unjustifiable confinement. A powerful figure who put himself at risk to aspire to great heights, he was reduced, as it were, to powerlessness.

Objectively, Steve's life bore no obvious signs of truncation or paralysis; his reach was wide-sweeping, his chains were invisible. Unlike Prometheus, Steve moved freely around the world, and continued to provide support and inspiration for all variety of people, including his rapidly growing son, his students, and his extended family. Like the character in the movie that he told me he loved, Steve was a faithful "keeper of the fire," which, thanks to his conscientious efforts, had certainly not gone out. And yet, he was on my couch feeling bound, and, moreover, afraid to be unbound.

Not coincidentally, during one of our sessions, he reported a sudden migraine: "A piercing pain just shot through my forehead." On that occasion, we had been speaking of his longstanding dream of buying a piano and learning how to play, a form of careless pleasure that fell outside the frame of his responsible life. "This is dangerous," he said, warning us that I had suddenly been transformed from being a kindred spirit and understanding therapist into a seductive snake with a pronged tongue. "My foot fell asleep; that is why I am limping." He got off the couch awkwardly, and we said our good byes. "Two weeks." When a foot falls asleep and it begins to revive, the pins and needles make movement awkward, and the sensations are uncanny. But what about the vital organs: do they pierce and burn like shrapnel when they are awoken from their semi-stupor?

The spark of individual ambition, the pleasure of unproductive play, the pride of personal accomplishment, had been cast as bit players in Steve's emotional theater. He had given them few lines to speak, claiming that their voices were a distraction from the serious drama that was being played out on the world's stage. Time and again I had been struck by the irony of how a man so committed to confronting the hard truths of broken bridge lights, yard work, and core curricula could be so blinded to certain elementary truths about emotional matters.

Anxious as I was to reach out to Steve on his own terms, I had once tried to convey to him the idea that the reality principle, of which he was a staunch proponent, was grounded on the pleasure principle. (He was familiar with basic psychoanalytic concepts and, with amusement, had, from time to time, used them in conversation himself.) Consequently, I argued, that it would be as negligent and foolhardy for him to ignore his desires as it would be for him to scrap his cherished core curriculum in favor of more esoteric subject matter. But while I was certain that he had caught the mischievous twinkle in my eye as I waged my argument in support of desire, he responded gloomily and veered off onto the next real-life problem. How do I speak Steve's language without joining him in his cut-off world of abstract principles, the world in which, chained down to a foundation without feelings, he is a bare rock in danger of crumbling into sand?

"I dream of sitting in my arm chair in the evening reading just for pleasure, but I don't. I feel ecstasy listening to the Bach cantatas in the car, but it is only on long car rides that I feel free to listen to music. . . . 'Cultivate your own garden': I have a big problem with that." Having returned from a recent trip, Steve described the other passengers in the airport who were docilely moving through the airport security systems. "Like cows in a herd, they just follow along complacently without questioning anything. That has been the problem throughout history."

"Yes, of course you are right," I thought to myself, though I was frustrated by the disheartening conclusion he drew, which was that he must remain continually vigilant lest he become docile himself. I felt like reading to him the passage from the Bruno Schulz story "Dead Season" that I have quoted in the epigraph to this chapter, so as to warn him against becoming a "monstrous hairy steel blue horsefly furiously circling and knocking blindly against the walls of the shop." "Stop kicking against the walls of the shop, Steve; fly out. It is time for a siesta; listen to the dance music outside." In my mind I returned to my theme of the moment: my brother's keeper. I was trying to keep Steve well by encouraging him to loosen the knots within himself and to care, not less about his fellow sisters and brothers, but more about himself. Could he unbind himself and strike an equitable compromise with the gods on mount Olympus without betraying his commitment to be a benefactor of mankind?

The kaleidoscope has turned somersaults in my mind numerous times over the two years that I have seen Steve, and fortunately it has turned in his mind as well. Steve has brought to our sessions highly condensed and colorful images from dreams and memories: cars racing out of control, foundations leaking and houses under water, bloody accusatory creatures, mythical women flying through the air. "Steve, do you dare to join me?" one beckons. Is interpretation even necessary? Snatches from romantic ballads and Big Band music of the thirties come back to him, and, like sirens, call us both back to a happier space and time before he was born, before Cain inaugurated murder and engraved his mark on the history of humankind. Back there in Eden, where love was innocent and adult sexuality was like a swing dance, we stumbled upon an image Steve had of himself as a little boy watching his beloved helium balloon slip from his fingers and fly off into the sky.

This story of the lost helium balloon has become an emblematic cautionary tale, one of those screen memories that Freud speaks of that holds within it a multi-layered treasure of meaning. We have referred to this image of lost potential on many occasions when Steve has slipped into a swamp of despondency. "Keep careful watch lest your dreams be lost forever," is the moral of the story. And so, keeping close watch has been a non-negotiable principle and guiding light in Steve's life. The watchman, who doubles as Steve's prison guard, lives within shadows, however, on the look-out for thieves. A defender of the law, he is intransigent when it comes to negotiating with unruly desires that cross his path.

Having learned caution from his experience with his beloved helium balloon, as well as from his parents' debilitating dives into depression, Steve has kept a tight grip on his feelings, good and bad, except when, under the cover of sleep, they have been unleashed in dreams – a veritable carnival, lighting up the night. As a diversion from our rational and plodding conversations concerning the disastrous state of the world and the pernicious decline of traditional values, Steve's dreams have served as oases of humor, terror, color, and confusion. If he could leave behind him, if only for an hour a week, the grey and even landscape of duty through which he soldiers day after day, would that be enough to lighten up his face and allow his spirits to take flight?

The mysterious pleasures of free association! A waste of time or the most meaningful hour of the day? Sometimes when we wandered beyond the farthest reaches of rational thought and practical reality, Steve would experience a sudden irrational panic and begin to question the value of our calculated disregard for ordinary logic. What did these intricate, cobbled-together stories from dreams and childhood say about the larger picture? his critic prodded irritably. What was he placing at risk when he turned his finely tuned microscope in upon himself? Usually by the time the hour had come to a close, such questions about therapy's significance had evaporated into thin air, however. Hollow words and bloodless sentiments couldn't compete with highly saturated feelings.

Although Steve had to bind himself back up before getting on the road, crossing the infamous bridge, and returning to his office, after having unraveled his coiled-up memories and unchained his imagination, I gathered that he breathed easier, felt more connected to himself and his history, and was less weighted down by his burden of care. Indeed, the last time he was flying to a conference and missed his connecting flight on account of the weather, he was pleased to note that, although he was frustrated, he did not feel the usual tightness in his chest. Am I being too presumptuous to think that something internal had been unclogged, and the anxiety of blocked connections had been cleared away?

From a therapeutic perspective, this change in Steve was certainly a desirable outcome, whatever its origin. His spirits were lighter and yet not soaring unrealistically, and, more significantly, he was starting to catch himself whenever he poked pins in his favorite balloons. But how do I evaluate these changes from an ethical perspective, and, in the long run, how will he? This is literally not my business; nonetheless, I wonder how therapy is likely to affect Steve's sense of bearing responsibility for keeping close watch over his less-than-conscientious or less capable "brothers." Will he succumb to the culture of narcissism that he derided months ago? Will he come to resemble his cohorts (on the road and at department meetings) who fly recklessly through intersections, without heed for you or me, as if their wishes made them entitled to do so? Does the one kind of good cancel out the other?

In the case of Steve, I would argue that it hasn't, despite the eradicable contradictions that continue to exist within him. After all, even though Steve has freely associated for one hour each week for over two years, and admitted into our conversations all sorts of crazy thoughts and images, his connections to other people have not suffered from neglect. To the contrary, new, less frustrating connections have been forged, and the clogged feelings that had separated him from the pulse of life have begun to flow more freely. Less cut off from his own emotions and history, he feels, ironically, less subverted by other people's insufficiencies. His commitment to an ethic of unselfishness has not been lost by having turned his gaze inward; rather it has surrendered its selfishly autocratic claim on reality. This more balanced, more democratic form of life must be good, I conclude, ready to defend my bias. The golden rule is golden only because it takes measure of everyone, Steve as well as his sisters and brothers.

The Keeper of Accounts: The (Mis) Calculation of Love

> "And whenever the idea struck him, as it often did, that it all came of his never having lived as he ought, he thought of all the correctness of his life and dismissed the strange idea. . . ."
>
> Leo Tolstoy, *The Death Of Ivan Ilyitch*

Shamefaced, Iris confessed how she hoarded her food when her bulimic step-daughter Susie was at the house: "Why have it go to waste? Literally, it is just pouring my money down the toilet." In defense of having resorted to what sounded, even to her, like rather outlandish tactics, such as hiding her favorite food in the car overnight, or placing a name tag on the leftover Chinese food she was saving for her lunch the next day, she complained that her husband Harry, Susie's father, didn't notice anything wrong with Susie's eating habits: "His head is in the clouds when it comes to his daughter's problems, maybe because he has plenty of his own addictive behaviors. He eats junk food though his cholesterol is dangerously high, and he smokes and drinks too much; when we were on the road with my daughter and her husband a couple of weeks ago I think he sneaked something into his coffee. I don't want to make a scene, so I don't say anything."

So what else should she have done, Iris asked plaintively, when Harry offered no support but, instead, angrily accused her of nagging when she documented the food that was missing from the refrigerator and pantry. "He says I make it all about me and that I am being just like my mother – he always hits me where he knows it hurts the most. He says we should be thinking about Susie, who is sixteen years old and has her own crazy mother to deal with. He doesn't care about my food disappearing; he just wants her to feel completely at home with us and loved unconditionally. He wants me to love him unconditionally, but is that right?"

As I watched Iris move from flashes of anger to sniffles and tears, and heard her stinging accusations turn into mumbled self-reproaches, I see-sawed back and forth between opposing points of view, empathizing not only with Iris's shame at having been seen as a wicked step-mother but also with Harry's guilt at being been seen as an inadequate husband and father. And then of course there was Susie, who was in the middle, the odd man out, who furtively took care of herself through her nightly binges and purges.

"So, why do I feel I have to count every cookie she vomits up, or track every movement she makes when I am supposed to be sleeping? I can tell you about what I am thinking when I go into her room in the morning, but I would never tell Harry: I feel embarrassed for being so selfish. Why does the three dollars for ice cream matter to me anyway?" A not unreasonable question, I thought to myself, though when we first began to talk she had posed it as an attack on herself, which, ironically, echoed the one Harry had launched the evening before, and I certainly didn't want to join forces with him.

"Selfish" is a loaded word, like the word "lazy," and whenever any of my patients uses either one to describe his or her feelings or behavior I insist we slow down and unpack its meaning. If it is *all* about Iris, as Harry claims, then I would agree, from both an ethical and psychological perspective, that this is a problem – though even then the word "selfish" would fail to capture anything more than the most superficial layer of experience. It would tell us nothing about the past origins or future aims of Iris's self-protective hoarding, or how it might have developed in relation to her family's dynamics, which seem to include secretive behavior on the part of everyone.

Moreover, as I watched Iris struggling, in a cracked whisper of a voice, to fight back her tears and return to her anger, which she directed first at Susie and then at Harry's blistering attack on her and her mother's characters, I asked myself whether her problem had not been the very opposite of what Harry and Iris had labeled selfishness. Indeed, maybe, over the years she had been too selfless, too easily drawn into ministering to people like Harry and Susie who were less capable of taking good care of themselves than she was. Perhaps her readiness to be a caretaker was taking its revenge.

Iris's first husband, Bruce, had died more than ten years earlier, and when she married Harry eight years ago she had made a concerted effort to blend her family, which included her son and daughter, with his. However, now that her children were grown and out of the house, and Susie's eating problems and Harry's ex-wife's failed mothering were dominating their marriage, Iris felt that she had disappeared and was herself in danger of starvation. She told me that she had been cast as the selfish step-mother whenever she asked Harry to place any limits at all on his daughter, and yet the image she saw in the mirror resembled more that of a neglected step-child who was pulling angrily at her father's shirt-tail: "I don't want to live on crumbs anymore. Set me a place at the table." Harry's reply confused her: "You are just stirring up problems; I can't do anything right with you." She came to me wanting to know what was real. Who needed support and who was being unsupportive?

So, as much as Iris's hoarding behavior looked simultaneously paranoid and self-abasing (it evoked the image of a hungry squirrel who watches furtively as she pushes her nuts into a hidden hole in the ground), I figured that I needed to gather more information before I settled on a diagnosis. Nobody in the family was a good keeper or was well kept. Stashing food might have balanced out flushing it down the toilet in Iris's mathematical computations, but where were they all going to end up if they continued to follow this logic?

"Harry doesn't want to confront Susie; he feels too guilty about the divorce. But we both know that she empties the cereal of all the raisins and, after we go to bed, picks apart the food I had saved for my lunch the next day. I tried putting a sign with my name taped to some leftovers, but that didn't stop her. Harry says, just eat something else, but that is not the point: I feel I have been violated. So I decided last week that I'd just have to hide what I need. Maybe Susie's counselor wouldn't agree, but I don't think we should be enabling her. And if Harry won't protect me, I 'm going to do it myself."

Violated? That sounded sexual. Protect herself from her sixteen-year old step-daughter's unregulated and illicit appetites? From Harry's attacks on her plea for support? As in Steve's case, I sensed that the logic of her explanation was deceptively simple and that I should listen carefully for what might lie beneath her words. I guessed that if we could plumb the depths of her psyche, we would discover conflicts about food and hoarding that were rooted in her childhood relationships with her two older, more aggressive brothers, if not in her infancy in relation to her mother. Nonetheless, whatever the originating source, from where I was sitting, Iris's world looked like an emotional wasteland, with the survivors scavenging through scraps of garbage. Watch your back, hold tight to your purse, avoid all eye contact, every man for himself. Each member of the family ran a parallel course, fearing that direct contact would be more treacherous than its absence. And yet, huddling in a corner and contemplating the next attack was obviously depressing and lonely, and Iris admitted that she envied all those normal people who did not feel the need to hide their food in their cars. "I have friends who have dinner parties and think nothing of offering their guests doggy bags with left-overs. They are not adding up the cost or keeping track. I wish I could be so generous."

My head was swirling as family systems theory and psychoanalysis vied for my attention. "Look at the triangulation and how Iris is using Susie as a scapegoat for her frustrations with Harry, who earns a lot less money than Iris does and eats and drinks and smokes too much!" "Listen for the echoes of Iris's father and mother. Harry may be right: her suspiciousness and feelings of not getting enough may have less to do with current reality than she makes it appear when she focuses all her attention on what is going into and out of other people's stomachs. Maybe she is vomiting up the undigested left-overs from her past." Although as usual I found myself listening to a cacophony of competing voices telling me to focus on different aspects of my patient's story, one theme rang out loud and clear: Iris's sense of deprivation was a breeding ground for suspicion, and suspicion had bred hiddenness and deception, and the cycle had assumed a life of its own. Everyone was a potential rival for scarce resources, nobody's source of nourishment was safe, and Iris's efforts to balance the accounts and accurately calculate levels of love coming in and going out were doomed from the outset.

Although Iris began her last session ready for battle, no doubt wondering if, after what she had told me, I too would be unsympathetic to her cause, she was clearly more saddened than angry. Indeed, after having delivered her prepared speech, her voice quavered, and when I saw her eyes begin to well up with tears I knew that, despite her reasoned arguments, her insightful analyses, and her aggrieved tone, she was as uncertain of her moral stance with regard to Susie as she was of the future of her marital relationship and the foundations of her love.

Her compulsive scrutinizing of Susie's every movement, her rifling through the kitchen garbage, and her withholding attitude toward both Susie and Harry all felt necessary and self-protective to Iris. And yet, these "bad behaviors" (which was what she called them) were no more attractive to her than they were to Harry or to me. As difficult as it was for Iris to give love unstintingly, it was even more difficult for her to take love in, as she was always on the look-out for counterfeits, which left her feeling voided of love and filled to capacity with envy and regret. A wicked step-mother? A neglected step-child? A law enforcement officer? An expert accountant? A high functioning professional woman married to a dysfunctional man who doubled as a guilty father? These are all true reflections of Iris, different versions of the tragic/comic story she tells of her life with Harry and Susie. And yet, adding all the fragments together, the center did not hold. Iris the person was missing from the picture: her suffering, her insight, her humorous asides, and, most significantly, her unflagging capacity for care.

The question of how much our experiences are reasonable responses to present-day life circumstances and how much they are shadowy repetitions from the past is impossible to answer. We would like to be able to make clear distinctions, but if we are honest with ourselves there is inevitable blurriness. Psychotherapy is, ironically, the place where we acknowledge the ambiguities that arise from the interpenetration of present and past and yet also insist on seeking clarity. So, when Harry told Iris, "You are just like your mother in being suspicious and critical; it's not me or Susie who is to blame for your feelings," she called it "psychobabble," but then she asked me, whether she should believe him. Her mother was suspicious and critical, and, Iris admitted, this was not the first time she had been told that she was too. (What a struggle she had with her daughter Flora when Flora was growing up!) Nonetheless, as if I were her judge, prosecuting attorney, and jury rolled into one, she asked me pleadingly whether it was fair to relieve Harry of all the responsibility for her hurt feelings.

"He smokes, he eats garbage, and he hasn't gotten to the book shelves he promised to make for me last spring; he says 'I love you' when I head up to bed at night, but stays up much later than me and often falls asleep on the living room couch." What would be a reliable measure of his care, and how was she to determine if the sum of all the parts made them good enough to stay married? Iris, the meek younger sister of two successful doctors, whose emotionally absent father had cheated on her mother, didn't want to feel ripped off, exploited, or invisible. "Never again will I accept crumbs from a man. I don't want to make the mistakes my mother did." Who can blame her?

By adding up the hours Harry devotes to yard work and the other chores she assigns him, subtracting the cost of the dinners and ice cream that end up in the toilet, and dividing the remainders between the three of them, Iris had hoped to arrive at the proof she needed to make a judgment and deliver her just sentence. "Proof?" I asked. I was speechless. What slippery substance was being measured or mis-measured? Its form and content changed from moment to moment. And what was the price she was willing to pay for certainty? Stashing food in the car and cutting coupons for food she didn't like seemed an exorbitant price to me.

After years of therapy, Iris has continued to harbor doubts about Harry's love and whether her emotional stinginess is justified, by his behavior or not. Who is generous and who is selfish, who is acting responsibly as a parent and who is behaving like a child: these seem to be the unanswerable and recurrent questions she poses each week, regardless of the answers we had arrived at, albeit tentatively, in our previous session. Her uncertainty has seemed to me less of an opening up to possibilities and more of a clamping off and shutting down.

I confess that after years of being a therapist I still find myself surprised and disappointed when I encounter, yet again, what appear to be self-destructive, life-negating forces. Those shapeless desires to return to the old and familiar suffering, which lie in wait beyond the pleasure principle and which Freud haplessly named the death instinct (for want of any scientific or religious explanation), seem to be stubbornly entrenched and to draw on ever-renewable sources. One week Iris concludes her session with a tearful epiphany, and her resolution to stop her constant measuring, in food or money or hours raking leaves, sounds insightful and heartfelt. But then, the following week it all begins again. I have come to see her repetitive and retaliatory skirmishes with Harry as her personal version of the Israeli-Palestinian conflict. Cease-fires are followed by new hostilities, which are followed by new overtures toward reconciliation. Then one rock, one stray bullet at the border, and hopes for peaceful co-existence are dashed once again. "See what happens when you let down your guard? You can't trust . . ." Iris has her own ways to fill in the blanks. Divorce or stay married? (A two state or one state solution?) Or the status quo of documented suspicion and incubated doubt?

Over the years, the casualties mount up, but there is hope as long as the Israelis and Palestinians keep talking (officially and behind the scenes), and Iris keeps coming to therapy. Though at this stage of the game I do not expect the interminable battle between change and repetition to be adjudicated once and for all, the battle continues and I cannot be impartial.

Curses from the Ground: Angry Gods and The Return of the Repressed

> "And the Lord said unto Cain, 'Where is Abel thy brother?' And he said, 'I know not: *Am* I my brother's keeper?'
> And he said, 'What hast thou done? The voice of thy brother's blood crieth unto me from the ground.
> And now art thou cursed from the earth, which hath opened her mouth to receive thy brother's blood from thy hand;'"
>
> (Genesis, 4:9-11)

As the biblical story suggests, when we are not our brothers' keepers, but instead have betrayed our brothers, out of envy or selfishness, a sense of injustice or a desire for favor, we doom ourselves. Their blood cries out to us from the ground. But if the prohibition against fratricide is delivered authoritatively by the voice of God, when it comes to figuring out what we are supposed to do with the envy that is so often justifiable or the selfishness that is a natural and hence eradicable extension of life itself, God is silent and we have no firm ground to stand on. In a letter to Marie Bonaparte, Freud wrote: "I always envy the physicists and mathematicians who can stand on firm ground. I hover, so to speak, in the air." When faced with the conflict between care for one's own body and spirit and care for another's, most of us hover in the air as well.

In his later, more philosophical writings, Freud described what he saw as the ultimate ethical paradox, one that is not comprehensible without a psychoanalytic understanding of unconscious processes. He argued that, contrary to the entire Christian tradition, when we try to love our neighbors as ourselves we end up creating more, not less, human strife. Feelings of love and hate are rooted in early, inchoate bodily experiences and, in contrast with behavior, are not transformable through reason, will, or the passage of time. Indeed, psychoanalytic insight into the dialectical nature of the human psyche suggests that aspiring to an ideal that is by our very nature unattainable fosters the very destructiveness it aims to eliminate. Faced with the impossibility of successfully exorcizing forbidden feelings and desires from our unconscious, we invent ingenious lies. Denial, repression, and projection of our selfish sexual and aggressive impulses onto others are the psychological mechanisms that underlie the universal tendency to find and invent scapegoats. By these circuitous routes, we temporarily manage to allay our anxiety and preserve our love for our immediate neighbors, but only by turning our envy, disgust, and hatred onto an ever renewable stream of outsiders, and this creates fertile breeding ground for violence.

Freud's antipathy toward all religious solutions to the problem of human aggression stemmed from his belief that they were not only founded on illusions but also were dangerously unstable. This did not mean, however, that he gave up on Eros or on civilization, despite its discontents. He was no romantic or utopian, nor did he subscribe to the Buddhist ideal of selflessness and detachment from transient desires; but neither was he a nihilist. Because we do care about love and life beyond the pleasure principle and the immediacy of the moment (whether we want to care or not), we are destined to wrestle with the eternal riddle of how to love honestly, which means how to love fully but with full recognition of love's limits.

The Golden Rule is an attempt to strike a just compromise between me and you, between the reality of our essential separateness and essential interrelatedness. It encourages us to do unto others as we would have others do unto us, but without obliging us in actuality to care as much as we would like to think we should. And yet, on close examination, even with the best intentions, this seemingly practical suggestion does not readily translate into real-life relationships. What I want may not be at all what you would want, and, what's more, I may be incapable of knowing from one day to the next what is really best for my well being, let alone for yours. How to care for a self that is, by its nature, divided and hidden and changing with every new encounter is the problem that self-help books pretend to solve but seductively paper over. Metaphors of care are too often idiosyncratic and not subject to reason; my patient Iris is by no means unique in having invented a personalized accounting system of love that fails to register three-quarters of her loved ones' deposits.

Even when we imagine that unconditional love is what everyone deserves and all that anyone could ever wish for, we discover that it too has a dark underside. Who hasn't been warned against the dangers of co-dependency, or admonished not to enable the alcoholic or all variety of seductive and self-destructive personalities? And who can't point to a situation in which jumping in to rescue a brother, husband, friend, colleague, or child may not only not enhance his life or life generally but prevent everyone involved from flourishing?

Educators are now saying that excessive praise may not only be unhelpful for learning but even damaging to a child's self esteem. If everything a child does is deemed wonderful, then whatever he does has no significance one way or the other, in which case, neither does he! Indeed, a constant stream of positive reinforcement, a term I associate with rats in a maze, can, in the short run, encourage the performance of certain targeted behaviors, but in the long run foster over-dependency on external responses and discourage the development of intrinsic motivation. In essence, if a child links his good behavior to rewards, in their absence, he figures, "Why do it?" It has no inherent value, but then, neither does he!

The story of the Good Samaritan has universal resonance, but he is hardly a figure worth emulating if he turns out to be either the victim of a scam or of his own rescue fantasies. Moreover, putting aside our doubts concerning the existence of free will, most of us still like to think that we are masters of our fate and that with sufficient pluck and self-reliance can overcome adversity. So, even when we agree that we should be our brother's keepers and suppress, if not exorcize, the jealousies and selfishness that prevent us from acting on our principles, we are honestly confused when we encounter the proverbial brother on the side of the road, who stops us in our tracks and pitifully asks for more than the usual amount of help. (Don't we reflexively wonder, on occasion, "Couldn't he help himself?")

Steve epitomizes the contradiction of values of which I speak. He does not wear a threadbare jacket in winter or question whether he should buy shoes for thirty-five dollars or give the money to the homeless, but, no less than my patient Kevin, Steve is acutely sensitive to the well-being of others and feels responsible for doing everything in his power to help promote it. And yet, he applies different rules when it comes to accepting help for himself. He resists hiring someone to do his extensive yard work or fix his plumbing or paint his ceiling, and follows a rigorous, unforgiving work ethic. The two clusters of values, both of them deeply rooted in his family and religious traditions, have lived uneasily in opposition, entangled with one another, clogging up his digestive track if not his arteries.

In considering the anger and resentment that Steve and Iris feel as a result of seeing themselves as the only responsible adults in a playground filled with impulse-ridden children, I think back to Kevin who, when speaking of Mother Teresa, asked me, "Where do you draw the line Dr. Block, between giving too much and too little?" Against the backdrop of the news of Mother Teresa's death, the question was posed as an ethical challenge. However, folded within the invitation to reflect with him on what it means to live a saintly life, was Kevin's unconscious plea for clemency. ("Can you let me off the hook doctor?")

As I was not Kevin's friend, his priest, or a classical Freudian analyst, I did not wish to tease him out of his moodiness, as his bar buddies attempted to do, or counsel him to proceed along the difficult path towards salvation. Nor could I bring myself to hide protectively behind the blank screen of professional neutrality. Instead, I found myself trying to reconcile the moral implications of selfless devotion with various psychological and personal theories I held about the formation, consolidation, and dissolution of the self.

Kevin's provocative question had put me on the hot seat where he was accustomed to perch, albeit precariously. Whether he had intended to or not, he had thrown me off balance and made me uncomfortable. Psychoanalysts speak of projective identification when a person relieves his anxiety by transferring it onto someone else, and my father used to say that "misery loves company," and added, with a bitter gleam of irony, that he suffered far too much from loneliness. But regardless of how I choose to describe the phenomenon, psychoanalytically or in the language of common sense, experience tells us that sharing pain is one of the most enduring forms of connection; it is a universal currency of intimacy, though not necessarily of tenderness, recognition, respect, or care. How brilliant, then, was Kevin's maneuver!

Looking back, I remember how Kevin's ears and nose were red from the cold, his jacket was worn thin at the elbows and frayed at the edges, and how he had come to my session ten minutes late, only to linger uneasily at the door when the time was over. So, while he had explicitly invited me to engage with him in abstract philosophical rumination, I gathered that he wished as much as I did to jump over the fence of verbiage he had masterfully erected and be rescued from a life of rationalized self-denial.

"Of course, if everyone were like Mother Teresa the world would be a better place, and then nobody would have to do what Mother Teresa did, but, Kevin, that is not the point! "

"But then, what is the point, Dr. Block?" he may have well asked, had I actually given words to my latest rescue fantasy. If life has to have some point or larger purpose in order for him or any of us to feel reasonably happy, didn't therapy have to take that into consideration? And are there words adequate to capture something so elusive as "larger purpose"? As Kevin was slowly defrosting, my burning wish to warm this young man up to the pleasures of life seemed the only clear or worthwhile purpose in sight, and at the moment I knew I had to settle for that. ("Go for it," a sympathetic voice inside my head urged me, as a smile, which I hoped might be contagious, crept across my face. But then another, sterner voice cautioned, "Let him figure it out himself, don't meddle.")

Though it is not in my job description to adjudicate the conflict between ethics and happiness, I cannot consider the one meaning of "good" apart from the other, as in my mind health and happiness are in some unquantifiable way inextricably linked to a person's ability to care lovingly and unselfishly for other human beings.

Sitting with a patient who has entrusted me with his care, I am aware of how my beliefs inadvertently color my interpretations and guide the way that I practice. I am not an objective third party, even if my patients like to believe that I am. And though I suspect that my close friends and family would be surprised at how non-judgmental I am in response to patients, I do have my prejudices, and one is that I abhor the postmodern dalliance with the idea that anything goes, that everything is performance and there are no hierarchies of value worth embracing. The ultimate paradox of being a psychotherapist is that whenever I do allow my own moral sense of right and wrong to shape my image of what a mentally healthy human being should look like, I feel a twinge of guilt. (Those classical Freudian analysts on the ceiling keep close watch over me, and I feel their reproachful glances whenever I forget my place and start to sound preachy.)

And yet, why should I feel guilty when I try to reconcile ethics with happiness, given the fact that people have been wrestling with this conundrum since the beginning of history? Moral integrity should certainly not be confused with emotional integration, but compartmentalizing the two meanings of the term "good" seems as dishonest and unhealthy to me as blurring the distinctions between them. I am a therapist but I am also a human being, so how could it be therapeutic to exclude the human values of care and responsibility from our conversations about how to live?

Whether Kevin's solicitous response to the timid woman at his church, with whom he was directing a play, was true to the spirit of Mother Teresa, is impossible to say. What was certain, however, was that his solicitude for her fragile ego, at considerable cost to his own desires to be heard, did not make him feel sanctified or sane or foster an atmosphere of authentic communion with her or within his church congregation. Ironically, even though his analyses of moral corruption in the commercial art world and at the local bar seemed idealistic and worthwhile, they were delivered with a spirit that was scarcely more generous than the one in which Iris made her mathematical calculations. Both his idealizations and her banal computations had emptied care of feeling and their lives of meaning. So, how could that be good in any sense?

"Love, oh Love, oh Careless Love. . . Oh See What Careless Love Can Do"

Driving up the coast of California with my sister and my husband Henry, we got into a conversation about whether a mutual friend of ours should give his son and daughter-in-law money for a down-payment on a house and help them out with the mortgage for as long as they needed it. Our friend's excitement over the plan had been contagious for me, and I wished to spread the good feelings. It sounds like a wonderful plan in which everyone wins, I argued, noting, out of the corner of my eye, my sister's wary look. Our friend wants to help, I continued, and his son could not possibly afford to buy a house on his own, so why on earth not? Moreover, we all knew that the relationship between father and son had been through some rough patches and that, finally, it had reached a new level of trust and intimacy. Future visits with grandchildren were happily on everyone's horizon.

However, as I had suspected, my certainty about the benefits of helping out was by no means shared by Diana and Henry. They foresaw myriad complications and troubles that I did not. "He would be too much in the mix of his son's life, and, what's more, his son needs to learn to stand on his own feet and live within his budget," my sister interjected, with obvious support from Henry. The three of us disagreed, and as we went round and round looking at the very same picture from different angles, it became evident that the facts were just facts and there was no hope of changing each other's minds. The tone of our conversation was mostly friendly, as we all knew that each of us wanted what was best for both our friend and his son. But I could sense a stew of feelings beginning to simmer within me as I filed the conversation away for future reference.

What if it were one of our daughters who had asked for our help under similar circumstances? I asked myself later on that night when everyone was sleeping peacefully. I can imagine how our tempers would flare when I discovered good reasons to help her out while Henry discovered good reasons not to:

"She works so hard and is so responsible. It would be my pleasure to be able to help her a little."

"She's a grown woman; you baby her; she needs to figure it out herself."

"It's not babying, it is simply caring."

"If we lay out that kind of money we won't be able to travel as much as we want to; it's not all about her. Nobody paid our rent for us when we were her age"

No doubt, in this imaginary conversation, Henry would have seen me as over-indulgent, enmeshed, and ultimately unhelpful to our daughter and uncaring toward him, whereas I would have seen myself as loving just the right amount to build a good foundation for her future and our developing relationships. Both Henry and I want the best for our children and our marriage, but I know that he can be as skeptical about my expressions of love and my conceptions of what is fundamental and life-affirming as I can be about his.

Embedded in our arguments for and against offering an additional helping hand to a child, a colleague, a street musician, or, in some cases, a patient are unconscious fears, wishes, and memories of being cared for or not cared for in particular ways. "I supported myself when I was a kid in college . . . nobody was there to hold my hand," Sam boasts at family gatherings, as his children shift uneasily in their seats, anticipating the moralizing endnote to what has now become a familiar Horatio Alger story. "It was not only good enough for me but in the long run I am better off for it," is the conclusion that Sam wants us to draw from his experience. Having to make it on his own made him strong, confident, and successful, and so he deliberately transfers this mode of caring to his care for his children.

In contrast to Sam, however, Julius's memories of having had to fend for himself from an early age have left a bitter taste of deprivation in his mouth, and I see him literally choking up on what his mother used to tell him: "Bastard, you owe me; if it weren't for me, you'd be in jail. I made you strong." And while he does not argue that he did develop certain qualities of character because he had nobody to depend on from an early age (an ability to endure pain, a photographic memory, and a belief that he is "bigger" than other people and can handle anything), he has told me that he wished he hadn't had to be so strong, if that is what it can be called, and that he envies those who are less careful and more careless than he. Susie, his unfaithful girlfriend, could walk into a room of strangers as if she owned the place, he told me, uncertain what to make of it. She acted on her impulses without considering his feelings or worrying about the consequences for the future; she's on her third marriage, she bounces back (like Steve's self-serving colleagues or Iris's husband Harry?). Who's got it right?

"I had no one looking out for me; I was running the streets and working at age ten. I bought my own clothes at eleven and opened up a bank account. My sisters tell me, 'Mama loved you; she bragged to the neighbors that you could walk barefoot on glass you were so strong. 'Maybe she did love me, but I didn't feel it." Of course he didn't feel it: Julius could walk barefoot on glass and didn't register any of his feelings, I thought glumly, as I forced myself to soak in his tortured expression and bear witness to his urgent desire to document every microscopic splinter he had stepped on that past week. What I could I do to soothe this grown man's suffering? I wondered, not altogether unselfishly, as sometimes I felt bombarded and then numbed and restless with the repetitions in his stories. How could I induce him not to repeat his history of first caring too much and then hardening his heart?

Over the course of a lifetime, Julius had developed strategies to hide, heal, and possibly even erase the scars of his mother's brutalizing care. Without intending to, he continually impressed me with tales of how he regularly functioned as a Good Samaritan – stopping to help a stranger stranded on the road in a snowstorm, spending hours in emergency rooms with neighbors and friends, steering them safely through medical crises that were overwhelming to them. Indeed, there has been no other patient I have seen who has gathered around him a wider circle of friends, people who consider him an integral part of their family. Everybody is fighting to have Julius for Thanksgiving dinner. And yet, paradoxically, he feels invisible for the very same reasons that he feels indispensable.

Although Julius could not be less like his mother, who responded with disdain when he shared his pizza with his buddies or accepted help from the Puerto Rican grocer down the block who offered him advice as well as a chance to make his own money, he is riddled with doubts as to whether his circle of care is legitimate: an honest expression of love or the lifeless remains from an experience of lovelessness, a calculated performance or an authentic connection. Until he knows for certain what real care is and what is just performance, he won't be able to decide whether he should continue shoveling all of the neighbors' driveways and then driving across town to shovel his best friend's mother's steps and her elderly sister's steps around the corner. Is his thoughtfulness and consideration for others a glaring reminder of feeling un-cared-for and unknown? The woman next door brought him a plate of home cooked enchiladas one evening to show her appreciation for his help with the snow, but Julius didn't want it, he confessed to me, and went out for Burger King instead. Having someone return his care is an unfamiliar, unpredictable, and dangerous experience for Julius, who both wants and does not want to remain invisible. What will she expect in return? Will they both discover he's just a beggar dressed up as the Good Samaritan?

"A lot of women say I am different from other men because I listen and think deeply. I don't like that. It makes me feel docile. I think they don't know who I really am." I can understand why women would feel that way about Julius, and yet also understand his uneasiness and disbelief. We both know that he is far more complicated and contradictory than he appears to be. As he has said, he hides in plain sight. And though Julius is undoubtedly the best neighbor ever, and a father figure to a flock of fatherless men, women, children, and step-grandchildren, he is also a suspicious and lonely man, who is painfully self-conscious about his clothes, his speech, his skin color, and his intelligence. He greets strangers with a smile, chats with every waitress and salesclerk, and, with little regard for what he is actually feeling at the moment, tries to make other people feel considered. Who is he really? The question is meaningless, though the very fact that it plagues him is itself highly significant. Julius looks at me guiltily; he is ashamed by his confusion. He hates hoarding his love, hiding his love, and faking his love, but, worst of all, he would hate to lose his love forever by carelessly throwing it away.

The other day, Julius had what he described as his "first love affair," and it was with a painting. We smiled and shared the understanding that, at this point in his life, it was an excellent choice, though not in keeping with either Jun' the Bum, Jun' the Bomb, Julius the Savior, or Julius the token black casualty of systemic racism. A painting cannot betray his trust, or take advantage of his irrational devotion. Art is itself a child of the irrational, so together they can play. Moreover, unlike his mother and sisters, a painting will not taunt him for having tender feelings or wishing to fly like Superman.

This had been Julius's first trip to the local museum. It was for a college class assignment (after twenty five years away he had returned to finish his degree), and he was flooded with conflicting emotions – intense happiness and intense fear. In one ear he heard his professor's whisper of encouragement to move in closely, take his time, and soak up the experience. But in the other, he heard his mother's scornful refrain: "Move your feet, you bastard. Don't think you're better than your raising." For some reason that afternoon, the whisper was louder, and Julius penetrated the barrier that would have ordinarily separated him from the work of art and from his feelings. What's more, he allowed himself to be penetrated.

"Pherklempt," a Yiddish word he picked up somewhere (he cannot recall where or when), was how he described his experience of that afternoon. It means choked up with feelings, he informed me, surprised that I didn't know the term (didn't I know everything that he did?). I suspected that it was not accidental that Julius used a foreign word to capture his unfamiliar experience of joyfully penetrating connection.

My daughter Vera's paintings, expressionistic portraits in bold colors, hang on my office walls. Now that he had had a brush with love, he was ready to ask me who the painter was and what she meant: "Do you know what she is saying? I am envious." I hesitated before responding, as I realized that the actual question he was asking was an entirely different one from the one he had explicitly posed. It was a question about wanting and daring to express something deeply personal. And it wasn't actually a question at all, but a declaration of independence from the bondage of not daring to want. Julius wants so much to *want* and then to take the next step and have the courage to express himself. Only then will his love feel legitimately carefree (as opposed to careless); only then will it no longer be entangled with memories of envy, self-abasement, and shameful need.

"Dr. Block, Dr. Block . . . Joyce . . . I think of you when I am not here. What are you like? What do you do in your free time? Are you making turkey for Thanksgiving? I feel embarrassed telling you this; is it okay? You know, I saw you on the street walking, but I didn't know if I should say hello; I wanted to but . . ."

I am another voice in the crowd of voices informing Julius of the pleasures and risks of asking questions and wanting answers, of accepting help from the kindly stranger passing by. In grade school he never dared to raise his hand, he told me with a regretful look on his face. And though he had taught himself the basic notes on the recorder, he never showed his teacher or tried out for the school concert. "I envied Dwight Simpson whose mother went to PTA meetings and who always had his hand up and never stopped talking. In the plays he always got the leading parts."

In contrast to my question and answer sessions with Kevin, concerning the problem of how much to give if one isn't as saintly as Mother Teresa, I was happy that Julius had taken the liberty of asking me a direct question. This was no maneuver on his part to transfer his anxiety onto me or to breach some professional boundary in order to provoke a rejecting response. Indeed, that day in my office Julius had taken the risk of including himself in a circle of care from which he had been excluded. By asking me a question, he was in effect saying that he too could be someone's brother, not just a brother to someone, that he had been his professor's brother and the artist's brother in the museum earlier in the week, and although he hadn't been able to be Dwight's brother when they were ten years old, he could be my brother at fifty-two.

"Through Two Points Only One Straight Line Can Pass (A theorem in geometry) "

(Yehuda Amichai, 1958)

"While I am away I will be checking my messages periodically. If you would like me to call you back, please leave a number where you can be reached and I will get back to you as soon as I am able. If this is an emergency, you may call the emergency crisis hotline or go to the nearest hospital emergency room for immediate attention."

I don't get many calls when I am on vacation, and it is rare that I speak with patients outside of our scheduled appointments, even though both my office and home telephone numbers are printed on my business cards. Once in a while, someone will call my home on the week-end, and in these instances, I have felt gratified that he or she was able to reach out to me in a moment of crisis and that I was able to respond with something that was helpful in a completely intangible yet meaningful way.

One exceptional experience stands out, however, in which an extremely guarded, middle-aged female patient, whom I had seen only five or six times, accidentally telephoned my home one Saturday afternoon. Stumbling for words, speaking in a timid little girl's voice that I had never before heard, Grace was evidently so embarrassed at having entered into my personal space unsolicited that she called me the first thing on Monday morning at my office to say that she would not ever be coming back. "It was completely unacceptable what happened," she repeated fiercely, despite my reassurances to the contrary. Grace was a woman who had been so uneasy revealing anything about herself to me that she had refused to give me her date of birth or place of work, and had emphasized during our first hour that I needn't worry as she wouldn't be telling me anything that I would need to report to the police. Of course, having said that, she had revealed far more about her inner life than most people do in a month of intentional self-disclosure, but that contradiction was the essence of her dilemma: she wanted my help, but she did not want to want it, much less to express it in a manner that was visible to me.

Because during our sessions Grace routinely stood rather than sat, peppering me with questions that she followed up with sarcastic remarks about my minimalist taste in art and my professional competency, the "accidental" phone call to my home was ripe for interpretation. (I might add, moreover, that the art work on my walls is anything but minimalist!) As much as she kept me at a distance and purposely misrepresented what she saw and felt, she unconsciously wished to get closer. The abrupt termination of treatment was a measure of how terrifying it was for her to expose her wish for contact and how crucial it was for her to avoid all possible temptations to fulfill it. Given the freighted tone of our connection, I confess that I was relieved when she precipitously cut it off.

Her response to therapy was an extremely naked illustration, however, of an all too common conflict that people have between wanting help and not wanting to want it, or, worse yet, to need it. The frame of the psychotherapy relationship, within which help is offered, but only in a limited amount and with an uncertain mix of ingredients, is a perfect arena in which to negotiate a compromise between these opposing desires. ("Can I accept less than what I wish for without feeling too angry or humiliated?" is the unconscious question that hovers in the background.) Yet, even under these experimental conditions, negotiations are conducted subliminally, with patients generally favoring expressions of self-sufficiency over dependency regardless of what is going on beneath the surface.

So, typically, they thank me for my offer to speak after hours if something particularly disturbing should arise, but do not take me up on it. Thanks, but no thanks. In most cases, I do not think that it is my sincerity that is in doubt or that my modest offer is being dismissed as inadequate or unhelpful. Rather, I think that most people are proud (maybe too proud) of their ability to manage on their own and accept no more than the standard portion of care. This has to do with not wanting to feel weak and dependent, as well as not wanting to feel out of control or even crazy, and, significantly, all these experiences are lumped together and require a lot of intricate work to sift apart.

But again there are the exceptions, times when what I offer, in session or out of session, has been explicitly derided as not only not good enough but as painfully meager and unjustifiably constricted. Indeed, one patient repeatedly challenged me to prove to him that the therapy relationship was something more than just a standardized form of care, empty of real feelings. ("If I didn't call you, you wouldn't care enough about me to call me to just see how I am doing.") He insisted that I was treating him as a scientific specimen I was observing and dissecting, and that this so-called care was the very opposite of what he needed to move ahead with his life. To him, my failure to feel for him in a personal way, which was evidenced by the limits I placed on my support and availability, repeated his damaging experiences from childhood. Moreover, he argued that as I understood him more than anyone else in his life, it was my professional responsibility to act on what I knew and provide him with something different – not simply insight (he could read a book), but a "corrective emotional experience." How can he learn to value himself when obviously I value him so very little?

When I am confronted by someone who is both asking me for help and rejecting the help I am giving him, claiming that it is at best too little and at worst counterfeit, I find myself confused. This is because I tend to see myself as someone who is, if anything, too emotionally engaged rather than too detached. And yet, clearly, this person is seeing me very differently and his perceptions tap into my own uncertainties about what it means to be a responsive person and how that corresponds with being a responsible psychotherapist. One of the most difficult lessons I have had to learn over and over again, both professionally and in my personal life, is that there is no sense in arguing with subjective experience. You don't need to be a strict Freudian to know that when someone tells you, "I feel mistreated, unloved, diminished, and unknown," it often cannot be reasoned away.

I remember how my first therapist, whom I saw very briefly as an adolescent, tried to make me feel better by telling me how smart and pretty I was. "You're a jewel," she said, and she probably meant it sincerely and in a motherly kind of way. Even at sixteen, however, I knew that her comment, however well meaning, was absurd and that she had no clue whatsoever about how to help me change my experience of who I was. "Through two points only one straight line can pass," the Israeli poet Yehuda Amichai wrote, but outside of geometrical theorems, the lines that connect you and me, my experience with yours, are invariably squiggly, and when we try to draw straight lines we often cut out significant details in the space that lies between us.

Putting aside the philosophical problem of subjectivity and the psychoanalytic insight that we are all subject to defensive distortions, I should note that when a patient of mine feels that my form of helpfulness is inadequate, insensitive and even damaging, I am uncertain as to how to rectify the situation. I have assumed that I have extended my circle of care to include this person, but he is telling me that I have left him out in the cold. What I am to do when my compass does not correspond with his?

"Could you turn off the ringer on the phone?" Nathan asked me the other day with a hurt and irritated tone in his voice; and then, "How do you go from one person to the other without a break? How many patients do you see in a day?" And even Julius has, on occasion, turned the microscope on me, hinting that perhaps I too will prove to be a disappointment: "This time you are late, Dr. Block . . . just kidding. Do you always carefully choose what you wear, like those sandals you brought back from Israel or those purple pants you wore last Thursday? Or do you just throw anything on?" What is Julius saying when he lets me know that he remembers and notices everything about me, and questions my intentions just as I question his? Is he wondering if I take as much care with myself and with him as he needs me to? Does anybody in this world care enough for him to feel safe (justified) caring?

And if Iris keeps track of every time Harry comes home late, adds up his cigarettes, beers, and calories, and then subtracts her step-daughter Susie's purges from his share of their household budget, why should I be surprised that one day she should try to quantify my worth to her and hers to me? "My insurance pays for the therapy now, but what if it runs out? I should take care of myself, shouldn't I? What is your regular fee?" When she said this, Iris looked forlorn and we were both unsure about what she really meant when she spoke of taking care of herself. Did it mean making the investment in herself by coming to talk or saving her money and keeping her own counsel? The universe can be a pretty cold place sometimes, but, as I speculated about Iris's internal struggle, I also asked myself what the range of my responsibility was and what were the limits of my desires to keep Iris (or any of my patients) warm.

"If you wish to continue and feel it is helpful to talk, we can work out a fee that you can reasonably afford." Anxiously, I wanted to reassure Iris as well as myself that I was not one of those imposters in the caring professions who only cared about her own time and money. Nonetheless, as usual, I was not certain how to determine what "reasonable" would mean, and whether we would make the same calculations of value. Kevin's admiration for Mother Teresa, and his question to me about how much to give and where I draw my ethical boundary lines, had returned in yet another form. If Iris's insurance ended and she had to pay for therapy herself, would she ask too much of me or too much of herself? Would I offer her more than what she needed in the way of support ("Anything you can afford") and inadvertently confirm her sense of deprivation in my attempt to relieve it? Moreover, what should I do to allay the anxiety I sensed behind Nathan's question, his worry that he was just one of too many patients in my busy schedule and that my attention would be on that other person who had just left the office? Figuring out what kind and what amount of help is good enough as a therapist is as complicated as figuring out what kind is good enough as a mother of a spunky two-year old or a sulky adolescent, a wife of a recovering alcoholic or an unrecovered workaholic. The uncertainty is the same as that of the stranger who passes a different beggar every day in the subway.

Re-reading Freud's case studies and his lectures concerning unconscious fixations and transference resistance, I have periodically reassured myself that I am not alone in wrestling with the problem of how to respond when a patient insists that if only I care for him genuinely, as a human being (or maybe a transitional mother or lover), his calcified feelings of lovelessness will dissolve, and he will finally be able to move on with his life. But knowing that even the most astute and empathic therapists have been the target of unreasonable attacks on their characters does not resolve my ethical conflicts. Therapy as a practice comes with its own implicit assumptions about healthy ways of relating and how much stretching and bending each one of us should do to accommodate the wishes and needs of other people. Ironically, however, the essence of therapy is to question all assumptions about how to live, even the assumptions of psychotherapy.

So, if I am the target of Grace's scorn, Nathan's feelings of neglect, or Iris's fears of deprivation, I feel that I should be neither disheartened and self-reproachful nor impervious and self-satisfied. In other words, I should tolerate the ambiguities inherent in the meaning of care and not simply reduce the problem to his or her unconscious resistance to cure that is being acted out in the transference. If I am to feel okay about being seen as the latest in a series of disappointing, insensitive, and punishing people, I have to be certain that I have not failed to be sufficiently responsive. Following the letter but not the spirit of therapy's written and unwritten rules is certainly not good enough.

And what is that spirit? Ideally, as a therapist I should be without an agenda of my own – meaning that I should have no personal stake in getting Julius or Kevin, Judy or Iris to live the kind of life I think would be best for them or for me. And though I should be empathic and understand their experience without making judgments on it, I should also be sufficiently detached from their experience so that I can weather the most violent and mysterious emotional storms. But these are ideals. I have my prejudices just as anyone does, and they determine what kinds of wishes and needs I believe are healthy and should be validated and even gratified within the therapy relationship and what kinds of wishes and needs are not.

Where I draw the line between addiction and attachment, between a neurotic displacement of childhood wishes and frustrations onto adult relationships and a healthy expression of these wishes and frustrations, is probably not precisely where Susan, my colleague in the office across the hall, might draw it, or my sister, or my husband Henry. It certainly was not where my patient Grace drew it when she hung up the phone that Sunday afternoon and slammed the door on any further contact first thing Monday morning.

Thus, after we have succeeded in un-burying the remains from a person's past in the hope that he will no longer be buried along with them, we are faced with the problem of how to integrate his unrequited and forbidden wishes into present-day life. When old frustrations are revived and add contaminated fuel to new ones, relationships inside and outside the office can become explosive. The twinned realities of desire and limitation are at the source of life itself, but how they can be creatively balanced is uncertain and perpetually subject to reinterpretation.

As I help patients tease apart what they want from what they want to want, what they have received in the way of care from what they may receive in the future if they only stop repeating themselves, they help me figure out what is best for me to give to them. Inviting a stranger into a space where no one else has previously entered is risky, though perhaps less dangerous than inviting an intimate, who assumes he knows you, but does not know you completely. I feel privileged when someone decides to take that risk with me. Following a different set of rules from those that structure ordinary life, we wander through a labyrinth of words, sensations, and images until we arrive at one of those rare and precious moments when our two points connect together with one straight line. When this happens we look around us and, in astonishment, see that we are surrounded by lines and shapes we hadn't seen before: constellations in the sky.

CLOSING(S) WITHOUT CLOSURE

> "We used to be complete wholes in our original nature, and now 'Love' is the name for our pursuit of wholeness, for our desire to be complete."
>
> Plato's *Symposium*

Analysis: Terminable or Interminable?

Through a fog of misunderstanding we grope, we make connections, we enter into a secret covenant that promises to bind us together (forever and ever as childhood blood sisters), but then . . . time runs out, the session is over, and there is no closure. How naive we were to believe that we should be able to close the circle around us and weave together all our ridiculous loose ends! Even as we set our next appointment and share our usual good bye rituals, I start to feel the familiar itch of incompleteness – yours, mine, and ours – of unasked, unanswered, and unanswerable questions. "What was Rebecca wanting from me when she showed me her photographs? And why did I choose to fulfill rather than analyze our unspoken desires to draw closer?" On reflection, I realized that I felt a vague anxiety about disappointing Rebecca, but, then again, was that my issue or a faithful mirror of her anxiety about being disappointing or disappointed? It may have been my counter-transference that was governing my responses to her unsettledness or it may have been an unconscious reminiscence of her relationship with her disappointed mother.

If I let myself, I can spiral endlessly round in circles and become dizzied by the possibilities. But just as my synapses begin to overload and my eyes threaten to glaze over in protest, I hear a sympathetic voice urging me to let it go! "Enough is enough! It's irrational, not to mention grandiose, to think that you or she or even Freud himself could be able to tease apart all those strands, let alone weave them back together again seamlessly, forever after. Be grateful that there will always be fresh material to work with next week, more knots that unravel into loose ends, which can be woven and re-woven into infinitely more complex and original designs and textures."

So the moment passes, and we reconcile ourselves, one way or another, to the fact that we can never fully capture it, let alone re-capture it when we meet again the following week. For me, writing is an effective palliative. Ambiguities are miraculously resolved when I am in solitary dialogue with a blank piece of paper. And when I find the "perfect" string of adverbs and draw a graceful conclusion to an awkward sentence, my appetite for closure is momentarily sated. I am ashamed to say it, as I would choose life over art as a matter of principle, but the written word sometimes provides a more solid form of nourishment than the inconsistent nibblings I get from a face-to-face encounter with an ever-changing living presence.

In psychotherapy as in the rest of life, we get to a clearing only to watch the fog rolling back in. Loose ends are what we are left holding. Loose ends are what draw us back together, what give us a purpose, what tangle us up in knots, what keep therapists in practice. They are the manna that fills our empty bellies as we wander like the Jews in the desert, suspended in exile, no longer slaves to Pharaoh, but still transients without permanent shelter, in search of a homeland.

A woman in her mid-seventies, she comes to me as she discovers in her encounter with aging that when relationships end, bodies fail, and conversations break off inconclusively, without the meeting of hearts and minds that was still hoped for in middle age, closing can mean anything but closure. Doors shut, but feelings and memories continue to leak in and out unpredictably through a labyrinth of invisible openings. On the one hand, this can be an encouraging sign because, contrary to the rumors that circulate about little old ladies, this stooped-over old woman's brain has not turned to mush and her life juices are still ebbing and flowing. On the other hand, however, as I listen to her stories, what sounds normal and healthy in theory can feel corrosive and unhealthy in practice.

Rebecca comes to me distraught and literally shaking about having to make a decision to move from the apartment in which she has lived since her husband suddenly died more than ten years before. Her health has been deteriorating and she has landed in the Emergency Room on two separate occasions, so the current arrangement seems untenable. But after we speak about the concrete specifics – her three children and the various options of where she can live – she veers off, with my encouragement, onto other adjoining branches that take us backwards and sideways through her distant and recent past. Listen to her story:

> For most of my life I felt utterly blessed. I had wonderful parents. When I was growing up my mother was always more progressive and understanding than my friends' mothers, and though I'm embarrassed to say it, my father was just about a saint. I always felt extremely lucky to

have had the family I did, and then I married a wonderful man whom everyone loved and whom I can honestly say was still my best friend after forty-five years. I never want to brag about my children, and I want you to know that I'm really not taking any credit for it, but they all grew up to be very special human beings too. My daughters-in-law tease me; they say I think my sons are perfect; I don't. I love them with all their imperfections. I had Susan when I was nearly forty, and we call her our "miracle child."

Before Lenny died, we were making plans to enjoy our retirement. Both of us loved to travel and we didn't feel old. With our savings and his pension we were finally free to do some of the things we couldn't do when we were younger. Lenny had dropped out of school when he was a teenager to help support his mother and brother after his father died, but he had gone back and finished his degree at sixty-five. I made a big graduation party for him, and everybody we knew came; it was a real celebration. He had never had much luck with money – I think he was too trusting to be a good businessman – but at that point he was finally able to work just a few hours a week and at something he really loved.

Back then, I was very disciplined and doing my art. I even had a few gallery shows. I saw a doctor maybe once a year for a check-up, and the only pill I ever took was a multi-vitamin. It seems like another life, but ten years ago I biked to get my groceries. Which one is the dream? Now I can't walk more than half a block even with this

> horrible contraption. I feel hideous and there is this ridiculous trembling inside of me; it's different than the Parkinson's; nobody can see it, thank God, but no matter what I say to myself, I can't control it. When you look the way I look, all bent over, people talk over you, it's as if you're not there. Since Lenny died I feel incomplete. I hate to whine and I don't want to be a burden, but whoever thought up aging didn't think it through very well; it comes at the worst time. It's a cruel joke to play on humanity.

Rebecca's life is drawing to a close, but not as she had hoped and thought it would, with vitality and a spirit of gratitude and equanimity (as it was once promised to her when she was a child, with subtle looks and gentle touch, before she had the words to say otherwise). Instead, she feels incomplete and ashamed, invisible and misunderstood, defective and out-of-step with the natural order of the universe (and she has always assumed that there is one). And then, she asks, not in words but with an apologetic look in her eyes, how much time is there left to rectify matters anyway?

"I look freakish; my swollen ankles are grotesque," says Rebecca, eyeing me for a response, wondering if I share her repulsion, challenging me to contradict her perceptions. And, as if that weren't bad enough, she adds, "I'm afraid I'm not a very interesting patient. If I don't have anything new or positive to say, I'd rather just listen. I feel like a burden, though my daughter has forbidden me to use that word. I know I shouldn't be closing myself off, but lately I start shaking at the thought of going out to lunch with friends I've known for over thirty years; I feel guilty to say it, but I'm relieved to get back home and be by myself."

Unable to seal over the cracks that have betrayed her dreams of completion and exposed the insufficiency of the past and the present, she apologizes for her existence and assumes the lion's share of the responsibility for the holes left in the fabric of her life. Ritualistically, she asks for forgiveness for unnamed crimes and mundane mishaps. Like a dutiful child, she attempts to defer to those who are supposed to know (I being the latest of the series) and respectfully disappear from sight. Perhaps, by swallowing her pride and quarantining her bitterness, she had once hoped to be blessed (as good children are), and, once blessed, granted the miracle of closure, by way of enclosure. What happened?

Had she acted in "bad faith" by holding onto false hopes, or had she taken a "leap of faith" into the unknown? And now, suspended as she was, with no direction home, was she simply losing courage? Is she a master of the art of dissembling or the loyal devotee of an ethic of renunciation? What is the most helpful interpretation? How different is this unsung heroine of domestic life from your ordinary passive bystander of history who is afraid to die because she has never really lived? Fifty years ago "masochism" was the popular term that was bandied about and applied to self-abasing (self-sacrificing) women; today, on daytime television talk shows, it has been replaced by the terms "enabling" and "co-dependency." However, when I notice Rebecca's sensitivity to any shifts in my posture that might signal discomfort, and when I notice how anxious she is not to inconvenience me by running late for our sessions, I am nauseated by the triteness of such labels. The descriptions readily available on daytime television talk shows offer "closure," but in exchange they commit yet another injustice. (As a woman and a diagnostician I cannot use words as binders but remain stubbornly at loose ends.)

Earnestly, Rebecca argues that discretion, modesty, and loyalty are essential virtues for creating harmony, living peacefully, and, most important, sustaining hope for this life, if not for the uncertain life hereafter. Moreover, she offers an abundance of concrete examples that demonstrate the practical wisdom of her ideals. And yet, neither of us is thoroughly persuaded. Her stomach is churning, her throat is constricted, and her voice sounds as if she were a Lilliputian. Feeling patronized and forgotten, she also feels pathetic and unmemorable. Forgiveness for her burdensome existence from friends and family (if that is what she has earned by her exemplary manners and solicitous behavior) has not proven to be a source of vitality or a sense of deep connection, and dissimulation as a protective filter transforms her gratitude into restlessness and boredom. Balled up and tucked hastily away, the unsightly loose ends remain; only now they are tangled up mixed in with guilt and shame.

Out of desperation and at the request of her daughter, who is burdened by her mother's apologies and confused by the evermore frequent lapses in her dissemblings of cheeriness, Rebecca has turned to me. "I'm twisted inside, straighten me out, but only if you guarantee that this can make me loveable," is what she seems to be saying. And yet, despite the regularity with which she keeps her appointments, and despite her generous compliments at the conclusions of every hour, I sense that her faith in psychotherapy is less than she would ever dare admit to me. (Who is she to openly challenge the expert, or cast a pall over the aspirations of her more liberated and sophisticated daughter?)

So, when she expresses gratitude for my patience and admiration for my insights, I remind myself that she may be suffering from too much gratitude and admiration directed toward others as well as too little directed toward herself. Moreover, it wouldn't be like her to tell me if she thought my "talking cure" was good for other, more verbally facile people, but not for her. She wouldn't want to embarrass me or herself by exposing the gaps in our already tenuous connection by suggesting that the practice of self-expression, rooted as it is in an ethos of "self-fulfillment," may actually amplify the conflict she is hoping to resolve. Her wish to open up, speak out, and be noticed seems unrealistic and dangerously seductive when she knows she needs to wind down, close in, and peacefully say goodbye.

"Why do I have to make things so complicated?" Rebecca's question nags at me, for I too am ambivalent about open-endedness and closure (echoes from my past, no doubt, of a mother who sealed off too much and a father who closed off too little). Does she manufacture trouble by ruminating, regretting, and straining to find answers to unanswerable questions? Or does her problem stem from the fact that she had naively wished for things to be simpler and more rounded off than they actually are? Would it be wiser to attain closure by closing in, sacrificing, and surrendering to the mysteries of life or not?

Knowing that I have a bias in favor of complication and find her contradictions stimulating, I try to resist the temptation to impose my tastes (or psychotherapeutic ethos) upon Rebecca. Psychoanalysis emerged when Freud rejected the hypnotic method, which relied on the power of suggestion. While he argued that hypnosis was, in the long run, ineffective, as it never addressed the underlying, unconscious conflicts that were the origin of the patient's symptoms, his rejection had ethical overtones as well. The goal of psychoanalysis was for the patient to live in awareness of reality, and to be able to make conscious choices in the face of competing strains within his personality. The kind of therapy I do is influenced by this ethos of freedom and compromise. Insofar as I exploit my patients' faith in me and my authority, and encourage rather than analyze idealizations and dependencies, I am in danger of betraying this ideal.

Ironically, as Rebecca has lost faith in Faith itself, she has become both more eager for, and less open to, any simple, rounded off answers to the complex questions she raises. She wants desperately to trust, and hints that she might even like it were she capable of being transported by religious feelings, but, nonetheless, she holds on tenaciously to her doubts. Her attendance at synagogue is ritualistic and limited to the Jewish High Holidays, and one hour a week in my office is not enough to anchor her securely as she moves reluctantly toward the darkening horizon.

When I bear witness to the anxiety that Rebecca associates with her unrelenting indecisiveness about even the most trivial things, such as writing a thank-you card or having lunch with an old friend, I wonder whether, despite her obvious suffering, doubt is serving some hidden purpose for her. After all, when she doubts she questions, and when she questions she expresses her individuality. After having been modest and deferential most of her life, Rebecca may be making a stab at freedom, and perhaps even establishing some healthy boundaries between her mind and the minds of others. Or is she? I can't know for sure if doubting reflects an aborted attempt to escape her desires and not express clearly what she wants, or whether it is her nod of recognition directed toward those desires, albeit one that, at this early stage, resembles a nervous tick.

The experience of uncertainty has been a relatively recent element in Rebecca's emotional repertoire, and this had made it all the more unsettling. As long as she was a wife and mother, Rebecca was the responsible party when it came to practical decision making. She was unswerving in her commitment to her family's well being, and though she described herself as having been excruciatingly shy as a child, as the woman of the house she was known to be tough and "very opinionated." Rebecca's eyes lit up briefly with the memories of good-natured tussles with her children and teases from her husband.

Her characteristically embarrassed and troubled look returned quickly, however, when she noted that the person she was then is not the person she is now. There are those dreaded mornings when she is startled to find that her dead husband Lenny is not lying next to her in bed ("He's more present now that he is absent"). She cannot shake the uncanny feeling of life lived in absentia, and so that feeling of uncanniness shakes her from within for the remainder of the day. Since becoming a widow, she has felt like "half a person"– she, who had always prided herself on being an untraditional and independent woman, having marched with the younger generation for civil rights, peace, and birth control. That middle-aged Rebecca, though not the woman sitting across from me on a straight wooden chair because of the chronic pain in her back, never felt envy for the friends whose husbands were much smarter in business than Lenny, and had retired them to the suburbs where they were privileged to be protected from those who were not as fortunate. Indeed, doing without the extra comforts was a sacrifice Rebecca had been proud to make as long as she felt blessed in the intangibles that really mattered. (I can imagine her singing the *dayenus* at the Passover Seders welled up with tears of gratitude as she looked around the table at her husband and children repeating "it would have been enough. . . ." But now Lenny is missing from the head of the table, and her back has given out so that she has to withdraw to the couch in the middle of the service, at which point it isn't enough anymore.)

Rebecca's admission of incompleteness is laced with moral overtones. Indeed, her failure to feel whole is more a mark of shame and guilt, linked to a message of betrayal, than it is a plea for help or understanding. Since it has been revealed to her that she is neither especially blessed nor eternally grateful, as she once presumed she was or hoped to be forever, she must have been a fool to have believed that everything in her life would work out for the best in the end – the joke's on her, everybody now knows, but nobody thinks it is funny ("Aging is cruel joke to play upon humanity . . . "). Ironically, in order to remain faithful to her youthful ideals, Rebecca would have to live out the remainder of her days as a performer. Living as if, despite her losses, her disappointments, her petty crimes against humanity (envy, suspicion, anger), she can will herself to rise like a phoenix, undamaged by the flames that threaten to consume her from within.

But what if this charade is impossible to pull off and the mask no longer covers what lies beneath its unnatural smile? Moreover, masquerading may be too great a sacrifice to ask of her at this late stage of life, when the curtain is about to fall and she has not yet done justice to her feelings. "Maybe I should have been angry when Lenny died, but everyone was wonderful to me, the medical staff, my friends, the children; I didn't feel angry then and I don't feel angry now, just pathetic. . . Really, who am I to complain? I've had such a good life, and who is there to be angry at anyway, God? My sister-in-law is also a widow, and since my brother-in-law died two years ago she's been traveling all over the country and has a new male friend. I guess she knows how to live, but it seems kind of callous; I don't do death well."

Because Rebecca's voice rises at the conclusion of the sentence, I know that the sentence is unfinished and that she has not arrived at a final verdict about her sister-in-law's uncanny resilience, or how she, Rebecca, should respond to death. She hooks me in by her expressions of incompleteness, hoping perhaps that I'll draw a conclusion about what it means to "do death well" and what it would look like for her to do life well without becoming a different person altogether, someone who is calloused (or would that simply be well-adjusted?).

Although an experience with death (the final closing) is what brought Rebecca to a point of crisis, she rarely speaks of death in our sessions, and does not seem particularly overwhelmed when contemplating its inevitability. Rather, she shudders uncontrollably at the incompleteness of her past and present lives and at the contradiction of being finished and unfinished simultaneously (closed without a sense of closure; finality without a closing statement). Unsolicited, she brings to my attention recollections of the innumerable sacrifices (or compromises) that she has offered up throughout the years, out of love and respect, honor and fear. The arguments she didn't wage (despite her reputation for being so opinionated), the gambles she never even considered taking, the responsibilities she embraced, the whims she exiled into fantasy. Apparently, as she amasses evidence for her case, and lays the facts before me, these acts of faith, which were once a source of pride and confidence, have assumed new meanings. They represent little deaths, abortive endings, holes that were hastily sealed over, hiding leaky foundations that may now be too late to repair. Her life no longer seems blessed and part of a continuous whole, but comprised of a series of cut-off still photographs.

So, what might Rebecca do differently to finish up her remaining days with a greater sense of dignity, creativity, and completion? What happy and unhappy feelings must she filter out, sift through, or assimilate in order to feel whole and wholly human? Are there words she should repeat, inspirational verses she should commit to memory, more painful sacrifices she should offer up, if not to God, then to reality, if she is to still her inner trembling?

Not offering religious counsel, or any counsel at all, for that matter, I ask myself whether psychotherapy is supposed to reunite her with her long lost "other half" (resuscitate the infant twin whose premature death was never properly mourned) or help her learn to live without that phantom figure that will always be missing, dangling, and by nature unfinished? Can she become hopeful if she has no hope of completion? Can she arrive at a sense of closure that is good enough without closing too much of herself down? Nirvana is the end of desire, the Eastern sages tell us, but if desire is what distinguishes death from life, what should this Western woman do with the loose ends that disrupt the peace and keep her desires burning? A child of the Depression, a wife, mother, and artist who found her voice echoed in the freedom and protest movements of the 1960's, Rebecca has found that her dreams are closing in on her. As an interpreter of dreams and a defender of dreaming, I am wondering how can we foster her capacity to dream without having the dreams turning into nightmares.

The Chosen People and the End(s) of Human Sacrifice

> "And Abraham was an hundred years old, when his son Isaac was born unto him.
> And Sarah said, God hath made me to laugh . . .
> And it came to pass after these things, that God did tempt Abraham, and said unto him,
> Abraham: and he said, Behold, *here* I *am*.

And he said, Take now thy son, thine only son Isaac, whom thou lovest, and get thee into the land of Moriah; and offer him there for a burnt offering . . . "

Genesis, 21:5-6; 22:1-2

"Religion promises to turn the needy incomplete being into a being as secure as the gods are seen to be. It does not work."

Martha Nussbaum, *The Therapy of Desire* (1994)

A miraculous birth, a test of faith, a people without a nation-state, a covenant that binds and shelters, an omnipotent and enigmatic God. The Abraham and Isaac story in Genesis tells of desires thwarted and promises fulfilled, of extraordinary blessings and extraordinary debts of obligation. A sanctification of sacrifice, which at the same time marks the end of human sacrifice. The story is rife with contradictions and cries out for interpretation. "What is it to be God's Chosen?" the philosopher Soren Kierkegaard asks in *Fear and Trembling,* his examination of the Abraham and Isaac story. But Kierkegaard's answer is posed as another question: "Is it to be denied in youth one's youthful desire in order to have it fulfilled in great travail in old age?"

If the answer to this timeless question is transparent to Abraham, who sired his only child with his wife Sarah when he was a hundred years old, and to his descendants who were miraculously delivered out of Egypt to become the people of The Book, it is not to those outside the faith who also want the reassurances and privileges of being chosen (and who doesn't?), but who question the legitimacy of God's covenant as well as the presumption of chosen-ness and its roots in a tradition of hardship and submission, exile and sacrifice.

Indeed, since Freud became a spokesman for the Unconscious, which is the voice of the *un*-chosen (the troublesome "it," or Other, that, from the beginning, we have alienated ourselves from), the value of sacrifice and submission to a distant, paternalistic figure of authority has plummeted, and to this day remains unstable. From a classic psychoanalytic perspective, sacrifice is not sublime. At best it is a sublimation of parricide, incest, or castration. Submission to the Law of the Father is the hefty price we have to pay for "civilization and its discontents." On the worst account, however, sacrifice is an expression of childish superstition and idolatry, an anachronistic relic of our collective past. As much as we need to resist the temptations of the flesh, we also need to refuse the tyranny of repressive morality if our instincts for love and life are to prevail over our instincts toward destruction and death.

Too much renunciation is a pernicious source of neurotic misery, my kindhearted therapist intimated, not in words but by the understanding and non-judgmental expression I saw on his face. I drank his perspective in thirstily and took it to heart. Renunciation is a dubious attempt to outwit nature by displacing desire, denying our mortality, or turning aggression inward; but the magic trick doesn't work, the dismembered body is alive and angry, and with its phantom limbs it is hammering beneath the trap door! This father figure of mine, my therapist Amos, who was named after one of the Hebrew prophets, did not favor blind devotion. Rather, in prompting me to connect to my own thoughts and feelings, he warned against a universal childlike willingness to offer up – as Abraham offered up his son on Mount Moriah. Ironically, I follow Amos' lead in not allowing myself to be led too much. The sacrifice of one's personal will might fulfill an ancient covenant, but it would have bound me, a twentieth-century woman, as it bound Abraham, to a narcissistic, if not outright sadistic, god (parent, priest, superego, or partner) whose rule could continue only with my complicity in the kingdom of the imagination.

Expanding on her father's theory, in her book *The Ego and the Mechanisms of Defense,* Anna Freud suggests, moreover, that selflessness, or what she terms "altruistic surrender," is as much of an expression of unconscious desires for sexual and egoistical gratification as any other behavior. In reading her analysis I confess however, that I feel uneasy and harbor doubts: "Is anything sacred? Don't we wish more than anything else to fall in love and surrender lovingly?" When nothing is what it is touted to be, and opposites collapse and prove to be identical within the realm of the unconscious, the notion that we choose freely appears as ridiculous and self-serving as the notion that we can secure a happy future if we prove ourselves worthy of being chosen. But where does that leave us when we are faced with choices on how to live?

Postponing gratification builds strength of character, and altruism serves the common good. There is no arguing with experience. It is only too much sacrifice that bleeds into codependency and masochism, perfectionism and guilt, too much self-mastery doubling as self-abnegation that turns a virtue into an affliction (or addiction) which we then impose first on ourselves and then, inevitably, upon the other. Shameful legacies of our ancestors' primitive fantasies of God's justice and man's sinfulness, our efforts to be good often turn against us and make us bad.

But if twentieth-century psychology, along with philosophy and science, has challenged but not successfully supplanted traditional religious dogma that previously monopolized conversations about who gets chosen, who gets to choose, and how, it has, in its most honest moments, cleared the space for irony, humility, and ethical reflection. For if no one, not even your analyst, can claim neutrality when it comes to defining the good-enough life and how best to care for a soul, then all hierarchies of value are fair subjects for dispute, including his, and only death can deliver on the promise of final closure. Ironically, the post-modernists might argue that the in the twenty-first century the Chosen People are permanent wanderers in a spiritual diaspora, who, in contrast to their ancestors, the people of the covenant, refuse to place a value on sacrifice or take refuge in inviolable commitment to a higher power. Instead, these people, without a home or fixed identity, rest their hopes on the possibility of endless transformation and are willing to sacrifice the shelter of a single tradition for the infinite maze of open-endedness. There is no getting around sacrifice, however, as much is given up for the embrace of uncertainty.

Rebecca is approaching eighty, and though she lives in the twenty-first century and had always liked to consider herself a modern woman with an open mind, she was born and raised on the borders of another time, a time of greater certainty. To be sure, God had been declared dead and Freud had discovered the unconscious years before she was born, but her faith in her family's religious and cultural traditions, and in the possibility of social and scientific progress, had not come to an end (sorry Jane). So, for her, sacrifice once meant surrendering to a higher power and participating in an unknowable world of infinite possibility. It was connected to feelings of hopefulness, infinitude, and the sense of being among the chosen. But recently, the idea of sacrifice has accrued different layers of meaning. Freud's archeological metaphor comes to my mind. Nothing of her past is gone; it is just buried in fragments. When I hear Rebecca describing herself as incomplete and ashamed, I think that, perhaps, in her obedience to an abstract and distracted figure of authority, she secretly cordoned off too much of her essential self, which would explain why she feels incomplete, unformed, and only half a person, even though I, not knowing what is missing, don't see her that way. But is that interpretation too facile, just my twenty-first century psychological bias?

Who knows how to measure the value of sacrifice for the multitudes of Abrahams and Sarahs and Isaacs, climbing the slopes of Mount Moriah, and how that value has shifted for Rebecca as her shadow lengthens and then contracts, gradients rise, fall, and level out across the changing landscape of her life, where the horizon was disappearing from sight before finally closing in?

Presenting Problem: "Fear and Trembling"

> "When the child is to be weaned the mother has more solid food at hand, so that the child will not perish. Lucky the one who has more solid food at hand."
>
> Soren Kierkegaard, *Fear and Trembling* (1843)

> "For the possibility of irony opens up in the *gap* between aspiration, pretense, and reality . . . properly understood, psychoanalytic interpretation is a form of irony."
>
> (Jonathan Lear, *Therapeutic Action. An Earnest Plea for Irony* (2003)

As I listened to Rebecca speak, with a certain amount of bitterness, of how she reined in her desires and postponed gratification, deferred to the needs of others and respected the ethical precepts of her forefathers, the idea of sacrifice became a unifying and repetitive theme in our sessions. Rarely did either of us ever use the word explicitly, but the question of what sacrifice had meant to Rebecca, an agnostic Jew, before her hair turned white and her eyes turned inward, when her future still stretched before her and was more vividly present than her present, was implicit. How that concept was evolving as she confronted the death of parents, friends, and a husband, the death of dreams that were preserved but buried within those relationships, was the focus of many conversations. The dreams that she had relinquished in her assimilation into an ever-shifting reality lingered on stubbornly as memories of wishes, inchoate, incomplete, and unfulfilled.

Was she a favored child who had fallen outside the reach of favor? One of the Chosen People who had lost faith in the wisdom of her choices? She hinted that she may have been seduced into giving up too much and, consequently, had been left, at her advanced age, with too little to sustain her. But too much or too little of what? The vague, free-floating sense of loss she emanated was too abstract! And yet, even if we can identify specific missing pieces, was it realistic to believe that this seventy-eight year old woman could make other choices now, before it was too late, choices that would restore her spirits if not her faith in a protective Holy Spirit? What could we create and hold onto in our conversations that would provide her the courage (which Kierkegaard refers to as "solid food") to let go of what she has to let go of? Jonathan Lear refers to the gap that separates aspirations from reality, and I wonder if this gap, which figures as a veritable chasm for Rebecca, can ever be adequately bridged for any of us, or whether an ironic perspective on the empty space is the closest approximation to closure we can ever hope to attain?

It was Rebecca who first called my attention to the Abraham and Isaac story, which she described as a perversion of faith and sacrifice. She couldn't fathom how the God of her ancestors could be so cruel, why He, the All-powerful One, should so abuse his power. To her, the happy ending in which a ram is substituted for a son was meager compensation for the unnecessary suffering inflicted on Abraham, Sarah, and Isaac. "The whole family must have been permanently scarred by the experience," she says. "The next thing you hear of Sarah is that she has died. What kind of God is that? A cruel joke to play on humanity, isn't it?"

The irony is that Rebecca was making the joke, not God. It was a joke about her naive faith in her own chosenness, in miracles, and in a wise and beneficent Being. "He tested man and failed his own test!" Since Rebecca was shaking with insult and terror, however, there was no ironical relief, and any amusement we shared was short-lived. The gap that Jonathan Lear had referred to had become a grinning chasm that was taunting Rebecca: "Do you dare to attempt closure?"

This spontaneous outburst, concerning God's call to Abraham to sacrifice, as a burnt offering, his beloved son Isaac, occurred several months after I had started seeing Rebecca, and it was out of character, both in its form and content. I had gotten used to Rebecca reflexively apologizing for any minor disruptions she might cause – an adjustment to the chair to accommodate her crooked back, a change in the schedule, even her embarrassing compulsion to apologize. Therefore, I found myself pleasantly thrown off balance by the vehemence with which she offered, unsolicited, her critical analysis of the famous Bible story. Perhaps something significant was happening between us after all! Having dispensed with the customary rituals that bound us together as needy patient and knowing therapist, Rebecca had opened the door to something more personally problematic. She had momentarily dispelled her fear of my displeasure, and her inner trembling had ceased long enough for her to admit to bitterness and discord. Finally, she was taking the risk of rupturing her superficially harmonious connection to the world.

Since this was psychotherapy and not historiography or Talmudic commentary, it didn't much matter to me whether there was any actual textual connection between the Biblical Sarah's death and her son's near-death experience at the command of God and at the hands of his father. Rebecca was making a connection, and, moreover, it was one that signified to her that God's test was not a test that could be passed with due celebration, but rather one that spelled universal failure regardless of the outcome. Good faith and diligence were insufficient protection against disaster, and limitless love and sacrifice turn out to be lethal.

Reluctantly, Rebecca had closed the *midrash* her rabbi had lent her that was supposed to allay her anxiety and resolve the apparent moral inconsistencies. And if I sense that she is proud of her ability to draw her own connections, I also sense that she is horrified at having broken down traditional forms of connection, and hangs suspended – refusing closure despite her desperate hunger for it. The God of Abraham is unworthy of her devotion, she insinuates as she sneaks me a defiant look from the corner of one eye: "He set out to test mankind and failed his own test." And yet, if God's absence (like Lenny's) is more present in her consciousness than His presence, what then? "Incomplete," "hideous," was what she had become, in which case her relationship to the world was destined to be either superficial or parasitic, shamefully dishonest or shamefully exposed.

Rebecca never liked to bear grudges for broken promises. Her memory was irreproachable, but her anger never caught fire; even when her orthopedic surgeon admitted that he had "botched" the third operation he performed on her back, she was proud to have forgiven the mistake, and told her friends and family, who urged her to consider suing, that she was not the litigious sort. But the unforgiving light of disillusionment has exposed a gaping hole that extends over her horizon. Falling through the hole, untethered from binding obligation, ritualized convention, willing sacrifice, she regrets her newly discovered freedom. (Being free to choose but no longer chosen felt like being pagan. Would she be consigned to an endless exile, the wandering Jew without a Moses to lead her through the desert?) The transient pleasures of the unsheltered have provided an escape from obligation and an open door into emptiness.

At seventy-eight, Rebecca has choices she never hoped to have at fifty-five, and all are temporary fillers for what is permanently missing. Indecisiveness is the bane of her existence, she tells me, but it is also the lucky charm that protects her from the dangers of closing down, settling for too little, and surrendering up her will. She thrusts it toward me, saying, "Help me make the right decision," and then clutches the charm tightly to her breast. "I wouldn't really want anyone to tell me what I should do. My children would laugh and tell you, I always like to get the last word."

Loss of a husband or a mother, even the loss of bodily integrity, should not have to mean feeling entirely lost, says the voice of the "healthy- minded" therapist, the one who sides with nurture over nature when it comes to explaining unmanageable anxiety. (I am alluding here to what Ernest Becker calls the "healthy-minded" argument, which is that anxiety and fear of death are not essential to human psychology, but are instead the consequences of not good-enough provisions of care.) So, when I am speaking from that perspective, I too question why Rebecca has been so paralyzed by her losses. Why is she filled with "fear and trembling" when others, who have endured similar losses, are not? Do those well-adjusted others feel internally complete, despite the incompleteness of their current lives and the limits of life in general, because they had more sustaining childhood experiences? How are *they* managing to neatly fasten up their loose ends when clearly Rebecca was tripping over hers? Does equanimity come from living more or less fully and honestly, or is it the product of self-serving fantasy, the blissfulness that comes from ignorance, the blindness of denial?

Ironically, the more Rebecca sought the serenity of closure, the more she resisted her lifelong tendency to close off her messy feelings and close in upon her given life. Rebecca trusted, and because she trusted she leaped over temptation, only to have fallen out of faith indecorously, uncertain how and where to land. No longer one of the favored children or God's Chosen People, she is loosed upon the world, and to what end? "Next year in . . . " It is up to her to fill in the blanks. She cannot choose.

This year she has landed in psychotherapy and the promise of a temporary shelter as she decides how to feel at home in the life she inhabits in her aging body. Ironically, she would like to bind up her anxiety by placing her free-floating faith in me and in the interminable oscillation between unraveling and re-binding which is the process of psychotherapy. As my faith wavers in sympathy with hers, I ask myself what I can do to help her feel more completed without glossing over the missing pieces in her life. I want her to feel more entitled to have and to express her desires and preferences, but I do not want to imply that the future will offer her ways of satisfying them. What form of protection can psychotherapy provide when opening up and making choices may be the only form of closure possible?

The Remains from Sacrifice

> "Perhaps those eternal mourners have transferred their allegiance from the permanent to mourning itself. As if they are saying to themselves, as if the young poet believes that if nothing else lasts mourning can."
>
> Adam Phillips, *Darwin's Worms* (1999)

> "When my father died it was as if my mother threw herself on the pyre. I did everything I could but it didn't make a difference; it wasn't enough. She stopped eating and died a year and a half afterwards. I never want to do that to my children."
>
> (Rebecca's opening statement in her campaign against culturally prescribed but personally disastrous, premature closure.)

Rebecca's compulsion to apologize for every aspect of her existence, even her apologies, became a standing joke between us, but lest I conclude from her self-effacing language that she had always thought of herself as disposable, she assured me early on that she had never intended to throw herself on the pyre after Lenny's death as her mother did after the death of Rebecca's father. To the contrary, she was determined to make a leap of faith out of the kind of faith that had turned bad. That is to say, she was determined to break with an old family tradition that beckoned her "beyond the call of duty" into a world in which no sacrifice was too great to ask and no sacrifice proved great enough.

And if I needed further proof of her intentions, she reminded me that she was calling for a moratorium on human sacrifice.

"The God of Abraham asked too much," she had proclaimed on several occasions, and were *she* asked to take His test today she would boldly refuse – not for selfish reasons, but for reasons of principle! Her mother was an exemplary mother, wife, and human being who didn't deserve to die anymore than Sarah deserved to have her son Isaac sacrificed, or Abraham to have his faith tested by God. No one stood to benefit from their suffering; nothing served as justification for the attenuation of their lives.

"I would have given my mother anything she asked of me and more; it was never even a question. Lenny and I stopped going away week-ends because whenever we did, something would invariably happen and we'd get a call. I wanted her to pull through; I never saw her as so dependent on my father; but she starved herself." And Rebecca, her mother's favored child, her heir apparent, lost not only the mother she loved, admired, served, and hoped to restore to life, but her own appetite for sacrifice and its fragmentary remainders.

Which is why, when Lenny died and history threatened to repeat itself, Rebecca resolved not to heap waste upon waste and treat herself as if her life were nothing but a bargain basement remainder. There would be no golden years, no promised land, no perfect closure (the rabbis got it wrong, her mother had got that right), but she was a modern woman (a secular Jew) who could flourish better without the uncertain privileges of the Chosen, who could enjoy exploring the world beyond the suburbs or the *shtetl*. Indeed, in contrast to her mother's response to the loss of Rebecca's father, Rebecca would unleash her appetite, not tamp it down, and in this manner create for herself as well as for those she loved an ever-replenishing source of vitality and nourishment. The American dream of the limitless frontier, psychology's promise of self-actualization, the new religions of plentitude, freedom, and autonomy, would be the "solid food" she needed to sustain her spirit now that the maternal breast had disappeared in the ashes and God, the father of Abraham, was a distant voice echoing from within a book.

And so, in inclement weather, with a hired companion to help her navigate through the underground garage, she came to my office religiously every Thursday afternoon for eight months (ten minutes early). She was a soldier on a mission, courageously fighting a crippled back, a paralyzing sense of duty, and a powerful compulsion to repeat, all of which fall within the dominion of Freud's death instinct, which threatened to draw her backwards toward the pyre, toward the closure her mother found only through self-sacrifice and closing down.

But – and this oscillation is the driving force of psychotherapy – as soon as Rebecca had completed her introductory rituals, which included extended thank-you's for my having carried in from the waiting room a chair that gave her aching back some additional support, a pessimism reminiscent of Ecclesiastes would seep into our conversations, reminding us both that this striving of ours might ultimately be for naught; for "All is vanity" (including this process we call psychotherapy). As the polite talk, the expressions of gratitude, and the sunny self-affirmations stuck in Rebecca's throat and she groped clumsily for words, I could hear the chorus of dissonant voices inside Rebecca's head accusing her of naivete or, even worse, dishonesty. Frustrated and embarrassed by her failure to make progress with her trembling, or at the very least entertain me with a funny story at her expense, she wondered aloud whether her temporary aphasia was a sign of dementia (she didn't think it was, but what did I think?) or a punishment for her untold sins: childlike obedience, blind optimism, and an embarrassingly superior ability to not say all of what she meant.

Maybe the cracks in her voice, her staccato-like speech were a wake up call, like the piercing sound of the *shofar* she had first heard more than seventy years ago, when it was blown by her grandfather on Yom Kippur, the Day of Atonement. Perhaps it was a warning that she should not try to fill the gaping holes in her psyche with coffee-*klatch* conversations! The Book of Life is about to close with a bang, and Rebecca has not yet divulged, even to her therapist, let alone her rabbi, all of her guilty secrets. Should she? Tempted by the ethos of psychotherapy and its faith in the restorative properties of exposure, she alternates between disclosure and closure, shameful immodesty and choreographed dissimulation.

"She only pretended to move on after Lenny died," one voice accused unforgivingly. "She tried her best, but how long can she keep up the charade?" another responded more sympathetically. And then there are the voices inside my head: "Rebecca's body has failed her repeatedly, along with modern medicine, Lenny, and her mother, so who are you, Joyce, a healthy, fifty-two year old psychologist, to presume that she should be able to feel happier with her lot in life, that she will be able to bridge the widening gulf between what she aspired to and what actually lies in store for the future? If her imagination has failed to buoy her spirits, why should yours succeed?" inquires the analyst/philosopher inside my head, who claims to represent reason and the Reality Principle, or what Ernst Becker refers to as the "morbidly minded" argument. There is only repetition and disintegration that remains, openings and makeshift closures, laborious joinings and the inevitable unravelings. This is life without illusion and, one way or another, we all have a moral obligation to face it, not spin it into something more palatable.

"And yet, the past eleven years could not have been just an act," Rebecca replies in her own defense, and in defense of her faltering belief in women's liberation. Somebody resembling Rebecca had painted pictures that were shown in obscure European art galleries not that many years ago. *Somebody* traveled half-way across the country three months after major surgery to celebrate a grandson's Bar Mitzvah, and that somebody is currently attending a continuing education class at the local university, where she and the professor engage in lively conversations about Renaissance painting.

But – and once again, Rebecca stumbles for words – that somebody is not, and perhaps never has been, a complete person unto herself. Confused, as I followed Rebecca's trail of arguments and circled back to where we had begun forty-five minutes earlier, I wondered what she meant when she insisted that something unnameable was missing (indeed had been missing all along without anybody having known it). We were stumbling together, searching, but who knows for what? Rebecca suggested that her faith in herself and her ability to make decisions was broken after her encounters with the unwanted and unexpected: when both of her parents ended their days in nursing homes, despite their unambiguous wishes to die in their own beds, when Lenny collapsed into a coma, despite the doctors' reports that his by-pass surgery had been a success, and when she became a patient with visible, life-altering disabilities, despite her precautions not to follow in her mother's footsteps and fold up prematurely. However, despite the obvious causes of her current state of despondency, Rebecca repeatedly wove us back to more distant memories, and intimated that the origins of her current experience of incompleteness and disfigurement, of being less than whole and more "holey" than normal, had tangled roots in early childhood experiences. (As I write, I am struck by the homonyms "wholly," "holey," and "holy," and wonder whether, in the language of Rebecca's unconscious, her aspirations to holiness are connected to her experience of being full of holes and of not being whole. I also am aware that as a therapist I have a bias towards the "healthy minded" argument, and am always listening for echoes from the past within the chorus of contemporary voices.)

Growing up in what she described as a "nearly perfect" family, in which the boundaries of self-sacrifice were never drawn, the dangers of faith were never acknowledged, and the value of harmony was always ranked above the value of dissension, Rebecca wondered whether she had failed to grow some essential organs. Maybe a certain part of her brain had never developed because not only had she not needed to think for herself she had never wanted to think only of herself. Were her hands not only arthritic but also Lilliputian because she could always rely on helping hands to fix and guide her? Was her backbone never firmly formed because she had developed an extraordinary flexibility, out of love and the desire to defer to those who had themselves sacrificed so much?

"I wanted to please my parents, not because I was afraid of them but because I thought that they were about as perfect as you can get. When my father lost his job during the Depression, we stopped going out to Chinese dinners, but they made sure to protect me from worry and I never suspected that they could scarcely make ends meet. And when my brother David's kindergarten teacher yelled at him for being late, my mother went straight to the principal the next day and it never happened again. David was completely different from me, however, and would constantly get into tugs of war with my mother; everybody suffered from his stubbornness and I could never see the point. Secretly I felt more fortunate than my friends to have the family I did, and when I think of it now, I even felt more fortunate than David because I was what they used to call the 'easy child' and my life was really pretty easy." (The Chosen child within the Chosen family has a heap of gratitude weighing on her frail shoulders, I thought to myself, as I noticed her stooped posture and gently trembling lips.)

And yet, as we spoke, Rebecca said that she now suspected that she had paid a hidden price for her good nature and good fortune. "I was excruciatingly shy and never liked standing out, even for good things. When I was elected president of my eighth grade class and had to make a speech in front of the entire school I was so embarrassed. I remember sitting on the stage tugging at my skirt; I felt so self-conscious about my knees. Once in the third grade I saw a teacher pick a girl up by her collar and pull her half way across the room just for talking back. We all sat there frozen, just watching her scream and turn red. I was horrified but didn't do anything, and I still wonder about her . . . the only time I ever rebelled was when I married Lenny."

Lenny's father had died when he was a boy, and as his family was in need of money he had quit school after the eleventh grade and never went to college. And while Rebecca's parents were not social snobs, they worried that their sensitive, sweet-tempered, and artistic daughter would not be equipped to handle the struggles and sacrifices that promised to be part of a life with Lenny. Retrospectively, she could appreciate their wish to protect her from adversity, as it was the mirror image of her wish to protect them, particularly in their later years, when they could not adequately protect themselves. From today's vantage point, however, she realized that everyone failed the test: her safety net had holes, as did her parents', and she was falling through them, following, first her father, then her mother, and most recently Lenny.

But all this is confusing, she tells me with an ironic twist in her smile. As a young woman, her faith was her best friend – it had both sheltered and emboldened her. She trusted her instincts and, miraculously, everything did turn out for the best. Indeed, her risky choice to marry Lenny, despite her parents' qualms, was the defining moment in her life: it inaugurated her capacity to choose and resist, rather than simply surrender to being chosen. "It was a struggle, there were sacrifices, but we managed, for better and for worse. My parents ended up loving him, and it all worked out. I have three wonderful children." Until, of course, it didn't "work out," and death and disease and age ripped openings in the almost perfect circle, and left Rebecca, at seventy-eight, hanging half inside and half out, unfamiliarly unenclosed and pockmarked with holes.

Thus, it seems that once upon a time Rebecca was filled up with gratitude and enveloped by hope, whereas now she chokes with disappointment and is emptied of speech. She looks in the mirror, she listens to her voice quavering, and recoils, scarcely recognizing herself. ("The black and blue marks from my latest fall could scare little children. I look like a witch! ") Where is that slip of a girl who was not a burden to anybody because she felt blessed and had a reserve of confidence to draw from? "Keep your distance; she is cowering in the shadows!" Rebecca warns protectively. "This female monster whom you see before you has needs that are gargantuan; she looks puny, she wants to please, but beware, she is liable to devour her own 'wonderful' children."

What reparations can be made for the losses (if we can call them losses) that have resulted from Rebecca's naive faith in the transcendent power of love? Having lived her life as a devoted, self-sacrificing child, wife, and mother, how can she reconcile herself to a life without transcendence or devotion, a life in which bodily aches and pains are no longer sacrificial offerings but accidental happenings, or worse yet, punishments, life's way of balancing the scales of justice? We cannot erase the marks of hopeful innocence betrayed, or bring back the missing branches of the family that are gone forever, any more than we can solder together the disintegrating cartilage in her back. So how do we fill in the holes in her emotional repertoire without tampering with her memories of better days (before her fall from grace) or creating irreparable damage to the sense of wholeness that sustained her throughout the years? If we can't all that will remain of what was once a blessed existence will be ambiguous diagnoses, indeterminate prognoses, an open-ended future, and a gnawing sense of incompleteness and dependency. Given Rebecca's history, can she ever feel exposed and still enclosed, pockmarked with holes, but nevertheless, whole enough?

"But then," I asked myself impatiently, uncertain as to what was possible to do for Rebecca and what was not, "isn't this just the human condition which we all have to face sooner or later in one form or another when our irrational, if virtuous, faithfulness is revealed for what it is, a childlike fantasy?" After months of empathizing with Rebecca's immediate predicament, which included a mishandled medical procedure and a deteriorating and irreversible physical disability, and then taking detours through a trail of memories to repeated instances of happy and unhappy endings, we had come to an impasse. Life was not now, never was, and certainly never would be in the future what it should be! There was no getting around that. But wasn't there a way to salvage from the wreckage a sustainable measure of hope?

So I took a break from empathic listening and from ferreting around for the early childhood origins to her particular brand of suffering. Maybe it would help if she were to view her incompleteness as normal, an existential reality that even the Chosen people must endure. I took a risk, and said something like this:

"You were the favored child of "near-angels"; at least that's the phrase you used, Rebecca, when you described your parents. So, naturally you figured that you should grow up to be an angel too. But what happened? Instead, you're an old lady who needs a walker and whose hands are shaking, and then when you get embarrassed and angry because people are aware of it, you don't feel angelic at all. It's like grade school when your knees were showing and you couldn't pull your skirt down. It isn't that you are 'half a person,' Rebecca, it's just the opposite: you've become a fully real individual and you find that hideous! And then to add to your problems, you believe that you should pretend you can still fly even without your angel wings."

Retrospectively, I realize that I was feeling powerless in the face of Rebecca's despair, and was attempting to fill in our gaps with a lecture that included a playful sense of irony. But Rebecca was in no mood to play philosopher or ironist. Indeed, she resisted my invitation to find either solace or amusement in the universality of incongruity, limitation, and disappointment. "I'm nothing like an angel and I certainly hope I never expected other people to be; you're wrong if you think I've been a quiet and sugary-sweet sort of person; my children could tell you how opinionated and pushy I can get. During the Vietnam War I was taking them on marches . . . Was I over-protected as a child? Am I over-protective as a mother? I don't think so. But, then, I never understood the value of toughening kids up to prepare them for the cruelty in the world. I say give them all the love you can give them; that's the best preparation."

Rebuked by her bristly denial of my contention that her expectations for herself and her life might have been naively optimistic,

I had to wonder whether I had touched a sensitive nerve that triggered her defenses or if my amateurish, existentialist formulation about unrequited desires and human limitations was so broad that it missed the mark, and was more like the irrational attempt of a rationalist to bind up loose ends prematurely.

One criticism of psychoanalysis is that there is no way to disprove a particular interpretation, that psychoanalysts too readily assume that a patient's adamant denial is evidence of the interpretation's truth. Thus, I often find myself in a quandary when a patient of mine responds angrily or dismissively to what I have to offer, and this was the case, in this instance, with Rebecca. Her response may have reflected her desire to distance herself from her naive aspirations to perfection, or it may have been a reaction to being gravely misunderstood. Paradoxically, responses of this kind are often both. Rebecca had aspired to be angelic, but she had also seen herself as a rebel. She was not your conventional suburban housewife, she had insisted time and again, and in her circles Lenny was a far cry from the perfect "catch." So, perhaps she bristled because my understanding was partially true and partially false, a painful exposure as well as an overly simplified caricature of her experience.

In either case, whether I was right or wrong about Rebecca's youthful wish-fulfilling fantasies, obtuse or intuitive with regard to the origins of her sense of incompleteness, I learned my lesson: generalizations don't hold much weight in psychotherapy; the one-size-fits-all model is yet another form of closing without closure. Rebecca wanted none of it; my "pearls of wisdom" were indigestible; moreover, my mini-lecture only made her feel more ordinary, more forgettable, and more, not less, guilty of disappearing.

And so, the question remained as to whether psychotherapy could be of use to Rebecca, given the undeniable losses she had experienced and the undeniable limits of all human existence. Could her uneasiness about the absence of closure be soothed through open-ended conversations that demand disclosure? The only sealant I was prepared to offer her in response to her predicament was a bittersweet mixture of empathy and irony. Could that be a sufficient container for her to keep herself afloat?

"Aha": A Distant Opening in the Tunnel

One dismal winter afternoon, after I had reluctantly but faithfully done my usual thirty laps in the pool, I caught myself shivering uncontrollably and remembered Rebecca's trembling, her lapsed faith, and her outrage at God in the Abraham and Isaac story ("He asked too much! ") The echo that reverberated from her body to mine was the missing link I had been searching for. Her attack on God and faith was an attack upon the version of her self as a voiceless appendage (one of the chosen not one of the choosers). It was a projection of her propensity to surrender her will, and to sacrifice herself excessively for some untested faith in the greater good. God's inhuman demand for human sacrifice was but a mirrored version of the burden that she had so dutifully shouldered since childhood ("I never thought to rebel"), which in the end proved of no avail. "I tried everything; my brother lived across the country; we were always a phone call away; but my mother starved herself and we ended up having to put her in a nursing home."

Finally a crack in the case! After her parents' and Lenny's death, and then her own "botched" medical treatments, Rebecca had lost faith in the transformative properties of unconditional love and limitless sacrifice, in God's covenant with his Chosen

People, and in the marriage between sacrifice and self-actualization. Offering herself up to the extent that she did was not only not enough to carry her, Lenny, and her parents along to the Promised Land, but was dangerously disabling, self destructive, and therefore, morally as well as psychologically problematic. If Rebecca had demanded more and conceded less, the orthopedic surgeon or doctors in the emergency room might have taken her more seriously and responded to her less impersonally; she might have spared herself some of the unnecessary physical pain that she had assumed she had to bear, as well as the emotional pain of being an object of condescension. If she had not repeated her mother's history of selfless devotion and unself-conscious renunciation, she might not be feeling so pathetic and invisible now, so hideous and incomplete. And if she had not depended so much on Lenny . . .

"Nobody benefitted, everybody suffered," was how she interpreted her brother's rebelliousness in relation to their parents. But those were precisely the words she also used in reference to Abraham's sacrificial offering. As her therapist, but also as a fellow human being, I hoped that this was not the only conclusion she could write to the story of her life (not enough of a spirit of sacrifice or else far too much). And though I didn't know whether I would be able to convince her of that, I began to imagine another conclusion, one that might even provide her with a modicum of a sense of closure. I envisioned Rebecca opening up the colorful jars of spices in her cupboards – which glared out at her each morning as she reached for her instant oatmeal, saying, "You've forgotten us!" And I could see her uncovering the canvases in her basement studio, draped in old sheets, unfinished, collecting dust.

I was on a roll, and opened "the crack" wider as I rushed back to the office not to be late for our session. Rebecca used to feel more fortunate than her brother David, who never compromised and whose life was a series of unnecessary (avoidable) conflicts. But now she tells me that their fortunes have been reversed and that this may have something to do with Rebecca's propensity to yield too much and expect too little. She described herself unflatteringly as "just" a widow, a pleasant-enough conversationalist who dabbled with paint and did not take herself seriously, while he was a well-esteemed professor who, along with his accomplished musician wife, commanded an attentive audience at academic colloquia and family reunions. As far as Rebecca could tell, David never doubted the way he navigated through reality, nor worried about overshadowing his sister or failing to rescue their parents from life's inevitable iniquities. It wouldn't have ever occurred to him that he might be a burden or that he should shoulder more of the family's burdens. He felt no moral imperative to peacefully disappear.

As an advocate for a patient whom I admire but who, despite her endearing qualities and considerable accomplishments, repetitively apologizes for her existence, I am loath to say which one of the two has more claim on the good enough life. If Rebecca had lived like David and forced herself to be more of what the television therapists call "her own person," would she now be more complete or less, would she be better or worse off? What about her parents and her children, how would their lives have been different? What burdens would they have had to endure, what sacrifices would they have had to make? Would she be loved as much by everyone, including me?

These questions are the undercurrent implicit in our conversations, but when Rebecca looks to me imploringly for certainty I find myself miscast: I thought I was supposed to be an "archeologist of the mind," not the messenger of good news or a seer who can foretell the future. "No, there is no certainty as to which way is the better way to be," I answer without having to say the words aloud. To her credit, Rebecca doesn't press me for some "pearls of wisdom," as Izzy did. Indeed, I suspect that if I had presented her with some artificially rounded off answer ("You were wrong, David was right" or vice versa), she would have been even more disappointed with me than she already was, and would have politely made her excuses and been out the door after a couple of sessions.

Surprisingly, however, what I can offer Rebecca and myself in the way of good news is that there is a different form of hope in uncertainty than there is in certain faith, but it is hope nonetheless. The losses that come with death and aging are undeniable and irreversible, and nobody, not even her courageously bullheaded brother David, can escape them, but Rebecca's responses to the givens of her life, which include losses as well as what remains from those losses, can be endlessly re-negotiated. "Abraham passed the test, but the next thing you hear of Sarah is that she died . . . Nobody benefitted . . . everybody in the family suffered . . . God shouldn't need that kind of proof." After my "Aha" experience at the pool, I was prepared to argue that Rebecca could draw up another sort of covenant in her remaining years, one in which the blessed were not crippled by their sense of gratitude, and the Chosen (those singled out for special love, responsibility, and protection) need not sacrifice their freedom to choose or to refuse.

It was easy to fall into the same trap that Rebecca had fallen into, the trap of believing in forced choices that turn out to be false choices, like the choice between being a grateful, modest, patient, and "easy," person, like she typically saw herself, or being a spontaneous, arrogant, demanding, and "difficult" person, like her brother David. And yet, I did want to tip the balance between the pull backward toward repetition (her mother's tradition) and the push forwards toward renewal. The woman who marched alongside her children against the Vietnam War and for women's right to choose, still lives somewhere, I thought, therefore, her return was not unimaginable.

What energy could we generate with words and gestures to help the life instinct gain an edge over Rebecca's desire to close off and find closure by foreclosing yet more than she already had? How could I help Rebecca bind off the loose ends just enough but not too much, without strangling herself in the process?

Rescue Fantasies and Nightmares

When a patient asks me, "Is there anything I should do or think about before I see you again next week?", and then follows up as Izzy did with the question, "Are there any pearls of wisdom you can offer?" I stiffen in fear of the fear of having no closure. Both I and the patient who is asking me are feeling anxious about the session closing inconclusively, so if I run over the hour or attempt to scrape together a capsule summary of what we have talked about before we edge our way to the door, I know that I am sharing in a fantasy of rescue. "Why pick on me?" is what I would like to say on these occasions, and what the psychiatrist Harry Stack Sullivan reported having said to his patients when they asked him for advice. But sometimes I do not have the heart to crush their hopes that I have an answer or a fancy tool hidden in my tool box; at other times I do not have the nerve to face them without one. Instead, I ruminate, "What exactly am I being paid for anyway?" Or, "Am I doing enough?"

Because Rebecca reminds me of my own mother, who, like Rebecca, rarely demanded anything of anyone, I am particularly susceptible to such rescue fantasies, fantasies which are known to be contagious and easily turn to nightmares. Macy's bargain basement was my mother's favorite place to rummage, alone on a Saturday afternoon "shopping spree." Saturday was her "day off," and she'd always come home in the evening, just after twilight, in time to prepare dinner. Her arms would be filled with paper shopping bags of assorted items which she had carefully selected from among the mass of random clothes in bins ("seconds," overstocks) for me and my sister. But as much as I loved her modesty (affectionately we used to call her "little mommy") I wished that she wasn't always so diminutive, frugal, and easy to please. I wished that she would wear high heeled open-toed sandals like my best friend Bobsie's mother, with deep purple and royal blue pattern dresses, and not just her usual browns and olive greens or pastel floral prints from the "reduced for sale" rack. She died prematurely at sixty-two, under anesthesia, a medical mis-calculation that maybe could have been prevented. And so, in memory of my mother, whose minuscule, rose-shaped earrings remain fixed in my second ear piercing alongside the dangling earrings I alternate daily, I want to keep Rebecca safe by my side or, at the very least, relieve her of the burden of feeling like a burden. I want her to take up space; I want her to argue with all those who want to rescue her, and who assume with all benevolence that they know more about what is good for her than she does. I want her to take the risk of contradicting and offending me, and I want her to paint again, regardless of whether she'll ever sell another painting.

These are fantasies, and for the sake of both of us I hold them in check, and hold us to my already ample sixty-minute hour. And yet, with due respect to Freud and the jury of classically trained analysts who cast me warning glances from one of the corners of my office ceiling, I feel that I should not simply dismiss my wishes and fears for Rebecca as counter-transference, or treat them as I would rambunctious children who are distracting me from the serious work of treatment. To be sure, the deepest roots of my feelings lie within my own personal history, but my fantasies and memories about my childhood mother were catalyzed by Rebecca's living experiences of invisibility and incompleteness, of having sacrificed too much and having missed too many connections. Sometimes the haunting feelings that are dredged up from my own childhood during a session with a patient are a window into an unconscious reality that we can understand better by sharing it.

Ten years after Lenny's sudden death, and three years after the "botched" back operation that left her with permanent nerve damage, Rebecca landed in the Emergency Room twice in the space of six months. The first time, a mysterious dizzy spell turned out to be nothing more than the flu, but the second time she was admitted to the hospital for "paranoia" and confusion, a life-threatening and misdiagnosed side effect of the medication she had been prescribed for her chronic back pain. Since then, Rebecca's life had become a series of rescues, rescue fantasies, and rescue nightmares, so I figured that fantasies of rescue implicit within our therapy relationship mirrored her experiences with other relationships outside.

Sprawled out indecorously on her living room floor, strapped to a hospital bed for thirty-six hours as if she were a prisoner, unable to string together a coherent sentence, there was no denying that Rebecca was physically as well as psychologically incapable of saving herself. The doctors had various erroneous theories as to the origin of her symptoms, and if her daughter Susan, the "miracle child," hadn't been close at hand to testify that this bent over, housebound old lady, who couldn't speak articulately for herself, was neither hypochondriacal, demented, nor psychotically depressed, she might of slipped into unconsciousness as another faceless statistic, waiting for an angel of the Lord to appear and proclaim an end to (in)human sacrifice. Fortunately, on this occasion the case was settled in her favor – Rebecca's life was saved, and it was established that she was neither crazy, morally deficient, silly, nor demented; she was just an innocent victim of circumstance, and no one was to blame.

However, more than one year after being "honorably discharged" from the rehabilitation unit of the hospital, Rebecca's confidence remained shaken, and she, if no one else was unimpressed by her "innocence." The latest traumatic episode had concluded happily, and everybody had agreed that she should move on, but for Rebecca the findings were contradictory and inconclusive, and it became our job to uncover and tie up the invisible loose ends. Wasn't there a moral she was supposed to draw from the story? Just as sacrifice had assumed many shades of meaning for Rebecca, so had her return to sanity, to "life as usual," which she had always associated with her innocence. "Innocent," she blended in and people looked through her; innocent, she hadn't dared to voice any complaints or raise any questions about the side effects of medications. Innocent, the doctors patronized, ignored, and misdiagnosed her confusion. Innocent, she was indeed "crazy," if crazy means out of touch with reality. For in her innocence Rebecca had believed in promises that should not have been given and that had to be broken –

the promise her parents made when she was a small child, that they would live as long as she needed them, and the promise she made to her parents sixty years later, that she would safeguard their wishes to die as they had lived, in peace and with dignity. Fifteen years ago the experts had said that Lenny's bypass operation had fixed his heart problems, and she had had faith; five years ago she was riding her bicycle and planning another art exhibit. Innocent? No more, and no thank-you!

When Rebecca looked in the mirror she saw a kaleidoscope of shifting images: a witch in widow's weeds, a patient who was paranoid and needed to be restrained for her own safety and the safety of others, a crabby old lady who was crawling along, holding onto a walker, speechless like a baby but without a mother to translate unintelligible sensations into logical sentences. Trapped within a nightmare, a pitiful shadow of the woman she was, tethered to a "hideous" decaying body, she felt guilty when she exposed who she really was and what she was really feeling and thinking, and guilty when she tried to protect the public (friends and family, doctors and therapist) from the naked truth and masquerade as someone she was not. Which was why she shook at the mere prospect of having to choose from among her three children where to make herself a home. (Maybe her mother was right about the pyre.) As long as she felt condemned to live as either a sliver of a person (who asked for too little) or a grotesque monster (who desperately wanted what she could not have), she would be shamefully incomplete, not fully human, and could never hope to settle peacefully at home anywhere.

Wrestling with a Phantom "Angel"

Over time Rebecca and I had established a comfortable rhythm with each other, as, with my encouragement, she revealed that there was far more to her than what she once referred to as her "organ recital." Ancient relics of her prior incarnations as a timid child, an adoring daughter, a devoted wife, and an off-beat mother were all pieces in the colorful mosaic of her life we re-collected, which included a march on Washington in 1969, disturbing expressionistic portraits she had painted, as well as impressionistic landscapes which she hung in remote corners of her home, out of sight, or gave away to friends free of charge. Her recent Kafkaesque hospital experiences, and her unwritten, previously censored, editorials on a broad range of subjects, were just part of the weekly fare: sacrifice and the Abraham and Isaac story, the value of optimism and of mourning, and the ethical problems associated with self-expression and lying were themes that crystallized in our conversations.

A homespun philosopher who couldn't be satisfied parroting either the traditional or the contemporary cliches that circulated around her apartment complex, the rehabilitation center, or the synagogue, she seemed more than enough of a complete person to me. "When Lenny was alive and the kids were at home, I was very independent. I ran the whole house. I had dinner parties, I worked free lance, and I set aside regular time for my painting." Offhandedly, so as not to appear too proud, Rebecca once showed me a brochure with her name in it from a gallery show in England. "But now that life feels like a dream. I can't even answer my letters, or decide whether I should have lunch with my friends, and I haven't painted in over a year. It's pathetic, but I wish someone would sweep in and make all my decisions for me; everybody tells me I'd regret it in the end if anybody actually did, but to tell you the truth, sometimes I don't know."

"To tell you the truth . . . " Sure, you don't know, I thought to myself, having become well acquainted with Rebecca's inclination to surrender up her will (or as Adam Phillips says "escape into doubt"), as well as her resistance to doing just that. For embedded in Rebecca's baleful plea to be saved from having to make choices, is a warning that echoed the warning I heard from the phantom psychoanalysts hovering above me. "Do not patronize me by joining in my fantasies of rescue! Appearances are deceptive. I am not to be defined by my bent-over, crippled body or my lapses of memory; and I am not a baby, even if I can't find the words to express myself and am unsteady on my feet. I am a complete person with a mind of my own, and don't let me forget it!" And so, as she thanked me excessively for my patience and "extraordinary" insights, and apologized mindlessly because her walker was cumbersome and the bruise on her nose from her most recent fall was "frightening," I imagined that she was silently reproaching herself for being so obsequious, so deferential to one more figure of authority who she suspected would prove to be fallible. Perhaps she was even plotting when and if and how she should make excuses not to come back.

Rebecca was well accustomed to handing over the lead, or at least appearing to, but her generosity, if that is what it could be called, made us both uncomfortable. (Too much sacrifice!) "Take your time, Rebecca; complete your thought, and certainly don't let me interrupt you." And so, when I stubbornly insisted on giving the reins back to her, she galloped ahead, but only so far. Backwards and forwards in time she lurched: in one story she was twelve, in the next twenty-three; she tiptoed into dark corners and swept around in circles as I tried to follow close behind. The possibilities were endless, for there were always more details tucked away that could add life to her prematurely buried stories that had gathered dust for too long. And life is good even when it's bad, I surmised, as it was the only alternative to the nothingness that had swallowed up, first her father and her mother, and then Lenny, all too soon, without sufficient time for closure.

But then, as soon as she detected any sign that she might have given offense, exposed her insufficiencies of character, or, even worse, mine, Rebecca surrendered hold of her loose-ended narrative, and said, in effect, "You choose what I need to talk about, what I should be talking about; I can't decide!" In the hope of finding completeness from being a model psychotherapy patient, just as she had been a model student, daughter, wife, and mother, Rebecca closed off her spontaneity and deformed her self. The mindless repetitions, the ritualized apologies, the self-effacing jokes, held out a promise that nothing would change, that all would end well, but it was one more promise that could not be kept. Closure? Of a sort, but not without tremendous sacrifice – tedium, aborted connections, a blind leap into faith as Rebecca prepared to gracefully disappear onto the pyre.

When Rebecca brought to our sessions this repetition of closing herself off without a true sense of closure, we both sensed that something was missing from our relationship, which now felt as deformed and incomplete as she did. If I had let this pass and, as was her custom, pretended that I didn't notice what she was glossing over, the therapy would have gone smoothly, at least for the hour, but smoothly nowhere.

And so, I thought, if I were to challenge her angelic-like goodness and our "goodness of fit," what was there to lose? Her tendency to empathize with her children, accommodate her friends, defer to her doctors, and idealize me, felt warm and comfy in the moment, but in the long run it left her feeling fragmented and both of us feeling unconnected to the pulse of life. Should I dare to unravel this finely woven fabric that was already frayed along the edges and wearing thin at the center? What was the risk of doing irreparable damage?

If I refused to accept Rebecca's sacrificial offerings, and instead encouraged her to remember but not repeat her past memory of relationships, would she experience that as an attack on her precious dreams and deepest values, or would she see me as the angel on Mount Moriah, who swooped down, just in the nick of time, and substituted a sacrificial ram for Isaac? By introducing Rebecca to a contradictory and complementary set of dreams and values, wouldn't I be giving her permission to see herself as a completed human being, not simply a fallen angel?

On paper, the mathematics worked; it all made perfect sense! Recollecting was a version of re-collecting all the missing pieces that were missed only after Lenny, her better half, died and her back gave out. Through the process of slowly sifting through the half-forgotten scraps she had saved but never used, Rebecca could choose to salvage some and tuck others away as souvenirs of days gone by, before binding herself back together into a whole person. Actively choosing not just passively chosen – wouldn't this be what is meant by closure?

I knew that in my wildest, most grandiose fantasies, I cast myself as the angel on Mount Moriah who rescues Rebecca from her nightmarish dreams of having to surrender up her will and lose her mind in exchange for love and protection. Back in my office chair, face to face with Rebecca, who was waiting anxiously for me to fill in the silence as we had forty minutes left in the hour, I groped clumsily for something original to say. The pressure was mounting. We certainly couldn't bring Lenny and her parents back, or repair the nerves damaged from the last back operation that the doctors had "botched," and we probably wouldn't want to restore her blind faith in an all powerful Presence who demanded limitless self-sacrifice in return for the promise of unlimited protection. But connecting Rebecca to her banished feelings, and restoring color and shape to her faded memories, good and bad, might be sufficient to bridge, if not fill up, the gap that cries out for closure, and, with her permission, we could certainly do that. Too much to ask? Too little to offer? What is good enough?

Another fall, a multi-colored bruise, a worm-like crawl across the room to the nearest telephone, and the metaphysical problems that we had only begun to sink our teeth into –about the relationship between dependency and inadequacy, faith, hope, and submission, peace and self-sacrifice – seemed embarrassingly insubstantial and irrelevant in the face of the material realities of Rebecca's life demanding the decisiveness of concrete solutions. Rebecca was literally unsteady on her feet, and objectively incapable of managing essential aspects of her life without the nearly constant support of others. Moreover, I couldn't deny that her discolored nose, her swollen wrist, and her trembling hands were distracting and disturbing, and that though she insisted that she wasn't as disabled as she appeared, and that with medication the pain was quite tolerable, I felt worried and increasingly protective.

As we penetrated the fogs of misunderstanding – her self-deprecating apologies and my stubborn refusal to accept her offerings – she began to identify unspeakable terrors for the future and irreversible losses from the past. Three quarters of the way through our session, our empathy quotient peaked and then leveled off, as, when the hour was coming to a close, we reflexively turned away from the tangled feelings we had only begun to untangle, and took a couple of steps back into the false comfort of the fog. A strained smile and "See you next week" seemed the only "reasonable" way to go on with the day at hand.

Necessity can be the mother of invention, however, and Rebecca's latest medical crisis forced our attention back to Rebecca's presenting dilemma: all three of her children had, for years, been pressing Rebecca to close down the apartment she had made into her "little nest" after Lenny had died and the family home became inhabited with ghosts:"I rattle around; it's too big for one person, a waste of good space and good money," was how she had convinced them that she should sell the family home, move ahead, and create something suitable for a woman on her own. The plan was practical, but, more significantly, it represented a promise Rebecca had made to herself that she would wrest herself away from her maudlin, nostalgic longing for the past, become whole once again, and life would go on. But now that plan was no longer viable, her back had given out, and her hopes of becoming whole, in the way she had once envisioned, were shattered. She had to move into a residential community closer to one of her children, and she, who felt like she was only half of a person, a leaky container for dysfunctional organs, had to make the choice.

This was complicated for reasons that defied practical solutions and which she could not readily articulate. Fortunately, it turned out that our conversations about sacrifice, the Abraham and Isaac story, the Women's Liberation Movement, and her mother's premature death from self-starvation, were relevant referents. Rebecca didn't want any of her children to have to bear the weight of caring for a semi-crippled mother; however, she also did not want any of her children to feel less loved or less important because of her choice of where to live. Being chosen is an honor as much as it is a curse. Indeed, according to the Jewish tradition in which she and her family had been raised, the responsibilities and sacrifices which the Chosen People were given to shoulder were well worth the love and privileges they had been promised to receive in return. But Rebecca was duly skeptical, and remembered that she had explicitly promised herself that she would not repeat her mother's history. No one should have to sacrifice too much, if the story that began with Abraham and Isaac and continued with her mother's "burnt offering" was to draw to a happier conclusion and that included Rebecca. But what is "too much" and what is just the right amount to support a loving life? Thus, I imagined that secretly she asked herself, "With whom would I feel more burdened, with whom would I be more likely to close off my feelings, fade into the background, or even disappear altogether into the realm of loving memory?"

Not being able to choose between the values of self-expression and self-restraint only added to her embarrassment, however, as she added indecisiveness to the growing list of her crimes. "If I don't even know my own mind, but waver back and forth like a pathetic little worm, then something essential is missing inside me that most normal people have. There is a hollow space where my will is supposed to be. Was it accidentally buried with Lenny? Maybe a CT scan of my brain would find what is missing. What do you think?"

Should she place her faith in her brilliant, oldest son's impeccable logic, in her middle son's unwavering devotion, or in her daughter's generous heart? Should she pay heed to her trembling arthritic hands or to the sadness she dared not express for fear of drowning the world in the flood of her tears?

As I witnessed Rebecca's tortuous oscillations, I asked myself whether she should be recollecting the past and revisiting the memories of the person she was, as she seemed to enjoy doing when she came to her sessions, or whether she should turn her gaze to the future. Would excavating remains from the past eventually inspire the faith and courage to move forward or would she fall prey to regrets and sterile ruminations? The passage of time is inevitable, and her body was certainly deteriorating month by month, but we were both uncertain how much she should accept a natural attenuation of hope and desire, and how much she should resist it and reconfigure her self-image before it was too late.

Susan, "the miracle child," was single and without children, and Rebecca knew that an uncertain romance and an unfinished degree were weighing on her mind. Surely Susan's focus should be on herself, not on her aging mother! On the subject of Susan's self-fulfillment Rebecca voiced no doubts whatsoever, and if Rebecca had sought out my opinion, I couldn't have offered a consistent opposing argument. I know that I wouldn't want my daughters to have to focus their lives on me, were I to become old and frail, though, unlike Rebecca, I am rather poor at dissimulating even when I think it might be reassuring and protective of those I love. So, luckily, in contrast to my patient Kevin, she did not force me to confront the ethical question, but proceeded to describe the next impossibility:

Sam, the oldest and most confident of the three, was already saddled with responsibilities and chronically over-scheduled. And while he was adamant that she move out east where there would be a large Jewish community and the doctors were "undoubtedly better," when Rebecca got on the phone with him she could never get a word in edgewise. "He's done the research already, and to him the best solution is obvious – I'm not getting any younger, I'll fit right in, I always make dozens of friends, and, moreover, I need to move on." No wallowing in a pool of self-pity, no room for irrationality and insecurity, no time to waffle back and forth with Sam; time is running out, he has the facts at his fingertips, and he has to run. "Come along, Mom; don't worry, you're no burden."

And then Abe, the middle child, whose personality was most like hers ("He'll give the shirt off his back and cannot say no to anybody"). Lowering her voice, Rebecca guiltily confided in me her worries and her judgments. "I never say it to anyone because I wish I didn't see it, but I think Abe's wife and step-daughter take advantage of his soft-heartedness. She's a powerful woman who has had a rough life; she has learned to take care of herself and has an iron will, and he bends." (Like her, whose back is bent? Like her, whose own tendency was to bend too much for the greater good, to keep the peace, but at great sacrifice?) " Of course that's his business, and I have to stay out of it."

"Stay out of it?" An alarm went off in my head. Sure, she had to stay out of her children's marriage, her daughter's romantic involvements, and the competition she alluded to in an earlier session between her Catholic and Jewish daughters-in-law. No voice in the chorus of contemporary psychologists could argue with the wisdom of that. But for some reason I couldn't get the phrase out of my mind. How far "out of it" does Rebecca feel she has to stay in order to be included, loved, chosen? Moreover, how can she extricate herself from that logical paradox of being an insider by way of discreetly remaining outside? Abraham's sacrifice: "The next thing you know, Sarah died." Her brother David's rebellion:" Everyone suffered. "Two different messages for a widow who feels incomplete, having lost her better half.

Bursting with the realization that "staying out of it" was a pivotal metaphor for Rebecca's unsatisfying relationship to her own life, I was struck by the parallel dilemma that I was facing as her therapist: how freely should I speak my mind to her, and when should I restrain my desire to voice my opinion or offer a potentially disturbing interpretation of hers? If I stay out of it, I may be giving her the freedom she requires to be herself, which is good, but I may also be acting as a passive bystander to her self-imprisonment, which is not. As a therapist, I am always questioning how much I should confine myself to speaking behind the blank screen of therapeutic neutrality and how much I should make a live appearance in the room. I wish to be a catalyst for something new and life enhancing for my patient, but the question is how?

Maybe it was her multi-colored bruise that stubbornly refused to fade from sight, or the description of her latest hurried telephone conversation with Sam, but Rebecca's self-sacrificing accommodations frustrated me that afternoon, and so without my usual parsing of words, at the risk of crossing over professional boundaries, I spilled forth my question: "If just for an instant you put aside your worries about Susan's career and love life, Sam's over-booked schedule, or Abe's younger-brother submissiveness, where would you prefer to live? Where would you feel more complete and more at home?"

Rebecca looked startled, and for a fleeting moment she smiled with the relief that comes when a blister finally pops. But then her face clouded over, as she tried to hide the fire that was beginning to smolder behind her eyes. She reminded me politely, but steamily, that the last thing she wanted to do was to cast a pall over her children's lives and that it was impossible for her to separate her children's happiness from her own. She was certain that nobody wanted to hear an "organ recital" or get unwanted advice from an opinionated, antiquated, and over-protective mother, and she would have to be completely demented to think otherwise. Which of course was not what I had been proposing, but what she saw and heard in my immodest proposal to think, for once, about herself.

Was her response fair warning that I and my morally suspect therapy should stay out of her family business, that she preferred to handle things in her customary way, which meant not actively choosing at all but waiting anxiously to be (or not be) chosen? The president of her junior high school class, pulling her skirt down over her knees in embarrassment, the local artist who never pursued a gallery or got an agent, the queen of the family kitchen and headmistress of its clean up, a faithful daughter, sister, and wife, for better and for worse, until the bitter end. These images of Rebecca rapidly flitted across my mind as I listened to her reproaches. They were yellowed snapshots of her "antiquated" traditions that had ended abruptly, without closure or completion. From behind the cloud that now darkened her eyes, she asked me why I would be encouraging her to abandon these traditions and spread out as if her life were a new canvas and she were once again a young budding artist. "Can't you see, I am old and cracked and disfigured, and that in order to preserve who I am, I must roll the canvas up and tighten the caps on my paints, lest the colors spill out and spoil the spoiled picture of my life even more?"

And then Rebecca recalled a dream she had had during the year that her father was in a nursing home, her mother was inconsolable, and she and Lenny were on call twenty four hours a day. In the dream she and Lenny had gone off to Florida for a second honeymoon, having temporarily forgotten her ailing parents back home. Carefree, they were strolling down a boulevard lined with palm trees when suddenly she saw her mother on a gurney that was rapidly hurtling down a hill just beyond her grasp. She ran to catch it but she couldn't gain enough speed. She was desperate to save her mother, and at the same time terrified that she wouldn't be able to. She woke up trembling.

Aha, I thought. I may have poked around indelicately, and Rebecca may have resisted and smoked me out, but she has led me to an opening (dreams being the "royal road to the Unconscious"), and we had too much to lose if I were to ignore my inner rumblings and politely stay out! "So, if you take liberties and do what you want, you might forget the really important stuff, and then disasters can happen! And yet, I imagine it must have been a tremendous burden on you, loving your parents so much, feeling the responsibility to protect them as best you could, and putting your own life completely on hold. You must have longed to get away, as you did in the dream. Is that why you are still so burdened with guilt now, and so burdened by the worry of over-burdening your children? Surely, you don't want history to repeat itself or for anyone to have to sacrifice and suffer as you did when in the end it seemed to make no difference."

The fire that I had started earlier when I asked Rebecca to take a moment to think just about herself, began to rage behind the darkening cloud protecting Rebecca's eyes. Now I was the one who had taken too many liberties, and I was the one who had courted disaster. "I never felt it as a burden," she stated emphatically, letting a flash of light shine through the ominous cloud. And after a pause of around thirty seconds, "I have to tell you I'm angry that you don't understand that." No apologies, just shifting in her chair and silence.

This was the first time, and it turned out to be the last time, that Rebecca expressed anything other than appreciation for my insights and attentiveness. And this was significant because it was also the first time that I had emphatically suggested that she felt something other than appreciation and love for her "nearly perfect" parents. Smarting under her reproachful hurt gaze, wondering if I was completely off base in my interpretation of her unconscious wish to break loose from the burden of responsibility and follow her impulses and pleasures, I told her that I was glad that she let me know how angry I had made her feel, whereupon she confessed that saying it rather than covering it over was, indeed, a radical step for her to take.

Rebecca spent the remaining few minutes of the session explaining to me how wrong I was and how completely committed she had been to her parents' care. She insisted that she never would have wanted to be less available to them than she had been and that she is still plagued at the thought that maybe, if she had done something differently, there would have been closure. Could she have sacrificed more? Was she not responsive enough? Those were her questions, not how she could have sacrificed less or freed herself more from her binding obligations!

This was very confusing to me at the time as I recalled her uncharacteristically angry response to the Abraham and Isaac story "He asked too much. Everyone suffered." I wanted to go back to the epiphany we had shared a few moments earlier when she had disclosed her anger and we were both shaken but also pleased that she had not papered over our ruptured connection. But the hour was up and she was clearly finished. We had more questions than we had started out with. I was hopeful that the new openings would draw us closer together and that we would find better resolutions to her dilemma, but was she? Was the gap too wide?

And then, a few days later, a flu scare, a postponed session, followed by a note: "I think I'll take a rest from the hard work of studying my past. Thank you for your help, you were wonderful." Would I be reading too much into it if I concluded that Rebecca was frightened by her encounter with anger and frustration, inner contradiction, and interpersonal disjunction? Did she regret not "staying out" of the conflict and resent my pulling us deeper in?

What cracks in the foundation of her life would I discover and pry open next time?

Closure Without Closing

Four months later another letter arrived, and whereas the first had not invited a response, as it was brief and typed on a piece of plain white paper, this one did, being handwritten on decorative stationery. Apologizing for not having kept in touch, thanking me for the therapy and for my openness to her returning if and when she wished to, Rebecca proceeded to inform me of her "wonderful" news. Susan, that miracle child, had pulled off another miracle.

Since I had last seen Rebecca, about two months after she had accused me of misunderstanding her and the terrifying nature of her dream, Susan had shared with her mother her vision of a happy compromise that was not unlike the one I had imagined but could not negotiate on my own months earlier when Rebecca had spoken bitterly of inhuman forms of sacrifice, God's ungodly testing of Abraham, and Sarah's post-traumatic death. So I was pleasantly surprised by the tone of the letter which bore not a trace of Rebecca's tortuous ruminations about burdens and sacrifice. Indeed, miraculously, given our closing session, she sounded not only open but also eager to move forward with her daughter's proposal.

According to the plan, Susan and Rebecca would share a two-story rental apartment, which would save both of them money and, more importantly, relieve each of an excessive amount of uncertainty and anxiety. Susan wouldn't have to wonder upon going to bed whether or not her mother was lying on the floor across town, unable to crawl to the phone, and Rebecca wouldn't have to wonder about whether a symptom was serious enough for her daughter to have to drive through the snow in the middle of the night to bring her to the hospital. As Susan had made it perfectly clear to Rebecca that she had no intention of truncating herself in an heroic effort to rescue her, Rebecca felt released from her nightmarish dreams of truncation and rescue.

Because their connection was completely volitional, and yet, at the same time, completely inviolable, the knots we had been wrestling with, having to do with choice, chosenness, incompleteness, and sacrifice, had dissolved or else had become irrelevant. Susan's loving bluntness had set in place a different tone: "Don't tell me how much I should sleep, or how I should feel about my boyfriend or my job or my weight, and I won't tell you how many lunch dates you should make or how you should feel about needing a walker." Thus, together they added an eleventh commandment to the original ten: Thou shalt not disappear into the Other or surrender up the right to choose as a condition of being chosen.

As I read Rebecca's gleeful letter, I recalled her history of quiet rebelliousness, and wished that I could have let her know that I heard echos of her voice in the voice of her daughter: "You used to tell your children not to believe all of what they heard on television: fruit loops are sweet but they have no nourishment, you admonished gently but stubbornly. And you gleefully refused to send the pastel-colored Hallmark cards that all the other mothers sent for birthdays. You insisted on making your own because it mattered to you to be more creative even if it didn't to anyone else." No wonder this proposal of Susan's suited her taste, I thought, delighting in how Rebecca had unobtrusively handed down to her only daughter her sense of moral integrity. Susan's blend of sacrifice and its vigorous refusal was what

Rebecca had always dreamed of, married into, painted, but never completely translated into life after Lenny.

Neither she nor her daughter was expected to bear the burden of offering up too much out of love, guilt, and gratitude. Consequently, neither one was in danger of being left in fragments, holding onto too little to make a whole person. In this arrangement, no widows were to be hurled upon the pyre, and no children were to be used as sacrificial lambs. Although Rebecca's self remained incompletely whole, submission and self-effacement were not the conditions for finding completion or redemption.

And so Rebecca took the leap out of her indecision and signed on with Susan. She wished me a happy and healthy New Year, and thanked me once again for having been there. No longer feeling like half a person, she could put the past behind her and stop the restless searching for her phantom missing pieces. What had changed internally is difficult to say, but from how she sounded in her note Rebecca now felt sufficiently whole. She didn't mention it, but my guess is that the mysterious inner shaking had mysteriously abated.

But what about me her therapist? I am left with an endless stream of unanswered questions. For example, if Susan hadn't stepped in and saved the day, would Rebecca have submitted to living as a shadow, unknown and incomplete on the margin of her sons' and daughter's busy lives? If so, that would mean that the turn of events was just good fortune, a life-sized *deus ex machina,* and that the therapy had meant nothing. Or would Rebecca have continued, despite our fortifying conversations, to shake with indecision outside the protective space of my office, until finally her "brilliant" son Sam, who had no time or understanding for waffling, made the choice: "You're coming to Boston. It'll be easy; I'll make all the arrangements," which would have left Rebecca as well as Susan and Abe perennially indebted but also guiltily ungrateful.

And then there's more. What is the part I played or should have played in all of the unraveling and binding up that naturally takes place during the closing years of any life? Should I have done something differently that afternoon when Rebecca confided in me her terrifying dream and then got angry at my clumsy attempt to understand her unconscious wishes? There is no doubt that I broke our rhythm and disrupted the harmony of our connection when I suggested that she was not only afraid of being a burden to others but also of being burdened herself by her own unlimited hopefulness and solicitude.

Into her traditional tale of unconditional love and unwavering loyalty I had slipped an unscripted, free-spirited character, someone whom I supposed had expressed a side of Rebecca which she had neglected or maybe even banished from conscious awareness (her missing piece). In my hope of helping Rebecca feel complete, I wedged this woman in through the cracks that were left when her dream of escape to a Florida beach shattered and turned into a nightmare from which there was no viable escape. However, from Rebecca's unwelcoming reaction, I wonder now if I took too many liberties. I was offering Rebecca liberation from the twin burdens of too much care and responsibility, but it may not have been what she needed to create a happier, more coherent life story that could serve as an inspiring and reliable companion in the years remaining her. Indeed, Rebecca had no guarantee that if she trusted me and accepted my offer to reunite with her other half, she wouldn't end up sacrificing more of what she holds most dear – her wholehearted faithfulness which had been the key to her happiness since she was a small child. Who is to judge?

And so she got angry, she expressed her anger, and we celebrated her expressiveness and agreed to call it courage, but then she never came back. Enough free expression. Enough discontinuity with the past. Enough human sacrifice under the guise of human potential! Thanks for all your gifts but . . . no more.

I'd like to think that our irregular skirmishes with Freud, our archeological digs, and our collision over the ethos of self-fulfillment inaugurated the beginnings of something new, something she could use to provide a sense of closure, as we survived her anger, bore witness to her disappointments, and reconnected with her "illegitimate" sister who had been banished from consciousness into the world of dreams for as long as she could remember. The turning of the kaleidoscope that I call psychotherapy – the shifting and re-grouping of fragmentary pieces of experience – must have created a new and more intricate pattern that she could call her self, and it was that denser, more completed self that struck a satisfying compromise with Susan. Or at least this is the story I would like to believe.

After over a year my understanding is still incomplete, but, mysteriously, I too feel ready to conclude the hard work of studying her past. Rebecca had enough of my talking cure, but talking with her had opened me up to her traditional cures which as a young, modern, female psychologist I had turned my back on too precipitously. As a result of our relationship and its inconclusive conclusion, I am less certain about how I feel about human beings finding completeness through love or what adds up to mutual enclosure (it's not as bad as it used to sound when autonomy was the buzz word and self-actualization was conceived of as an individualized peak experience). Ironically, in that uncertainty about love and identity, self-completion and human incompleteness, I feel more whole, though more aware of the holes in my understanding, than I did before.

I keep Rebecca's file folder in my active file cabinet, though I doubt I'll ever see her again. Once in a while I look at the photographs she brought me of her paintings and read the letters she wrote me. I find that I feel more, not less of a sense of closure if I leave her file open (she is still active in my memory, alongside my mother, and this is consoling). Despite the usual protocol, I'll probably drop her a card around the New Year, hoping for a reply. I also hope that she will not feel burdened with guilt if she doesn't want to reply because I am a reminder of an unhappy time, or burdened by shame if she wants to write but, for some reason, is unable. Does more openness make for more closure or, is it the other way around, more closure makes for more openness? Another chicken and the egg dilemma, so who can say.

If the pursuit of wholeness and the desire to be complete is called Love then my work with my patients is a work of love and its sacrifice. In our uncertain experiments with meaning, we grope through a fog, imagine an ideal, and mourn when it disintegrates under the impressions of our hands. We flirt with new possibilities, wrestle with angels (prophetic and fallen), and soothe ourselves with the comfort of familiar rituals. Demanding the best, fearing the worst, and discovering, with a sigh of disappointment as well as relief, neither one, we get on and off the couch, sustained with the hope of creating a life that is always unfinished but, nevertheless, good enough.

AFTERWORD

After Kevin left for the Peace Corps I placed his wire sculpture of a tree on the end table near my couch. It shares the space with a box of tissues, a photograph of Freud's couch from the Freud Museum in London, and the hand-made ceramic plate that is the gift from an old friend in New York, the plate that served as a touchstone for me and Julius. Though I haven't heard from Kevin for several years, he comes to my mind each day as I look across the room at his skinny tree. Tilting somewhat precariously on its twisted wire base, it tumbles over from time to time. When it does, I rediscover how to balance it amidst the clutter, and wonder how Kevin is balancing his competing desires out in the world.

When Judy stopped coming to see me she was toying with the idea of serving again on the national board of her professional organization. She had been surprised at having been sought out and re-nominated, despite her reputation for being demanding and outspoken. At the time of our last session, whether she would continue to wade further into the messy realm of politics or to pull back and find less frustrating ways to spend her time and energy remained an open question. (Hope was sometimes, but now not always, a "four letter word.") Bill continued to pop in and out of her life, mostly by way of e-mail, but he had receded to the outer margins where he rightfully belonged. His unreliability and his flimsy commitment to their shared future might have spelled the end of all romantic commitments for Judy, but I hope that has not been how she has processed her disappointing experience. The Struggler was gone when we last spoke, but Judy's willingness to struggle for what she wanted had remained a value that she relied on for her sense of vitality. I hope, therefore, that she is continuing to struggle to not be quite so self-reliant.

Julius still suffers with deeply rooted feelings of sadness, betrayal, and anger, but these are different from what had been paralyzing doubt and depression; he tells me that he is filled with gratitude that he can feel, acknowledge his feelings, and talk about them honestly even outside my office. He has returned to school and is getting a degree in Spanish; perhaps this is his gift of love to the Puerto Rican candy store owner who took him under his wing at the age of ten and gave him his first job. He is always balancing the scales. He never forgets, though he still fears being forgotten. I still see Julius twice a week, and though forgiveness remains an ambiguous virtue in his book of ethics, he continually amazes me in his commitment to deepening his awareness of how love is embedded in hate, and to opening himself up to what he feels to be authentic human connections. The ability to walk on glass is a strength of sorts; it was a source of pride for his mother, but for Julius today it is not a good enough response to suffering; the life of selflessness is not a good enough answer to a life of selfishness and pain.

My daughter Vera no longer plays dress-up in the basement with her neighbor friends, though we still keep the basket of old fashioned dress-up clothes in a basement closet. I am hoping that some day there will be grandchildren who will squeal with delight as they invent stories for no practical purpose and without a care for the world outside. Vera has just completed her first year at an art academy and plans to become a painter. Her imaginative flights of fancy have found a purpose that I hope will make her happy.

Steve has taken on new responsibilities at work and, as customary, has extended his reach so far that he is inevitably running to keep his commitments. Recently, however, he has begun to laugh at his anxieties and poke fun at his unproductive tirades about stupidity and wastefulness; moreover, it has been over a year since I've seen him boil with frustration at the unnecessary impediments in life that used to take him off track and slow him down. Steve's equanimity confuses him, and he wonders aloud if he has become too complacent. The twinkle in his eyes suggests that he has not. Quite the contrary, less restrained and less burdened by the obligation to impose restraints upon himself, he seems less cynical and more open to the simple pleasures of life. Music is still a love he has neglected, for no rational reason, but recently, when he came upon a book of poems that he used to read when he was in high school, he decided to keep it close to him, on his desk in his office. An "unadulterated pleasure" is how he described his feelings upon reciting these poems quietly to himself; I hope he feels at liberty to enjoy them and not just wonder whether he should. We continue to explore that.

As for Iris, she continues with her meticulous calculations, and lives uncomfortably with the suspicion that her meager savings accounts are in constant danger of being depleted. And yet, if I am measuring her moods correctly, there have been times when she has been able to set aside her mathematical computations and see Harry as the man she married, the man who smokes and drinks too much, who has no patience for her neediness, but who also is eager to babysit her grand-daughter and buy her the special cake and flowers she wanted for her birthday.

I have heard nothing of Rebecca, and the card I sent her last year for the Jewish New Year was returned stamped "addressee unknown." Neither she nor her daughter is in the phone book, and I have to assume that she has either died or moved away. I keep her file in my active file cabinet so that I can look at the prints she gave me of her artwork when I want to do so. Paradoxically, closing her file up and placing it out of sight would deny me the sense of closure I feel by keeping it open.

I am tempted to offer my readers fresh morsels from the lives of my friends' son David or my daughter Saralena. And I would love to give the most recent update on the resolutions, predictions, and debates that have been cooked up for New Year's dinner at my friend Jane's. But I resist the temptation to add ever more details, as if they could either bring a final closure to these stories or else postpone such closure indefinitely. I close without closure and have to live with that.

The times are uncertain, but time's passing is not. How then do we live fully or peacefully or happily within the confines of such limitations? Repetition is an anchor amidst the tumult. It keeps us afloat, but at the same time hypnotizes us into believing that we float forever. When we repeat ourselves endlessly, we are tricked into feeling that time stands still, that we are immortal, and that there is always hope for a better tomorrow. Ironically, psychotherapy is a semi-real, semi-imaginary space that welcomes repetition, but also a space in which we are committed to breaking out of our trance. Is it better to live with "eyes wide open" as opposed to "in a stupor?" This is a choice the Israeli writer Amos Oz posed in his memoir *A Tale of Love and Darkness.* My patients and I wrestle with this question every day and the answer is not self-evident.

We are creatures of contradiction, according to Freud. However, as long as both sides of the conflicts that rage within us are acknowledged, *eros* will not have lost the battle to *thanatos* and that will have to be good enough.

Made in the USA
Middletown, DE
22 December 2014